The Essential
DIABETIC AIR FRYER
Cookbook for Beginners

1500 Days Easy, Delicious, Guilt-Free, Low-Carb Air Fry Recipes for Pre Diabetic, Type 2 Diabetes Boost Your Wellbeing Incl. 30-Day Meal Plan

Joseph Gentile

Table of Contents

INTRODUCTION

Hello there, I'm Joseph Gentile, and if you're here, you've likely walked the challenging yet rewarding path of parenthood. You understand those early mornings, late nights, and the constant desire to provide the very best for your family. Today, I want to share a deeply personal story with you- one that began with my unwavering love for my two sons and my determination to help others like me who've been diagnosed with diabetes.

Parenthood has been my journey too, as I've watched my sons grow, nurturing their dreams and cherishing the moments we've shared together. Like many children, they developed a taste for fried foods- those crispy, delightful indulgences that bring instant joy but come with long-term health concerns. That's when I embarked on a transformative journey, leading me straight to the heart of my home - the kitchen- and to the remarkable kitchen appliance that would change our lives: the air fryer.

In fact, I'm one of diabetic, but I refuse to let that limit my enjoyment of the magic of the air fryer with my kids. In fact, I've become obsessed with finding ways to make the air fryer work for our family's health and happiness. That's why I'm thrilled to introduce you to the 500 diabetic air fryer recipes that I am honored to share with you today. These recipes are more than mere instructions and ingredients- they symbolize hope, transformation, and the promise of a healthier, happier life.

Each recipe has been thoughtfully crafted, meticulously tested, and perfected not only to align with diabetes-friendly guidelines but also to tantalize your taste buds and ignite your culinary creativity. You see, I understand the desire to savor delicious meals with your loved ones while managing your health, and these recipes are here to make that possible.

But why did I decide to compile these recipes into a book? The answer is straightforward- I want to share the transformational power of the air fryer with you, my fellow parents, and anyone else on a quest for improved health. I've experienced the impact firsthand, and I'm eager for you to experience it too. I want you to wake up excited about your meals, eager to explore new flavors, and confident that your choices are paving the way to a brighter future for your family.

So, whether you're just embarking on your journey toward healthier living or you're a seasoned cook looking to expand your repertoire, I warmly invite you to delve into the pages of this cookbook. Let the air fryer become your trusted companion in the kitchen, your instrument for nourishing your family, and your gateway to a world of culinary possibilities that can transform your lives, just as it has transformed mine.

Together, let's embark on a journey that celebrates family, health, and the sheer joy of cooking. Take that first step towards a brighter, more flavorful future. Your loved ones, your taste buds, and your health will all be profoundly grateful.

CHAPTER 1
THE DIABETIC DIET 101

In its simplest terms, heart disease encompasses a range of conditions that impact the health and functionality of the heart. While the definition might appear straightforward, the intricacies of heart disease are anything but simple. This chapter is dedicated to unraveling the complexities of heart disease and shedding light on the vital role that a heart healthy diet plays in controlling its various forms.

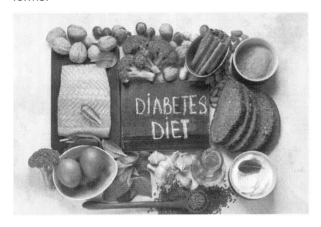

What Does a Type 2 Diabetes Diagnosis Mean?

For those of us unfortunate enough to be diagnosed with type 2 diabetes, it can be a scary and uncertain time. When we develop type 2 diabetes, our body can no longer efficiently process sugar. When we consume food high in natural sugars—like many fruits and grains—our body digests them down into glucose. Glucose then travels into our intestines and bloodstream, where it would naturally move around the body to power our cells. For glucose to power our cells, we need the hand of a hormone called insulin; unfortunately, for people with type 2 diabetes, our cells are resistant to insulin (Mayo Clinic Staff, 2020). Because of this insulin resistance, we have all of the glucose floating around in our blood, leading to a large amount of potentially life-threatening health conditions.

Helpful Methods and Tools for Diabetes

Sadly, there is no cure for type 2 diabetes. However, various methods make life far easier for us, massively lowering the chances of complications. For those recently diagnosed with diabetes, talk to

your general practitioner about what options you have going forward in regulating and controlling your diabetes. Keep in mind, everyone is different. Just because the medication works for one person doesn't mean it will work for another. Some people get by on diets alone; others rely on regular exercise. Experiment and find out what works best for you.

- **Medications**

Medication is the most widespread—and generally successful—method of type 2 diabetes. The goal of diabetes medication is to bring your blood sugar down to a stable and regular level. More often than not, insulin therapy comes after seeking medicine.

Insulin therapy is the next step for many of us after a course of medication. Although the name may come across slightly unnerving, insulin therapy is a natural and safe way of managing diabetes. In essence, we supply our bodies with extra insulin to help us combat the high blood sugar. The two types of insulin typically prescribed are basal (long-term) and bolus (short-term) (Editor, 2019).

Basal insulin helps control our blood sugar levels between meals and throughout the day; typically, basal insulin starts working under five hours and lasts up to 24 hours.

Bolus insulin, on the other hand, is taken before meals. By taking bolus insulin before we eat, we help control the spike in blood sugar levels we have after eating. Those of us on bolus insulin need to keep a particular track of our carbohydrate intake during meals, to know precisely how much insulin we're going to need; this type of insulin starts working in under 15 minutes and lasts up to five hours (Editor, 2019).

New medications and types of insulin drugs are being approved by the Food and Drug Administration (FDA) every month, so be sure to check with your doctor for new alternatives regularly.

Another useful tool for diabetics is the blood sugar monitor; being able to keep close tabs on our blood sugar levels is invaluable for those of us on insulin therapy treatments. It's especially helpful to check your levels while fasting, before meals, or two hours after a meal. This particular process allows us to see how food is affecting us and what action we may need to take.

- **Healthy Diet**

Another very useful method of type 2 diabetes is a simple diet change. Registered dietitians are the best source of credible and proven diet-based diabetic treatments. Medical nutritional therapy is a commonly recommended form of diet-based therapy for diabetes. This type of specifically designed diet helps diabetic patients lower their A1C hemoglobin percentage (Brown, 2019).

Remember: there is rarely only one way of doing things; several different meal plans and diets have shown to be very beneficial to people with diabetes. Consider researching and asking a medical professional about the Mediterranean, vegetarian, paleo, and DASH diets.

- **Physical Activity**

Physical activity is a key part of all diabetic health plans; following a structured workout plan has shown to have massive benefits towards general health as well as lowering our A1C hemoglobin levels. Ideally, adults with type 2 diabetes should aim for 150 minutes of exercise every week, spread over the course of at least three days (Mayo Clinic Staff, 2020). It's also recommended that we go no more than two days in a row without exercising. This may sound like a lot if you currently aren't exercising regularly, but don't worry: start off slow and build your way up. Some exercise is always better than none!

Nutrients and Diabetes

Just like with every living creature, we need certain nutrients to survive. For people with diabetes, it's important that we keep track of the nutrients we eat: too much of a good thing can certainly be bad for us.

Macronutrients

Macronutrients are nutrients which we need a large amount of to be healthy. The three which we'll talk about are carbohydrates, fats, and proteins (Avita Health, 2020).

- **Carbohydrates:** Carbs are the macronutrient that we have the most complicated relationship with as diabetics. Carbs are the densest source of glucose, which means too much can be unhealthy for us. However, carbs are also a very important energy source. Sugars, starches, and fiber are all types of carbohydrates. Starches and fiber are complex carbs, meaning that they're made up of a more complex chain of molecules. These complex carbs take longer to break down and digest. Sugars are simple carbs, therefore take far less time to digest and can cause dangerous spikes in our blood sugar levels.

Something to take into account when approaching carbs as a diabetic is the glycemic index and glycemic load. The glycemic index (GI) of food is how quickly it will raise your blood sugar levels. Foods are rated on a scale of 0 to 100, with white sugar given a rating of 100 (Higdon, 2003). Glycemic load (GL) on the other hand, paints a more complete picture of the carb content of foods because it recognizes exactly how many carbs are available in each serving of food. An example of this can be a watermelon which has a glycemic index of 72, but because of the high water content only has a glycemic load of four.

- **Fats:** Fat is often made out to be the villain in most diets, but fat can actually be very useful to us. Fat takes far longer to digest in our bodies than carbs or protein, which means it keeps us satisfied and feeling full for longer. Fat comes in two forms: saturated and unsaturated (American Heart Association [AHA], 2014). Unsaturated fats are broken down further into polyunsaturated and monounsaturated fats. These types of fats are the ones we want to include in our diet, as they're actually very healthy. Polyunsaturated fats are called essential fats because our body cannot produce them, but needs them to function properly.

Saturated fats, on the other hand, are a hotly debated topic among dietitians. Although they can be eaten in moderate amounts, we should look to replace them with unsaturated fats wherever possible. The most dangerous type of fat we can consume is trans-fat, a type of saturated fat. This is a manufactured form of saturated fat often found in creamer, margarines, and commercially baked goods.

- **Proteins:** Just like with carbohydrates, protein is an important source of energy for us, almost everything in our body relies on protein to function properly. Protein contains the same amount of calories as carbs but digests far more slowly. Most people don't know that there are in fact two types of protein, plant-based and animal-based.

Healthy forms of animal-based protein include: fish, grass-fed beef, poultry, cheese, and eggs.

Healthy plant-based proteins include nuts, lentils, seeds, beans, quinoa, and tofu.

Plant-based proteins are especially useful for people with diabetes as they are high in fiber and are more comfortable for kidneys to process.

Other Essential Nutrients

- **Vitamin D:** Vitamin D is a crucial nutrient for people with diabetes as it strengthens our immune system and promotes insulin creation. Fish, sunlight, and supplements are all great sources of vitamin D. Make sure to get your vitamin D levels checked to be sure that you're getting the right amount your body needs.

- **Magnesium:** Magnesium is one of the most important minerals in our diet; it helps with regulating blood pressure, strengthening bones, muscle growth, improving nerve function, and making the breakdown of glucose more efficiently. In short, magnesium is impressive. Luckily, it's effortless to increase our magnesium intake with peanuts, almonds, spinach, black beans, quinoa, avocado, and soy milk.

- **Sodium:** Sodium is a mineral necessary for keeping electrolyte balance in our body. Too much sodium can be highly detrimental to our health because high sodium levels have increased the risk of heart disease, stroke, and high blood pressure. As diabetics, we should look to reduce our sodium intake as much as possible: avoid processed foods and fast food as these are usually filled with sodium.

How to Succeed Keeping Healthy for Diabetic Diagnosed

- **Whole Health**

It's crucial when planning a diabetic diet that we look at the diet as a whole. Rather than just focusing on cutting out specific foods, we should look at balancing the bad foods with the good in a healthier way. Because no food is technically bad for you, we still need carbs for energy, and sugar tastes nice. At the end of the day, we just need to make sure we offset these troublesome foods with ones that will help us be healthy.

- **Educating Yourself**

Educating yourself is half the battle when trying to live with diabetes. We have to take special care of ourselves. For us to do that, we need to understand precisely what our bodies need. Therefore, the best thing I can recommend we do is to learn. Go and research different diets, techniques, tricks and methods. By adjusting our diets to meet our needs, we can make our lives so much easier. If you haven't consulted a dietitian yet, I highly recommend sitting down with one and discussing what you would like to do about your diabetes.

- **Counting Carbs**

Carb counting is a fantastic method of self-regulating your carbohydrate consumption. A basic guideline to carb counting is as follows:

To lose weight:
- **Men:** 45 to 60 grams of carbs per meal and 15 to 30 grams of carbs per snack.
- **Women:** 45 grams of carbs per meal and 15 grams of carbs per snack.

To maintain weight:
- **Men:** 60 to 75 grams of carbs per meal and 30 grams of carbs per snack.
Women: 45 to 60 grams of carbs per meal and 15 to 30 grams of carbs per snack (CDC, 2019).

The American Diabetes Association recommends that we do not eat less than 130 grams of carbohydrates daily. There has been some evidence to show that eating less than that can promote better blood sugar control. Try consulting your doctor or dietitian about a low-carb diet if you feel like you may need it.

• Reading Labels

Reading food labels is a critical tool in eating correctly as a person with diabetes. Food labels can contain a lot of information regarding the food you enjoy. Here is what I believe to be the most important details:

- **Serving Size:** This displays the size of what the manufacturer considers a typical serving. Be careful though: most of us eat more than one serving.

- **Calories**: This is the number of calories per serving, incredibly helpful for weight control.

- **Total Carbs:** Convenient for counting carbs; focus on the total carbs in a meal rather than the sugar. All carbs end up turning into sugar as we digest them.

- **Fiber:** Fiber is fantastic for lowering blood sugar and cholesterol; it also makes us feel full longer.

- **Sugar:** It's always good to take note of the sugar content of a meal alongside the carb content. Although carbs are more important to note, knowing whether a meal is heavy in sugar or not can still be vital in helping you eat healthily.

Watch What You Eat

As we've already learned, watching what nutrients we eat and what amounts is a crucial part of living a healthy life as a person with diabetes. In this section, we will go over some other useful points that help with building a healthy, diabetic diet.

• Portion Control

With over 70 percent of Americans being overweight or obese, portion control is a topic that must be addressed far more frequently in our lives (CDC, 2020). As diabetics, in particular, it is essential for us to not overeat and risk spiking our blood sugar levels. The best way for us to measure our portions is with a small food scale. Weigh all your ingredients before cooking and calculate the total calories; this will be a massive help towards staying healthy and losing weight if that's one of your goals.

• Alcohol

Contrary to popular belief, alcohol can slide straight into a diabetic diet. Dry wines and spirit liquors are incredibly low in carbs and sugars, making them adequate for people with diabetes to consume. Sweet wine and beer, on the other hand, tend to contain many more carbs. More carbs means if you do drink those, do so in moderation. Avoid mixers and cocktails at all costs: these contain sugary drinks or fruit juices, which can cause your blood sugar levels to skyrocket.

• Sugar Substitutes

On average, Americans consume 22 tsps. of sugar a day (Associated Press, 2009). As diabetics, that would be devastating to our blood sugar levels. Therefore, we need to look at alternatives. Sugar substitutes—known as artificial sweeteners—contain few to zero carbs or calories. Some commonly found artificial sweeteners are aspartame, acesulfame-K, neotame, saccharin, sucralose, and stevia.

• Sugar Alcohol

Sugar alcohols are chemically modified sugars that have less than half the carb content of normal sugars. Unlike artificial sweeteners, these can cause your blood sugar levels to increase. Typically, you will find these in sugar-free candies, syrups, ice cream, and baked goods. Some examples of sugar alcohols include sorbitol, mannitol, erythritol, and maltitol.

CHAPTER 2
DIABETIC DIET MADE AIR FRYER

Why Air Fryer?

Believe me, I get it. When I first heard about air fryers, I was skeptical too. How could something that claimed to make food crispy and delicious use so little oil? Was it just another kitchen gadget that would gather dust? But let me tell you, the air fryer is not just a passing trend - it's a game-changer, especially for those of us managing diabetes.

Here's why the air fryer became my kitchen superhero, and why I think it can be yours too:

- **Healthier Cooking, Less Oil:** The magic of the air fryer lies in its ability to create that coveted crispiness with a fraction of the oil used in traditional frying methods. For those of us watching our blood sugar levels, reducing unnecessary fats and oils is a big win.

- **Balanced Nutrition:** These recipes aren't just about ditching the frying pan - they're also about nourishing your body. The air fryer helps retain the nutrients in your food, keeping your meals rich in vitamins and minerals that contribute to your overall well-being.

- **Ease of Use:** Let's face it - not all of us are seasoned chefs. The air fryer is remarkably user-friendly. Just pop your ingredients in, set the time and temperature, and let it work its magic. No more standing over a hot stove for hours!

- **Time-Saving:** With our busy lives, convenience is key. The air fryer speeds up cooking times, ensuring that you can enjoy a home-cooked, diabetes-friendly meal without spending hours in the kitchen.

- **Versatility:** This little appliance isn't limited to just one type of dish. From crispy vegetables to juicy proteins and even baked goods, the air fryer's versatility will surprise you.

- **Less Mess:** Cleaning up after cooking can be a hassle. With the air fryer, you'll have fewer pots and pans to scrub - a true blessing after a long day.

- **Flavor Explosion:** The air fryer isn't just about health; it's about taste too. You'll be amazed at the depth of flavors that develop in your dishes, making every bite a delight.

- **Diabetes-Friendly Options:** Crafting recipes with diabetes in mind was my priority. The air fryer lets you create meals that are lower in carbs, sugars, and unhealthy fats, helping you manage your condition without compromising on taste.

So, if you're ready to take control of your diet, explore new flavors, and embrace a healthier lifestyle, I urge you to give the air fryer a chance. Let it be your partner in the kitchen, guiding you toward diabetes-friendly creations that are as delightful as they are nourishing. The air fryer is more than an appliance; it's a tool for transformation.

Remember, every small step you take toward healthier eating is a victory. And with the air fryer, those steps are not only easier but also more delectable than you could have ever imagined. So, join me in this air fryer journey, and let's savor the taste of health, one crispy bite at a time.

Air Fryer Functions on Diabetes

In your hands lies an appliance that's poised to revolutionize your culinary journey - the air fryer. This compact marvel boasts a range of functions that not only tantalize your taste buds but also play a pivotal role in managing diabetes.

Function 1: Frying with Less Guilt

The air fryer's ability to replicate the crispy textures of frying while using a fraction of the oil is a boon for those with diabetes. With traditional frying methods, the excessive oil can send blood sugar levels soaring. But with the air fryer, you can enjoy your favorite fried treats with significantly reduced oil content, mitigating the impact on your glucose levels.

Function 2: Roasting for Flavorful Satisfaction

Roasting is an art that an air fryer elevates to new heights. Imagine tender cuts of meat, succulent vegetables, and aromatic herbs - all roasted to perfection with minimal oil. This cooking method not only retains the natural flavors but also enhances the sensory experience of your meals. For those managing diabetes, this means a pathway to savoring delicious, low-carb dishes that keep blood sugar spikes at bay.

Function 3: Baking with a Healthier Twist

The air fryer is not just about savory dishes; it's your partner in creating healthier baked goods. From whole-grain muffins to almond flour bread, baking in the air fryer achieves the desired texture and taste with reduced carbohydrates. For individuals watching their sugar intake, this translates to guilt-free indulgence in treats that don't compromise on flavor.

Function 4: Grilling for Leaner Delights

Grilling imparts that smoky essence we all love, and the air fryer lets you achieve it with ease. With its grilling capabilities, you can enjoy lean proteins like chicken and fish with tantalizing grill marks and flavors, minus the heavy marinades or sauces that could spike your blood sugar. It's a gateway to leaner, protein-packed meals that are diabetes-friendly and delectable.

Function 5: Reheating with Crispy Revival

Leftovers often suffer a loss of texture and taste when reheated. But fear not - the air fryer rekindles their crispy glory. Whether it's a slice of pizza or a portion of roasted vegetables, reheating in the air fryer rejuvenates their crunch, giving new life to yesterday's flavors.

For those navigating diabetes, dietary choices are paramount. The air fryer bridges the gap between health-conscious cooking and tantalizing flavors. By reducing oil consumption, enhancing flavors, and offering versatile cooking methods, this appliance becomes a tool of empowerment in managing your condition.

Each crispy bite, each succulent morsel created in the air fryer carries the promise of keeping your blood sugar levels in check. It's a culinary journey that emphasizes pleasure without compromise, and it aligns perfectly with your diabetes management goals.

Master Your Air Fryer

Let's embark on a journey through the ins and outs of using your air fryer to craft delectable dishes that cater to your diabetes management needs.

Step 1: Preheating for Success

Just like a symphony needs a conductor, your air fryer needs preheating. Set the temperature to the desired level and let it warm up for a few minutes. Preheating ensures that your food starts cooking the moment it enters the appliance, ensuring even and efficient cooking.

Step 2: Prep and Season Your Ingredients

Prepare your ingredients with care, washing, chopping, and seasoning as needed. A light drizzle of heart-healthy oil - such as olive oil - can enhance the crispiness without compromising on health. Don't forget to add your favorite herbs and spices to infuse each bite with flavor.

Step 3: Choose Your Cooking Temperature

Select the cooking temperature based on your recipe's recommendations. Air fryers usually reach temperatures of 180°C to 200°C (360°F to 400°F), ensuring that your creations are cooked to perfection with that coveted crispy exterior.

Step 4: Set the Cooking Time

Set the cooking time according to your recipe's guidelines. Remember, air fryers work faster than conventional ovens, so be vigilant to prevent overcooking. As you gain experience, you'll intuitively adjust cooking times to achieve your desired results.

Step 5: Arrange Your Ingredients

Place your seasoned ingredients in a single layer in the air fryer's basket or tray. Ensure that each piece has ample space for the hot air to circulate freely, resulting in even cooking and a uniform crispiness.

Step 6: Monitor and Toss

During the cooking process, monitor your creation's progress. For dishes that require even browning on all sides, use tongs to toss, shake, or flip the ingredients. This simple action ensures that every inch of your dish achieves that delightful crunch.

Step 7: The Aroma of Success

As the cooking time approaches its end, your kitchen will be filled with tantalizing aromas. Keep a close eye on your creation, ensuring that it reaches the perfect level of crispiness that you desire.

Step 8: Savory Satisfaction

Once your dish is perfectly cooked, carefully remove it from the air fryer using tongs or a spatula. Give it a moment to cool down before indulging in the symphony of flavors and textures you've orchestrated.

Step 9: Cleanup and Care

After your culinary masterpiece has been enjoyed, let your air fryer cool down before cleaning. Most models feature nonstick surfaces, making cleanup a breeze. Ensure that all parts are properly dried before reassembling the appliance.

Step 10: Embrace Culinary Exploration

Your journey with the air fryer is a voyage of discovery. Embrace the experimentation, the learning curve, and the moments of culinary triumph. As you become more acquainted with your appliance, you'll unlock its full potential to create dishes that celebrate both your health and your taste buds.

With your air fryer cookbook as your guide, you're poised to whip up meals that marry health and flavor seamlessly. Get ready to savor each bite, knowing that your culinary creations are contributing to your diabetes management goals in the most delightful way.

Precautions for Safe Handling

As you dive into the world of air frying, it's essential to wield your newfound culinary power responsibly. While air fryers offer a host of benefits, adhering to a few precautions ensures that your cooking endeavors remain not only delicious but safe as well.

1. Location Matters

Place your air fryer on a stable, flat surface, away from flammable materials like kitchen towels and curtains. Adequate ventilation is crucial to prevent overheating, so avoid using the appliance against a wall or inside a cabinet.

2. Read the Manual

Every air fryer model has its unique features and operating instructions. Before embarking on your cooking journey, take the time to read the user manual thoroughly. This ensures that you're aware of the appliance's functions, safety guidelines, and maintenance requirements.

3. Avoid Overcrowding

Resist the temptation to pack the air fryer basket with ingredients. Overcrowding hampers proper air circulation, leading to uneven cooking results. Opt for a single layer or cook in batches if necessary.

4. Watch for Hot Surfaces

Air fryers become hot during operation. Use oven mitts or tongs when handling the basket or tray, and avoid touching the exterior while it's cooking.

5. Preheat with Care

While preheating is a crucial step, be mindful of the high heat generated during this process. Keep flammable materials and your hands away from the air fryer until it's fully preheated.

6. Protect Your Countertop

Place a heat-resistant mat or trivet under your air fryer to protect your countertop from potential heat damage.

7. Minimize Oil Splatters

Certain ingredients might release moisture during cooking, leading to oil splatters. Ensure your ingredients are as dry as possible before placing them in the air fryer to minimize splattering.

8. Monitor Cooking Progress

Though air fryers are relatively low-maintenance, it's important to keep an eye on your cooking. This not only ensures that your dish doesn't overcook but also prevents any unexpected incidents.

9. Handle the Basket with Care

When removing the basket during or after cooking, be cautious of the hot components. Using oven mitts or heat-resistant gloves is advisable.

10. Choose Appropriate Utensils

Use utensils made of heat-resistant materials when stirring or flipping ingredients within the air fryer. Avoid using metal utensils that can scratch the nonstick coating.

11. Mind the Cord

Keep the power cord away from the hot surfaces of the air fryer. Make sure the cord isn't tangled or positioned where it might get snagged or damaged.

12. Unplug When Not in Use

When you've completed your cooking, ensure that your air fryer is unplugged before cleaning or storing. This minimizes the risk of electrical hazards.

By observing these precautions, you're not only safeguarding yourself and your kitchen but also ensuring that your air frying experiences are a seamless blend of culinary creativity and safety. Happy and secure cooking!

CHAPTER 3
BREAKFAST

Zucchini Fritters

Prep time: 15 minutes, Cook time: 7 minutes, Serves 4

10½ ounces zucchini, grated and squeezed
7 ounces low-fat Mozzarella cheese
¼ cup whole wheat flour
2 eggs
1 tsp. fresh dill, minced
Salt and black pepper, to taste

1. Preheat the Air fryer to 360°F (182°C) and grease an Air Fryer basket.
2. Mix together all the ingredients in a large bowl.
3. Make small fritters from this mixture and place them on the prepared Air Fryer basket.
4. Bake for about 7 minutes.
5. Dish out and serve warm.

Nutrition Info per Serving:

Calories: 250, Fat: 17.2g, Carbohydrates: 10g, Sugar: 2.7g, Protein: 15.2g, Sodium: 330mg

Golden Avocado Tempura

Prep time: 5 minutes, Cook time: 10 minutes, Serves 4

½ cup bread crumbs
½ tsp. salt
1 Haas avocado, pitted, peeled and sliced
Liquid from 1 can white beans

1. Preheat the air fryer to 350°F (177°C).
2. Mix the bread crumbs and salt in a shallow bowl until well-incorporated.
3. Dip the avocado slices in the bean liquid, then into the bread crumbs.
4. Put the avocados in the air fryer, taking care not to overlap any slices, and air fry for 10 minutes, giving the basket a good shake at the halfway point.
5. Serve immediately.

Nutrition Info per Serving:

Calories: 190, Protein: 4g, Fat: 10g, Carbohydrates: 22g, Fiber: 5g, Sugar: 0.5g, Sodium: 410mg

Gold Avocado

Prep time: 5 minutes, Cook time: 6 minutes, Serves 4

2 large avocados, sliced
¼ tsp. paprika
Salt and ground black pepper, to taste
½ cup whole wheat flour
2 eggs, beaten
1 cup bread crumbs

1. Preheat the air fryer to 400°F (204°C).
2. Sprinkle paprika, salt and pepper on the slices of avocado.
3. Lightly coat the avocados with flour. Dredge them in the eggs, before covering with bread crumbs.
4. Transfer to the air fryer and air fry for 6 minutes.
5. Serve warm.

Nutrition Info per Serving:

Calories: 301, Protein: 8g, Fat: 18g, Carbohydrates: 29g, Fiber: 7g, Sugar: 2g, Sodium: 290mg

Veggie Pita Sandwich

Prep time: 10 minutes, Cook time: 9 to 12 minutes, Serves 4

1 baby eggplant, peeled and chopped
1 red bell pepper, sliced
½ cup diced red onion
½ cup shredded carrot
1 tsp. olive oil
⅓ cup low-fat Greek yogurt
½ tsp. dried tarragon
2 low-sodium whole-wheat pita breads, halved crosswise

1. Preheat the air fryer to 390°F (199°C).
2. In a baking pan, stir together the eggplant, red bell pepper, red onion, carrot, and olive oil. Put the vegetable mixture into the air fryer basket and roast for 7 to 9 minutes, stirring once, until the vegetables are tender. Drain if necessary.
3. In a small bowl, thoroughly mix the yogurt and tarragon until well combined.
4. Stir the yogurt mixture into the vegetables. Stuff one-fourth of this mixture into each pita pocket.
5. Place the sandwiches in the air fryer and bake for 2 to 3 minutes, or until the bread is toasted.
6. Serve immediately.

Nutrition Info per Serving:

Calories: 133, Protein: 4g, Fat: 3g, Carbohydrates: 24g, Fiber: 4g, Sugar: 5g, Sodium: 132mg

Indian Masala Omelet

Prep time: 10 minutes, Cook time: 12 minutes, Serves 2

4 large eggs
½ cup diced onion
½ cup diced tomato
¼ cup chopped fresh cilantro
1 jalapeño, deseeded and finely chopped
½ tsp. ground turmeric
½ tsp. kosher salt
½ tsp. cayenne pepper
Olive oil, for greasing the pan

1. Preheat the air fryer to 250°F (121°C). Generously grease a 3-cup Bundt pan.
2. In a large bowl, beat the eggs. Stir in the onion, tomato, cilantro, jalapeño, turmeric, salt, and cayenne.
3. Pour the egg mixture into the prepared pan. Place the pan in the air fryer basket. Bake for 12 minutes, or until the eggs are cooked through. Carefully unmold and cut the omelet into four pieces.
4. Serve immediately.

Nutrition Info per Serving:

Calories: 166, Protein: 13g, Fat: 11g, Carbohydrates: 4g, Fiber: 1g, Sugar: 2g, Sodium: 399mg

Supreme Breakfast Burrito

Prep time: 15 minutes, Cook time: 8 minutes, Serves 2

2 eggs
2 whole-wheat tortillas
4-ounces chicken breast slices, cooked
¼ of avocado, peeled, pitted and sliced
2 tbsps. low-fat mozzarella cheese, grated
2 tbsps. salsa
Salt and black pepper, to taste

1. Preheat the Air fryer at 390ºF (199ºC).
2. Whisk together eggs with salt and black pepper in a bowl and transfer into a small shallow nonstick pan.
3. Arrange the pan into an Air fryer basket and bake for about 5 minutes.
4. Remove eggs from the pan and arrange the tortillas onto a smooth surface.
5. Divide the eggs in each tortilla, followed by chicken slice, avocado, salsa and mozzarella cheese.
6. Roll up each tortilla tightly and set the Air fryer at 355ºF (179ºC).
7. Line an Air fryer tray with a foil paper and arrange the burrito in the prepared tray.
8. Place in the Air fryer and air fry for about 3 minutes until the tortillas become golden brown.

Nutrition Info per Serving:
Calories: 281, Fat: 13g, Carbohydrates: 15.4g, Sugar: 1.8g, Protein: 26.2g, Sodium: 249mg

Breakfast Zucchini

Prep time: 5 minutes, Cook time: 25 minutes, Serves 4

4 zucchinis, diced into 1-inch pieces, drained
2 small bell peppers, chopped medium
2 small onions, chopped medium
Cooking oil spray
Pinch salt and black pepper

1. Preheat the Air fryer to 350ºF (177ºC) and grease the Air fryer basket with cooking spray.
2. Season the zucchini with salt and black pepper and place in the Air fryer basket.
3. Roast for about 20 minutes, stirring occasionally.
4. Add onion and bell pepper and roast for 5 more minutes.
5. Remove from the Air fryer and mix well to serve warm.

Nutrition Info per Serving:
Calories: 146, Fat: 0.5g, Carbohydrates: 3.8g, Sugar: 5.5g, Protein: 4g, Sodium: 203mg

Pumpkin and Yogurt Bread

Prep time: 10 minutes, Cook time: 15 minutes, Serves 4

2 large eggs
8 tbsps. pumpkin puree
6 tbsps. banana flour
4 tbsps. nonfat plain Greek yogurt
6 tbsps. oats
4 tbsps. honey
2 tbsps. vanilla essence
Pinch of ground nutmeg

1. Preheat the Air fryer to 360ºF (182ºC) and grease a loaf pan.
2. Mix together all the ingredients except oats in a bowl and beat with the hand mixer until smooth.
3. Add oats and mix until well combined.
4. Transfer the mixture into the prepared loaf pan and place in the Air fryer.
5. Bake for about 15 minutes and remove from the Air fryer.
6. Place onto a wire rack to cool and cut the bread into desired size slices to serve.

Nutrition Info per Serving:
Calories: 212, Fat: 3.4g, Carbohydrates: 36g, Sugar: 20.5g, Protein: 6.6g, Sodium: 49mg

Spinach with Scrambled Eggs

Prep time: 10 minutes, Cook time: 10 minutes, Serves 2

2 tbsps. olive oil
4 eggs, whisked
5 ounces (142 g) fresh spinach, chopped
1 medium tomato, chopped
1 tsp. fresh lemon juice
½ tsp. coarse salt
½ tsp. ground black pepper
½ cup of fresh basil, roughly chopped

1. Grease a baking pan with the oil, tilting it to spread the oil around. Preheat the air fryer to 280ºF (138ºC).
2. Mix the remaining ingredients, apart from the basil leaves, whisking well until everything is completely combined.
3. Bake in the air fryer for 10 minutes.
4. Top with fresh basil leaves before serving.

Nutrition Info per Serving:
Calories: 287, Protein: 14g, Fat: 21g, Carbohydrates: 9g, Fiber: 3g, Sugar: 3g, Sodium: 626mg

Tofu and Mushroom Omelet

Prep time: 15 minutes, Cook time: 28 minutes, Serves 2

¼ of onion, chopped
8 ounces silken tofu, pressed and sliced
3½ ounces fresh mushrooms, sliced
3 eggs, beaten
2 tbsps. low-fat milk
2 tsps. canola oil
1 garlic clove, minced
Salt and black pepper, to taste

1. Preheat the Air fryer to 360ºF (182ºC) and grease an Air Fryer pan.
2. Heat oil in the Air Fryer pan and add garlic and onion.
3. Air fry for about 3 minutes and stir in the tofu and mushrooms.
4. Season with salt and black pepper and top with the beaten eggs.
5. Bake for about 25 minutes, poking the eggs twice in between.
6. Dish out and serve warm.

Nutrition Info per Serving:
Calories: 224, Fat: 14.5g, Carbohydrates: 6.6g, Sugar: 3.4g, Protein: 17.9g, Sodium: 214mg

Mustard Meatballs

Prep time: 15 minutes, Cook time: 15 minutes, Serves 4

½ pound ground pork
1 onion, chopped
2 tbsps. fresh basil, chopped
½ tbsp. low-fat cheddar cheese, grated
½ tbsp. low-fat Parmesan cheese, grated
1 tsp. garlic paste
1 tsp. mustard
1 tsp. honey
Salt and black pepper, to taste

1. Preheat the Air fryer to 395ºF (202ºC).
2. Mix together all the ingredients in a bowl until well combined.
3. Make small equal-sized balls from the mixture and arrange in an Air fryer basket.
4. Air fry for about 15 minutes until golden brown and serve hot.

Nutrition Info per Serving:
Calories: 110, Fat: 2.9g, Carbohydrates: 4.6g, Sugar: 2.7g, Protein: 15.9g, Sodium: 45mg

Cauliflower Hash Brown

Prep time: 20 minutes, Cook time: 10 minutes, Serves 4

2 cups cauliflower, finely grated, soaked and drained
2 tbsps. xanthan gum
Salt, to taste
Pepper powder, to taste
2 tsps. chili flakes
1 tsp. garlic
1 tsp. onion powder
2 tsps. vegetable oil

1. Preheat the Air fryer to 300ºF (149ºC) and grease an Air fryer basket with oil.
2. Heat vegetable oil in a nonstick pan and add cauliflower.
3. Sauté for about 4 minutes and dish out the cauliflower in a plate.
4. Mix the cauliflower with xanthum gum, salt, chili flakes, garlic and onion powder.
5. Mix well and refrigerate the hash for about 20 minutes.
6. Place the hash in the Air fryer basket and air fry for about 10 minutes.
7. Flip the hash after cooking half way through and dish out to serve warm.

Nutrition Info per Serving:
Calories: 291, Fat: 2.8g, Carbohydrates: 6.5g, Sugar: 4.5g, Protein: 6.6g, Sodium: 62mg

Spinach Omelet

Prep time: 10 minutes, Cook time: 10 minutes, Serves 1

1 tsp. olive oil
3 eggs
Salt and ground black pepper, to taste
1 tbsp. low-fat ricotta cheese
¼ cup chopped spinach
1 tbsp. chopped parsley

1. Grease the air fryer basket with olive oil. Preheat the air fryer to 330ºF (166ºC).
2. In a bowl, beat the eggs with a fork and sprinkle salt and pepper.
3. Add the ricotta, spinach, and parsley and then transfer to the air fryer. Bake for 10 minutes or until the egg is set.
4. Serve warm.

Nutrition Info per Serving:
Calories: 235, Protein: 18g, Fat: 15g, Carbohydrates: 3g, Fiber: 1g, Sugar: 1g, Sodium: 367mg

Luscious Scrambled Eggs

Prep time: 10 minutes, Cook time: 10 minutes, Serves 2

2 tbsps. almond butter
4 eggs
¼ cup fresh mushrooms, chopped finely
2 tbsps. low-fat Parmesan cheese, shredded
¼ cup tomato, chopped finely
Salt and black pepper, to taste

1. Preheat the Air fryer at 285ºF (140ºC) and grease a baking pan.
2. Whisk together eggs with salt and black pepper in a bowl.
3. Melt almond butter in the baking pan and add whisked eggs, mushrooms, tomatoes and cheese.
4. Transfer in the Air fryer and bake for about 10 minutes.
5. Remove from the Air fryer and serve warm.

Nutrition Info per Serving:
Calories: 254, Fat: 21.7g, Carbohydrates: 2.1g, Sugar: 1.4g, Protein: 13.7g, Sodium: 267mg

Avocado Quesadillas

Prep time: 10 minutes, Cook time: 11 minutes, Serves 4

4 eggs
2 tbsps. skim milk
Salt and ground black pepper, to taste
Cooking spray
4 whole wheat flour tortillas
4 tbsps. salsa
2 ounces (57 g) low-fat Cheddar cheese, grated
½ small avocado, peeled and thinly sliced

1. Preheat the air fryer to 270ºF (132ºC).
2. Beat together the eggs, milk, salt, and pepper.
3. Spray a baking pan lightly with cooking spray and add egg mixture.
4. Bake for 8 minutes, stirring every 1 to 2 minutes, until eggs are scrambled to the liking. Remove and set aside.
5. Spray one side of each tortilla with cooking spray. Flip over.
6. Divide eggs, salsa, cheese, and avocado among the tortillas, covering only half of each tortilla.
7. Fold each tortilla in half and press down lightly. Increase the temperature of the air fryer to 390ºF (199ºC).
8. Put 2 tortillas in air fryer basket and air fry for 3 minutes or until cheese melts and outside feels slightly crispy. Repeat with remaining two tortillas.
9. Cut each cooked tortilla into halves. Serve warm.

Nutrition Info per Serving:
Calories: 308, Protein: 16g, Fat: 15g, Carbohydrates: 30g, Fiber: 6g, Sugar: 2g, Sodium: 462mg

Air Fryer Breakfast Bake

Prep time: 15 minutes, Cook time: 25 minutes, Serves 2

4 eggs
1 slice whole wheat bread, torn into pieces
1½ cups baby spinach
⅓ cup low-fat cheddar cheese, shredded
½ cup bell pepper, diced
½ tsp. kosher salt
1 tsp. hot sauce

1. Preheat the Air fryer to 250ºF (121ºC) and grease a 6-inch soufflé dish with nonstick cooking spray.
2. Whisk together eggs, salt and hot sauce in a bowl.
3. Dip the bread pieces, spinach, ¼ cup cheddar cheese and bell pepper in the whisked eggs.
4. Pour this mixture into prepared soufflé dish and sprinkle with remaining cheese.
5. Transfer into the Air fryer basket and bake for about 25 minutes.
6. Remove from the Air fryer basket and let it rest for 10 minutes before serving.

Nutrition Info per Serving:
Calories: 249, Fat: 15.7g, Carbohydrates: 10.3g, Sugar: 3.4g, Protein: 18.2g, Sodium: 979mg

Delish Mushroom Frittata

Prep time: 15 minutes, Cook time: 17 minutes, Serves 2

½ red onion, sliced thinly
2 cups button mushrooms, sliced thinly
3 eggs
Cooking spray, as required
3 tbsps. low-fat Ricotta cheese, crumbled
1 tbsp. olive oil
Salt, to taste

1. Preheat the Air fryer at 330ºF (166ºC) and grease a 6-inch ramekin with cooking spray.
2. Heat olive oil on medium heat in a skillet and add onion and mushrooms.
3. Sauté for about 5 minutes and dish out the mushroom mixture in a bowl.
4. Whisk together eggs and salt in a small bowl and transfer into prepared ramekin.
5. Place the mushroom mixture over the eggs and top with Ricotta cheese.
6. Arrange the ramekin in Air fryer basket and bake for about 12 minutes.
7. Dish out and serve hot.

Nutrition Info per Serving:
Calories: 220, Fat: 17.1g, Carbohydrates: 6g, Sugar: 3.5g, Protein: 12.8g, Sodium: 332mg

Fluffy Cheesy Omelet

Prep time: 10 minutes, Cook time: 15 minutes, Serves 2

4 eggs
1 large onion, sliced
⅛ cup low-fat cheddar cheese, grated
⅛ cup low-fat mozzarella cheese, grated
Cooking spray
¼ tsp. soy sauce
Freshly ground black pepper, to taste

1. Preheat the Air fryer to 360ºF (182ºC) and grease a pan with cooking spray.
2. Whisk together eggs, soy sauce and black pepper in a bowl.
3. Place onions in the pan and air fry for about 10 minutes.
4. Pour the egg mixture over onion slices and top evenly with cheese.
5. Bake for about 5 more minutes and serve.

Nutrition Info per Serving:
Calories: 216, Fat: 13.8g, Carbohydrates: 7.9g, Sugar: 3.9g, Protein: 15.5g, Sodium: 251mg

Onion Omelet

Prep time: 10 minutes, Cook time: 12 minutes, Serves 2

3 eggs
Salt and ground black pepper, to taste
½ tsps. soy sauce
1 large onion, chopped
2 tbsps. grated Cheddar cheese
Cooking spray

1. Preheat the air fryer to 355ºF (179ºC).
2. In a bowl, whisk together the eggs, salt, pepper, and soy sauce.
3. Spritz a small pan with cooking spray. Spread the chopped onion across the bottom of the pan, then transfer the pan to the air fryer.
4. Bake in the preheated air fryer for 6 minutes or until the onion is translucent.
5. Add the egg mixture on top of the onions to coat well. Add the cheese on top, then continue baking for another 6 minutes.
6. Allow to cool before serving.

Nutrition Info per Serving:
Calories: 173, Protein: 12g, Fat: 11g, Carbohydrates: 7g, Fiber: 1g, Sugar: 3g, Sodium: 348mg

Lettuce Fajita Meatball Wraps

Prep time: 10 minutes, Cook time: 10 minutes, Serves 4

1 pound (454 g) 85% lean ground beef
½ cup salsa, plus more for serving
¼ cup chopped onions
¼ cup diced green or red bell peppers
1 large egg, beaten
1 tsp. fine sea salt
½ tsp. chili powder
½ tsp. ground cumin
1 clove garlic, minced
Cooking spray
For Serving:
8 leaves Boston lettuce
Pico de gallo or salsa
Lime slices

1. Preheat the air fryer to 350ºF (177ºC). Spray the air fryer basket with cooking spray.
2. In a large bowl, mix together all the ingredients until well combined.
3. Shape the meat mixture into eight 1-inch balls. Place the meatballs in the air fryer basket, leaving a little space between them. Air fry for 10 minutes, or until cooked through and no longer pink inside and the internal temperature reaches 145ºF (63ºC).
4. Serve each meatball on a lettuce leaf, topped with pico de gallo or salsa. Serve with lime slices.

Nutrition Info per Serving:
Calories: 272, Protein: 19g, Fat: 18g, Carbohydrates: 7g, Fiber: 2g, Sugar: 3g, Sodium: 574mg

Tomato and Mozzarella Bruschetta

Prep time: 5 minutes, Cook time: 4 minutes, Serves 1

6 small loaf slices
½ cup tomatoes, finely chopped
3 ounces (85 g) low-fat Mozzarella cheese, grated
1 tbsp. fresh basil, chopped
1 tbsp. olive oil

1. Preheat the air fryer to 350ºF (177ºC).
2. Put the loaf slices inside the air fryer and air fry for about 3 minutes.
3. Add the tomato, Mozzarella, basil, and olive oil on top.
4. Air fry for an additional minute before serving.

Nutrition Info per Serving:
Calories: 369, Protein: 16g, Fat: 21g, Carbohydrates: 30g, Fiber: 2g, Sugar: 3g, Sodium: 452mg

Tuna and Lettuce Wraps

Prep time: 10 minutes, Cook time: 4 to 7 minutes, Serves 4

1 pound (454 g) fresh tuna steak, cut into 1-inch cubes
1 tbsp. grated fresh ginger
2 garlic cloves, minced
½ tsp. toasted sesame oil
4 low-sodium whole-wheat tortillas
¼ cup low-fat mayonnaise
2 cups shredded romaine lettuce
1 red bell pepper, thinly sliced

1. Preheat the air fryer to 390°F (199°C).
2. In a medium bowl, mix the tuna, ginger, garlic, and sesame oil. Let it stand for 10 minutes.
3. Air fry the tuna in the air fryer basket for 4 to 7 minutes, or until lightly browned.
4. Make the wraps with the tuna, tortillas, mayonnaise, lettuce, and bell pepper.
5. Serve immediately.

Nutrition Info per Serving:

Calories: 291, Protein: 25g, Fat: 11g, Carbohydrates: 21g, Fiber: 4g, Sugar: 3g, Sodium: 339mg

Cheesy Greens Sandwich

Prep time: 15 minutes, Cook time: 10 to 13 minutes, Serves 4

1½ cups chopped mixed greens
2 garlic cloves, thinly sliced
2 tsps. olive oil
2 slices low-sodium low-fat Swiss cheese
4 slices low-sodium whole-wheat bread
Cooking spray

1. Preheat the air fryer to 400°F (204°C).
2. In a baking pan, mix the greens, garlic, and olive oil. Air fry for 4 to 5 minutes, stirring once, until the vegetables are tender. Drain, if necessary.
3. Make 2 sandwiches, dividing half of the greens and 1 slice of Swiss cheese between 2 slices of bread. Lightly spray the outsides of the sandwiches with cooking spray.
4. Bake the sandwiches in the air fryer for 6 to 8 minutes, turning with tongs halfway through, until the bread is toasted and the cheese melts.
5. Cut each sandwich in half and serve.

Nutrition Info per Serving:

Calories: 226, Protein: 11g, Fat: 9g, Carbohydrates: 28g, Fiber: 5g, Sugar: 3g, Sodium: 300mg

Veggie Salsa Wraps

Prep time: 5 minutes, Cook time: 7 minutes, Serves 4

1 cup red onion, sliced
1 zucchini, chopped
1 poblano pepper, deseeded and finely chopped
1 head lettuce
½ cup salsa
8 ounces (227 g) low-fat Mozzarella cheese

1. Preheat the air fryer to 390°F (199°C).
2. Place the red onion, zucchini, and poblano pepper in the air fryer basket and air fry for 7 minutes, or until they are tender and fragrant.
3. Divide the veggie mixture among the lettuce leaves and spoon the salsa over the top. Finish off with Mozzarella cheese. Wrap the lettuce leaves around the filling.
4. Serve immediately.

Nutrition Info per Serving:

Calories: 109, Protein: 9g, Fat: 5g, Carbohydrates: 10g, Fiber: 3g, Sugar: 5g, Sodium: 327mg

Heirloom Tomato Sandwiches with Pesto

Prep time: 20 minutes, Cook time: 16 minutes, Serves 4

3 tbsps. pine nuts
½ cup fresh basil, chopped
½ cup fresh parsley, chopped
2 heirloom tomatoes, cut into ½ inch thick slices
8-ounce low-fat Ricotta cheese, cut into ½ inch thick slices
½ cup plus 2 tbsps. olive oil, divided
Salt, to taste
1 garlic clove, chopped

1. Preheat the Air fryer to 390°F (199°C) and grease an Air fryer basket.
2. Mix together 1 tbsp. of olive oil, pine nuts and pinch of salt in a bowl.
3. Place pine nuts in the Air fryer and roast for about 2 minutes.
4. Put the pine nuts, remaining oil, fresh basil, fresh parsley, garlic and salt and pulse until combined.
5. Dish out the pesto in a bowl, cover and refrigerate.
6. Spread 1 tbsp. of pesto on each tomato slice and top with a Ricotta slice and onion.
7. Drizzle with olive oil and arrange the prepared tomato slices in the Air fryer basket.
8. Air fry for about 14 minutes and serve with remaining pesto.

Nutrition Info per Serving:

Calories: 559, Fat: 55.7g, Carbohydrates: 8g, Sugar: 2.6g, Protein: 11.8g, Sodium: 787mg

CHAPTER 4
FISH AND SEAFOOD

Crab Cakes with Sriracha Mayonnaise

Prep time: 15 minutes, Cook time: 10 minutes, Serves 4

For the Sriracha Mayonnaise:
1 cup mayonnaise
1 tbsp. sriracha
1½ tsps. freshly squeezed lemon juice
For the Crab Cakes:
1 tsp. extra-virgin olive oil
¼ cup finely diced red bell pepper
¼ cup diced onion
¼ cup diced celery
1 pound (454 g) lump crab meat
1 tsp. Old Bay seasoning
1 egg
1½ tsps. freshly squeezed lemon juice
1¾ cups panko bread crumbs, divided
Vegetable oil, for spraying

1. Mix the mayonnaise, sriracha, and lemon juice in a small bowl. Place ⅔ cup of the mixture in a separate bowl to form the base of the crab cakes. Cover the remaining sriracha mayonnaise and refrigerate. (This will become dipping sauce for the crab cakes once they are cooked.)
2. Heat the olive oil in a heavy-bottomed, medium skillet over medium-high heat. Add the bell pepper, onion, and celery and sauté for 3 minutes. Transfer the vegetables to the bowl with the reserved ⅔ cup of sriracha mayonnaise. Mix in the crab, Old Bay seasoning, egg, and lemon juice. Add 1 cup of the panko. Form the crab mixture into 8 cakes. Dredge the cakes in the remaining ¾ cup of panko, turning to coat. Place on a baking sheet. Cover and refrigerate for at least 1 hour and up to 8 hours.
3. Preheat the air fryer to 375ºF (191ºC). Spray the air fryer basket with oil. Working in batches as needed so as not to overcrowd the basket, place the chilled crab cakes in a single layer in the basket. Spray the crab cakes with oil. Bake until golden brown, 8 to 10 minutes, carefully turning halfway through cooking. Remove to a platter and keep warm. Repeat with the remaining crab cakes as needed. Serve the crab cakes immediately with sriracha mayonnaise dipping sauce.

Nutrition Info per Serving:

Calories: 382, Protein: 21g, Fat: 23g, Carbohydrates: 23g, Fiber: 1g, Sugar: 3g, Sodium: 621mg

Crispy Coconut Shrimp

Prep time: 15 minutes, Cook time: 8 minutes, Serves 4

For the Sweet Chili Mayo:
3 tbsps. mayonnaise
3 tbsps. Thai sweet chili sauce
1 tbsp. Sriracha sauce
For the Shrimp:
⅔ cup sweetened shredded coconut
⅔ cup panko bread crumbs
Kosher salt, to taste
2 tbsps. whole wheat flour
2 large eggs
24 extra-jumbo shrimp (about 1 pound / 454 g), peeled and deveined
Cooking spray

1. In a medium bowl, combine the mayonnaise, Thai sweet chili sauce, and Sriracha and mix well.
2. In another medium bowl, combine the coconut, panko, and ¼ tsp. salt. Place the flour in a shallow bowl. Whisk the eggs in another shallow bowl.
3. Season the shrimp with ⅛ tsp. salt. Dip the shrimp in the flour, shaking off any excess, then into the egg. Coat in the coconut-panko mixture, gently pressing to adhere, then transfer to a large plate. Spray both sides of the shrimp with oil.
4. Preheat the air fryer to 360ºF (182ºC).
5. Working in batches, arrange a single layer of the shrimp in the air fryer basket. Air fry for about 8 minutes, flipping halfway, until the crust is golden brown and the shrimp are cooked through.
6. Serve with the sweet chili mayo for dipping.

Nutrition Info per Serving:

Calories: 272, Protein: 23g, Fat: 13g, Carbohydrates: 17g, Fiber: 1g, Sugar: 6g, Sodium: 421mg

Breaded Hake

Prep time: 15 minutes, Cook time: 12 minutes, Serves 2

1 egg
4 ounces breadcrumbs
4 (6-ounces) hake fillets
1 lemon, cut into wedges
2 tbsps. vegetable oil

1. Preheat the Air fryer to 350ºF (177ºC) and grease an Air fryer basket.
2. Whisk the egg in a shallow bowl and mix breadcrumbs and oil in another bowl.
3. Dip hake fillets into the whisked egg and then, dredge in the breadcrumb mixture.
4. Arrange the hake fillets into the Air fryer basket in a single layer and air fry for about 12 minutes.
5. Dish out the hake fillets onto serving plates and serve, garnished with lemon wedges.

Nutrition Info per Serving:

Calories: 300, Fats: 10.6g, Carbohydrates: 23g, Sugar: 2.2g, Proteins: 29.3g, Sodium: 439mg

Sesame Seeds Coated Haddock

Prep time: 15 minutes, Cook time: 14 minutes, Serves 4

4 tbsps. whole wheat flour
2 eggs
½ cup sesame seeds, toasted
½ cup breadcrumbs
4 (6-ounces) frozen haddock fillets
⅛ tsp. dried rosemary, crushed
Salt and ground black pepper, as required
3 tbsps. olive oil

1. Preheat the Air fryer to 390ºF (199ºC) and grease an Air fryer basket.
2. Place the flour in a shallow bowl and whisk the eggs in a second bowl.
3. Mix sesame seeds, breadcrumbs, rosemary, salt, black pepper and olive oil in a third bowl until a crumbly mixture is formed.
4. Coat each fillet with flour, dip into whisked eggs and finally, dredge into the breadcrumb mixture.
5. Arrange haddock fillets into the Air fryer basket in a single layer and roast for about 14 minutes, flipping once in between.
6. Dish out the haddock fillets onto serving plates and serve hot.

Nutrition Info per Serving:

Calories: 497, Fat: 24g, Carbohydrates: 20.1g, Sugar: 1.1g, Protein: 49.8g, Sodium: 319mg

Fried Shrimp

Prep time: 15 minutes, Cook time: 5 minutes, Serves 4

½ cup self-rising flour
1 tsp. paprika
1 tsp. salt
½ tsp. freshly ground black pepper
1 large egg, beaten
1 cup finely crushed panko bread crumbs
20 frozen large shrimp (about 1-pound / 907-g), peeled and deveined
Cooking spray

1. In a shallow bowl, whisk the flour, paprika, salt, and pepper until blended. Add the beaten egg to a second shallow bowl and the bread crumbs to a third.
2. One at a time, dip the shrimp into the flour, the egg, and the bread crumbs, coating thoroughly.
3. Preheat the air fryer to 400ºF (204ºC). Line the air fryer basket with parchment paper.
4. Place the shrimp on the parchment and spritz with oil.
5. Air fry for 2 minutes. Shake the basket, spritz the shrimp with oil, and air fry for 3 minutes more until lightly browned and crispy. Serve hot.

Nutrition Info per Serving:

Calories: 198, Protein: 17g, Fat: 7g, Carbohydrates: 17g, Fiber: 1g, Sugar: 1g, Sodium: 744mg

Homemade Fish Sticks

Prep time: 15 minutes, Cook time: 10 to 15 minutes, Serves 4

4 fish fillets
½ cup whole-wheat flour
1 tsp. seasoned salt
2 eggs
1½ cups whole-wheat panko bread crumbs
½ tbsp. dried parsley flakes
Cooking spray

1. Preheat the air fryer to 400ºF (204ºC). Spray the air fryer basket lightly with cooking spray.
2. Cut the fish fillets lengthwise into "sticks."
3. In a shallow bowl, mix the whole-wheat flour and seasoned salt.
4. In a small bowl, whisk the eggs with 1 tsp. of water.
5. In another shallow bowl, mix the panko bread crumbs and parsley flakes.
6. Coat each fish stick in the seasoned flour, then in the egg mixture, and dredge them in the panko bread crumbs.
7. Place the fish sticks in the air fryer basket in a single layer and lightly spray the fish sticks with cooking spray. You may need to cook them in batches.
8. Air fry for 5 to 8 minutes. Flip the fish sticks over and lightly spray with the cooking spray. Air fry until golden brown and crispy, 5 to 7 more minutes.
9. Serve warm.

Nutrition Info per Serving:

Calories: 242, Protein: 21g, Fat: 5g, Carbohydrates: 29g, Fiber: 4g, Sugar: 1g, Sodium: 602mg

Lemony Tuna

Prep time: 15 minutes, Cook time: 12 minutes, Serves 8

4 tbsps. fresh parsley, chopped
4 (6-ounce) cans water packed plain tuna
1 cup breadcrumbs
2 eggs
4 tsps. Dijon mustard
2 tbsps. fresh lime juice
6 tbsps. canola oil
Dash of hot sauce
Salt and black pepper, to taste

1. Preheat the Air fryer to 360ºF (182ºC) and grease an Air fryer basket.
2. Mix tuna fish, breadcrumbs, mustard, parsley, hot sauce, canola oil, eggs, salt and lime juice in a large bowl.
3. Make equal-sized patties from the mixture and refrigerate for about 3 hours.
4. Transfer the patties into the Air fryer basket and bake for about 12 minutes.
5. Dish out and serve warm.

Nutrition Info per Serving:

Calories: 388, Fat: 21.8g, Carbohydrates: 31.7g, Sugar: 1.2g, Protein: 14.2g, Sodium: 680mg

Roasted Fish with Almond-Lemon Crumbs

Prep time: 10 minutes, Cook time: 7 to 8 minutes, Serves 4

½ cup raw whole almonds
1 scallion, finely chopped
Grated zest and juice of 1 lemon
½ tbsp. extra-virgin olive oil
¾ tsp. kosher salt, divided
Freshly ground black pepper, to taste
4 (6 ounces / 170 g each) skinless fish fillets
Cooking spray
1 tsp. Dijon mustard

1. In a food processor, pulse the almonds to coarsely chop. Transfer to a small bowl and add the scallion, lemon zest, and olive oil. Season with ¼ tsp. of the salt and pepper to taste and mix to combine.
2. Spray the top of the fish with oil and squeeze the lemon juice over the fish. Season with the remaining ½ tsp. salt and pepper to taste. Spread the mustard on top of the fish. Dividing evenly, press the almond mixture onto the top of the fillets to adhere.
3. Preheat the air fryer to 375ºF (191ºC).
4. Working in batches, place the fillets in the air fryer basket in a single layer. Air fry for 7 to 8 minutes, until the crumbs start to brown and the fish is cooked through.
5. Serve immediately.

Nutrition Info per Serving:

Calories: 289, Protein: 32g, Fat: 16g, Carbohydrates: 6g, Fiber: 3g, Sugar: 1g, Sodium: 463mg

Simple Salmon

Prep time: 5 minutes, Cook time: 10 minutes, Serves 2

2 (6-ounces) salmon fillets
Salt and black pepper, as required
1 tbsp. olive oil

1. Preheat the Air fryer to 390ºF (199ºC) and grease an Air fryer basket.
2. Season each salmon fillet with salt and black pepper and drizzle with olive oil.
3. Arrange salmon fillets into the Air fryer basket and roast for about 10 minutes.
4. Remove from the Air fryer and dish out the salmon fillets onto the serving plates.

Nutrition Info per Serving:

Calories: 285, Fat: 17.5g, Carbohydrates: 0g, Sugar: 0g, Protein: 33g, Sodium: 153mg

Swordfish Skewers with Caponata

Prep time: 15 minutes, Cook time: 20 minutes, Serves 2

1 (10-ounce / 283-g) small Italian eggplant, cut into 1-inch pieces
6 ounces (170 g) cherry tomatoes
3 scallions, cut into 2 inches long
2 tbsps. extra-virgin olive oil, divided
Salt and pepper, to taste
12 ounces (340 g) skinless swordfish steaks, 1¼ inches thick, cut into 1-inch pieces
2 tsps. honey, divided
2 tsps. ground coriander, divided
1 tsp. grated lemon zest, divided
1 tsp. juice
4 (6-inch) wooden skewers
1 garlic clove, minced
½ tsp. ground cumin
1 tbsp. chopped fresh basil

1. Preheat the air fryer to 400ºF (204ºC).
2. Toss eggplant, tomatoes, and scallions with 1 tbsp. oil, ¼ tsp. salt, and ⅛ tsp. pepper in bowl; transfer to air fryer basket. Air fry until eggplant is softened and browned and tomatoes have begun to burst, about 14 minutes, tossing halfway through cooking. Transfer vegetables to cutting board and set aside to cool slightly.
3. Pat swordfish dry with paper towels. Combine 1 tsp. oil, 1 tsp. honey, 1 tsp. coriander, ½ tsp. lemon zest, ⅛ tsp. salt, and pinch pepper in a clean bowl. Add swordfish and toss to coat. Thread swordfish onto skewers, leaving about ¼ inch between each piece (3 or 4 pieces per skewer).
4. Arrange skewers in air fryer basket, spaced evenly apart. (Skewers may overlap slightly.) Return basket to air fryer and air fry until swordfish is browned and registers 140ºF (60ºC), 6 to 8 minutes, flipping and rotating skewers halfway through cooking.
5. Meanwhile, combine remaining 2 tsps. oil, remaining 1 tsp. honey, remaining 1 tsp. coriander, remaining ½ tsp. lemon zest, lemon juice, garlic, cumin, ¼ tsp. salt, and ⅛ tsp. pepper in large bowl. Microwave, stirring once, until fragrant, about 30 seconds. Coarsely chop the cooked vegetables, transfer to bowl with dressing, along with any accumulated juices, and gently toss to combine. Stir in basil and season with salt and pepper to taste. Serve skewers with caponata.

Nutrition Info per Serving:

Calories: 377, Protein: 34g, Fat: 19g, Carbohydrates: 18g, Fiber: 4g, Sugar: 10g, Sodium: 312mg

Vegetable and Fish Tacos

Prep time: 10 minutes, Cook time: 9 to 12 minutes, Serves 4

1 pound (454 g) white fish fillets
2 tsps. olive oil
3 tbsps. freshly squeezed lemon juice, divided
1½ cups chopped red cabbage
1 large carrot, grated
½ cup low-sodium salsa
⅓ cup low-fat Greek yogurt
4 soft low-sodium whole-wheat tortillas

1. Preheat the air fryer to 400°F (204°C).
2. Brush the fish with the olive oil and sprinkle with 1 tbsp. of lemon juice. Air fry in the air fryer basket for 9 to 12 minutes, or until the fish just flakes when tested with a fork.
3. Meanwhile, in a medium bowl, stir together the remaining 2 tbsps. of lemon juice, the red cabbage, carrot, salsa, and yogurt.
4. When the fish is cooked, remove it from the air fryer basket and break it up into large pieces.
5. Offer the fish, tortillas, and the cabbage mixture, and let each person assemble a taco.
6. Serve immediately.

Nutrition Info per Serving:

Calories: 301, Protein: 29g, Fat: 9g, Carbohydrates: 27g, Fiber: 6g, Sugar: 6g, Sodium: 446mg

Wasabi Crab Cakes

Prep time: 20 minutes, Cook time: 24 minutes, Serves 6

3 scallions, finely chopped
1 celery rib, finely chopped
⅓ cup plus ½ cup dry breadcrumbs, divided
2 large egg whites
1½ cups lump crab meat, drained
3 tbsps. mayonnaise
1 medium sweet red pepper, finely chopped
¼ tsp. prepared wasabi
Salt, to taste

1. Preheat the Air fryer to 375°F (191°C) and grease an Air fryer basket.
2. Mix scallions, red pepper, celery, ⅓ cup of breadcrumbs, egg whites, mayonnaise, wasabi, and salt in a large bowl.
3. Fold in the crab meat gently and mix well.
4. Place the remaining breadcrumbs in another bowl.
5. Make ¾-inch thick patties from the mixture and arrange half of the patties into the Air fryer basket.
6. Bake for about 12 minutes, flipping once halfway through and repeat with the remaining patties.
7. Dish out and serve warm.

Nutrition Info per Serving:

Calories: 112, Fat: 4g, Carbohydrates: 15.5g, Sugar: 2.7g, Protein: 4.9g, Sodium: 253mg

Chinese Style Cod

Prep time: 20 minutes, Cook time: 15 minutes, Serves 2

2 (7-ounces) cod fillets
1 cup water
2 scallions (green part), sliced
¼ cup fresh cilantro, chopped
Salt and black pepper, to taste
¼ tsp. sesame oil
5 little squares coconut sugar
5 tbsps. light soy sauce
1 tsp. dark soy sauce
3 tbsps. olive oil
5 ginger slices

1. Preheat the Air fryer to 355°F (179°C) and grease an Air fryer basket.
2. Season each cod fillet with salt and black pepper and drizzle with sesame oil.
3. Arrange the cod fillets into the Air fryer basket and air fry for about 12 minutes.
4. Bring water to boil and add coconut sugar and both soy sauces.
5. Cook until sugar is dissolved, continuously stirring and keep aside.
6. Dish out the cod fillets onto serving plates and top each fillet with cilantro and scallions.
7. Heat olive oil over medium heat in a small frying pan and add ginger slices.
8. Sauté for about 3 minutes and discard the ginger slices.
9. Drizzle the hot oil over cod fillets and top with the sauce mixture to serve.

Nutrition Info per Serving:

Calories: 433, Fat: 23.4g, Carbohydrates: 7.6g, Sugar: 4.2g, Protein: 48.2g, Sodium: 2001mg

Paprika Shrimp

Prep time: 10 minutes, Cook time: 10 minutes, Serves 2

1 pound tiger shrimp
2 tbsps. olive oil
½ tsp. smoked paprika
Salt, to taste

1. Preheat the Air fryer to 390°F (199°C) and grease an Air fryer basket.
2. Mix all the ingredients in a large bowl until well combined.
3. Place the shrimp in the Air fryer basket and air fry for about 10 minutes.
4. Dish out and serve warm.

Nutrition Info per Serving:

Calories: 173, Fat: 8.3g, Carbohydrates: 0.1g, Sugar: 0g, Protein: 23.8g, Sodium: 332mg

Crunchy Air Fried Cod Fillets

Prep time: 10 minutes, Cook time: 12 minutes, Serves 2

⅓ cup panko bread crumbs
1 tsp. vegetable oil
1 small shallot, minced
1 small garlic clove, minced
½ tsp. minced fresh thyme
Salt and pepper, to taste
1 tbsp. minced fresh parsley
1 tbsp. mayonnaise
1 large egg yolk
¼ tsp. grated lemon zest, plus lemon wedges for serving
2 (8-ounce / 227-g) skinless cod fillets, 1¼ inches thick
Vegetable oil spray

1. Preheat the air fryer to 300°F (149°C).
2. Make foil sling for air fryer basket by folding 1 long sheet of aluminum foil so it is 4 inches wide. Lay sheet of foil widthwise across basket, pressing foil into and up sides of basket. Fold excess foil as needed so that edges of foil are flush with top of basket. Lightly spray the foil and basket with vegetable oil spray.
3. Toss the panko with the oil in a bowl until evenly coated. Stir in the shallot, garlic, thyme, ¼ tsp. salt, and ⅛ tsp. pepper. Microwave, stirring frequently, until the panko is light golden brown, about 2 minutes. Transfer to a shallow dish and let cool slightly; stir in the parsley. Whisk the mayonnaise, egg yolk, lemon zest, and ⅛ tsp. pepper together in another bowl.
4. Pat the cod dry with paper towels and season with salt and pepper. Arrange the fillets, skinned-side down, on plate and brush tops evenly with mayonnaise mixture. (Tuck thinner tail ends of fillets under themselves as needed to create uniform pieces.) Working with 1 fillet at a time, dredge the coated side in panko mixture, pressing gently to adhere. Arrange the fillets, crumb-side up, on sling in the prepared basket, spaced evenly apart.
5. Bake for 12 to 16 minutes, using a sling to rotate fillets halfway through cooking. Using a sling, carefully remove cod from air fryer. Serve with the lemon wedges.

Nutrition Info per Serving:

Calories: 385, Protein: 40g, Fat: 16g, Carbohydrates: 16g, Fiber: 1g, Sugar: 1g, Sodium: 537mg

Blackened Salmon

Prep time: 10 minutes, Cook time: 5 to 7 minutes, Serves 4

For the Salmon:
1 tbsp. sweet paprika
½ tsp. cayenne pepper
1 tsp. garlic powder
1 tsp. dried oregano
1 tsp. dried thyme
¾ tsp. kosher salt
⅛ tsp. freshly ground black pepper
Cooking spray
4 (6 ounces / 170 g each) wild salmon fillets
For the Cucumber-Avocado Salsa:
2 tbsps. chopped red onion
1½ tbsps. fresh lemon juice
1 tsp. extra-virgin olive oil
¼ tsp. plus ⅛ tsp. kosher salt
Freshly ground black pepper, to taste
4 Persian cucumbers, diced
6 ounces (170 g) Hass avocado, diced

1. For the salmon: In a small bowl, combine the paprika, cayenne, garlic powder, oregano, thyme, salt, and black pepper. Spray both sides of the fish with oil and rub all over. Coat the fish all over with the spices.
2. For the cucumber-avocado salsa: In a medium bowl, combine the red onion, lemon juice, olive oil, salt, and pepper. Let stand for 5 minutes, then add the cucumbers and avocado.
3. Preheat the air fryer to 400°F (204°C).
4. Working in batches, arrange the salmon fillets skin side down in the air fryer basket. Air fry for 5 to 7 minutes, or until the fish flakes easily with a fork, depending on the thickness of the fish.
5. Serve topped with the salsa.

Nutrition Info per Serving:

Calories: 301, Protein: 35g, Fat: 16g, Carbohydrates: 4g, Fiber: 2g, Sugar: 1g, Sodium: 484mg

Quick and Easy Shrimp

Prep time: 10 minutes, Cook time: 5 minutes, Serves 2

½ pound tiger shrimp
1 tbsp. olive oil
½ tsp. old bay seasoning
¼ tsp. smoked paprika
¼ tsp. cayenne pepper
Salt, to taste

1. Preheat the Air fryer to 390°F (199°C) and grease an Air fryer basket.
2. Mix all the ingredients in a large bowl until well combined.
3. Place the shrimps in the Air fryer basket and air fry for about 5 minutes.
4. Dish out and serve warm.

Nutrition Info per Serving:

Calories: 174, Fat: 8.3g, Carbohydrates: 0.3g, Sugar: 0g, Protein: 23.8g, Sodium: 492mg

Herbed Haddock

Prep time: 10 minutes, Cook time: 8 minutes, Serves 2

2 (6-ounce) haddock fillets
2 tbsps. pine nuts
3 tbsps. fresh basil, chopped
1 tbsp. low-fat Parmesan cheese, grated
½ cup extra-virgin olive oil
Salt and black pepper, to taste

1. Preheat the Air fryer to 355ºF (179ºC) and grease an Air fryer basket.
2. Coat the haddock fillets evenly with olive oil and season with salt and black pepper.
3. Place the haddock fillets in the Air fryer basket and roast for about 8 minutes.
4. Dish out the haddock fillets in serving plates.
5. Meanwhile, put remaining ingredients in a food processor and pulse until smooth.
6. Top this cheese sauce over the haddock fillets and serve hot.

Nutrition Info per Serving:

Calories: 751, Fat: 65.5g, Carbohydrates: 1.3g, Sugar: 0g, Protein: 43.5g, Sodium: 176mg

Appetizing Tuna Patties

Prep time: 15 minutes, Cook time: 10 minutes, Serves 6

2 (6-ounce) cans tuna, drained
½ cup panko bread crumbs
1 egg
2 tbsps. fresh parsley, chopped
2 tsps. Dijon mustard
Dash of Tabasco sauce
Salt and black pepper, to taste
1 tbsp. fresh lemon juice
1 tbsp. olive oil

1. Preheat the Air fryer to 355ºF (179ºC) and line a baking tray with foil paper.
2. Mix all the ingredients in a large bowl until well combined.
3. Make equal sized patties from the mixture and refrigerate overnight.
4. Arrange the patties on the baking tray and transfer to an Air fryer basket.
5. Bake for about 10 minutes and dish out to serve warm.

Nutrition Info per Serving:

Calories: 130, Fat: 6.2g, Carbohydrates: 5.1g, Sugar: 0.5g, Protein: 13g, Sodium: 94mg

Green Curry Shrimp

Prep time: 15 minutes, Cook time: 5 minutes, Serves 4

1 to 2 tbsps. Thai green curry paste
2 tbsps. coconut oil, melted
1 tbsp. nonfat coconut milk
1 tsp. fish sauce
1 tsp. soy sauce
1 tsp. minced fresh ginger
1 clove garlic, minced
1 pound (454 g) jumbo raw shrimp, peeled and deveined
¼ cup chopped fresh Thai basil or sweet basil
¼ cup chopped fresh cilantro

1. In a baking pan, combine the curry paste, coconut oil, coconut milk, fish sauce, soy sauce, ginger, and garlic. Whisk until well combined.
2. Add the shrimp and toss until well coated. Marinate at room temperature for 15 to 30 minutes.
3. Preheat the air fryer to 400ºF (204ºC).
4. Place the pan in the air fryer basket. Air fry for 5 minutes, stirring halfway through the cooking time.
5. Transfer the shrimp to a serving bowl or platter. Garnish with the basil and cilantro. Serve immediately.

Nutrition Info per Serving:

Calories: 185, Protein: 24g, Fat: 8g, Carbohydrates: 1g, Fiber: 0g, Sugar: 0g, Sodium: 395mg

Scallops with Capers Sauce

Prep time: 15 minutes, Cook time: 6 minutes, Serves 2

10 (1-ounce) sea scallops, cleaned and patted very dry
2 tbsps. fresh parsley, finely chopped
2 tsps. capers, finely chopped
Salt and ground black pepper, as required
¼ cup extra-virgin olive oil
1 tsp. fresh lemon zest, finely grated
½ tsp. garlic, finely chopped

1. Preheat the Air fryer to 390ºF (199ºC) and grease an Air fryer basket.
2. Season the scallops evenly with salt and black pepper.
3. Arrange the scallops in the Air fryer basket and air fry for about 6 minutes.
4. Mix parsley, capers, olive oil, lemon zest and garlic in a bowl.
5. Dish out the scallops in a platter and top with capers sauce.

Nutrition Info per Serving:

Calories: 344, Fat: 26.3g, Carbohydrates: 4.2g, Sugar: 0.1g, Protein: 24g, Sodium: 393mg

Cod Cakes

Prep time: 20 minutes, Cook time: 14 minutes, Serves 6

1 pound cod fillet
1 egg
⅓ cup coconut, grated and divided
1 scallion, finely chopped
2 tbsps. fresh parsley, chopped
1 tsp. fresh lime zest, finely grated
1 tsp. red chili paste
Salt, as required
1 tbsp. fresh lime juice

1. Preheat the Air fryer to 375°F (191°C) and grease an Air fryer basket.
2. Put the cod fillet, lime zest, egg, chili paste, salt and lime juice in a food processor and pulse until smooth.
3. Transfer the cod mixture into a bowl and add scallion, parsley and 2 tbsps. of coconut.
4. Mix until well combined and make 12 equal-sized round cakes from the mixture.
5. Place the remaining coconut in a shallow bowl and coat the cod cakes with coconut.
6. Arrange cod cakes into the Air fryer basket in 2 batches and bake for about 7 minutes.
7. Dish out in 2 serving plates and serve warm.

Nutrition Info per Serving:

Calories: 165, Fat: 4.5g, Carbohydrates: 2.1g, Sugar: 1g, Protein: 27.7g, Sodium: 161mg

Sesame Seeds Coated Tuna

Prep time: 15 minutes, Cook time: 6 minutes, Serves 2

¼ cup white sesame seeds
1 tbsp. black sesame seeds
1 egg white
2 (6-ounces) tuna steaks
Salt and black pepper, as required

1. Preheat the Air fryer to 400°F (204°C) and grease an Air fryer basket.
2. Whisk the egg white in a shallow bowl.
3. Mix the sesame seeds, salt, and black pepper in another bowl.
4. Dip the tuna steaks into the whisked egg white and dredge into the sesame seeds mixture.
5. Arrange the tuna steaks into the Air fryer basket in a single layer and air fry for about 6 minutes, flipping once in between.
6. Dish out the tuna steaks onto serving plates and serve hot.

Nutrition Info per Serving:

Calories: 450, Fat: 21.9g, Carbohydrates: 5.4g, Sugar: 0.2g, Protein: 56.7g, Sodium: 182mg

Orange-Mustard Glazed Salmon

Prep time: 10 minutes, Cook time: 10 minutes, Serves 2

1 tbsp. orange marmalade
¼ tsp. grated orange zest plus 1 tbsp. juice
2 tsps. whole-grain mustard
2 (8-ounce / 227 -g) skin-on salmon fillets, 1½ inches thick
Salt and pepper, to taste
Vegetable oil spray

1. Preheat the air fryer to 400°F (204°C).
2. Make foil sling for air fryer basket by folding 1 long sheet of aluminum foil so it is 4 inches wide. Lay sheet of foil widthwise across basket, pressing foil into and up sides of basket. Fold excess foil as needed so that edges of foil are flush with top of basket. Lightly spray foil and basket with vegetable oil spray.
3. Combine marmalade, orange zest and juice, and mustard in bowl. Pat salmon dry with paper towels and season with salt and pepper. Brush tops and sides of fillets evenly with glaze. Arrange fillets skin side down on sling in prepared basket, spaced evenly apart. Air fry salmon until center is still translucent when checked with the tip of a paring knife and registers 125°F (52°C) (for medium-rare), 10 to 14 minutes, using sling to rotate fillets halfway through cooking.
4. Using the sling, carefully remove salmon from air fryer. Slide fish spatula along underside of fillets and transfer to individual serving plates, leaving skin behind. Serve.

Nutrition Info per Serving:

Calories: 342, Protein: 40g, Fat: 14g, Carbohydrates: 14g, Fiber: 1g, Sugar: 9g, Sodium: 233mg

Lemon Garlic Shrimps

Prep time: 15 minutes, Cook time: 8 minutes, Serves 2

¾ pound medium shrimp, peeled and deveined
1½ tbsps. fresh lemon juice
1 tbsp. olive oil
1 tsp. lemon pepper
¼ tsp. paprika
¼ tsp. garlic powder

1. Preheat the Air fryer to 400°F (204°C) and grease an Air fryer basket.
2. Mix lemon juice, olive oil, lemon pepper, paprika and garlic powder in a large bowl.
3. Stir in the shrimp and toss until well combined.
4. Arrange shrimp into the Air fryer basket in a single layer and roast for about 8 minutes.
5. Dish out the shrimp in serving plates and serve warm.

Nutrition Info per Serving:

Calories: 260, Fat: 12.4g, Carbohydrates: 0.3g, Sugar: 0.1g, Protein: 35.6g, Sodium: 619mg

Pecan-Crusted Tilapia

Prep time: 10minutes, Cook time: 10 minutes, Serves 4

1¼ cups pecans
¾ cup panko bread crumbs
½ cup whole-grain flour
2 tbsps. Cajun seasoning
2 eggs, beaten with 2 tbsps. water
4 (6-ounce/ 170-g) tilapia fillets
Vegetable oil, for spraying
Lemon wedges, for serving

1. Grind the pecans in the food processor until they resemble coarse meal. Combine the ground pecans with the panko on a plate. On a second plate, combine the flour and Cajun seasoning. Dry the tilapia fillets using paper towels and dredge them in the flour mixture, shaking off any excess. Dip the fillets in the egg mixture and then dredge them in the pecan and panko mixture, pressing the coating onto the fillets. Place the breaded fillets on a plate or rack.
2. Preheat the air fryer to 375ºF (191ºC). Spray both sides of the breaded fillets with oil. Carefully transfer 2 of the fillets to the air fryer basket and air fry for 9 to 10 minutes, flipping once halfway through, until the flesh is opaque and flaky. Repeat with the remaining fillets.
3. Serve immediately with lemon wedges.

Nutrition Info per Serving:

Calories: 531, Protein: 39g, Fat: 27g, Carbohydrates: 25g, Fiber: 4g, Sugar: 1g, Sodium: 476mg

Cajun Fish Fillets

Prep time: 15 minutes, Cook time: 6 minutes, Serves 4

¾ cup whole wheat flour
¼ cup yellow cornmeal
1 large egg, beaten
¼ cup Cajun seasoning
4 (4-ounce / 113-g) catfish fillets
Cooking spray

1. In a shallow bowl, whisk the flour and cornmeal until blended. Place the egg in a second shallow bowl and the Cajun seasoning in a third shallow bowl.
2. One at a time, dip the catfish fillets in the breading, the egg, and the Cajun seasoning, coating thoroughly.
3. Preheat the air fryer to 300ºF (149ºC). Line the air fryer basket with parchment paper.
4. Place the coated fish on the parchment and spritz with oil.
5. Bake for 3 minutes. Flip the fish, spritz it with oil, and bake for 3 to 5 minutes more until the fish flakes easily with a fork and reaches an internal temperature of 145ºF (63ºC). Serve warm.

Nutrition Info per Serving:

Calories: 220, Protein: 18g, Fat: 5g, Carbohydrates: 27g, Fiber: 3g, Sugar: 0g, Sodium: 600mg

Thai Shrimp Skewers with Peanut Dipping Sauce

Prep time: 15 minutes, Cook time: 6 minutes, Serves 2

Salt and pepper, to taste
12 ounces (340 g) extra-large shrimp, peeled and deveined
1 tbsp. vegetable oil
1 tsp. honey
½ tsp. grated lime zest plus 1 tbsp. juice, plus lime wedges for serving
6 (6-inch) wooden skewers
3 tbsps. creamy peanut butter
3 tbsps. hot tap water
1 tbsp. chopped fresh cilantro
1 tsp. fish sauce

1. Preheat the air fryer to 400ºF (204ºC).
2. Dissolve 2 tbsps. salt in 1 quart cold water in a large container. Add shrimp, cover, and refrigerate for 15 minutes.
3. Remove shrimp from brine and pat dry with paper towels. Whisk oil, honey, lime zest, and ¼ tsp. pepper together in a large bowl. Add shrimp and toss to coat. Thread shrimp onto skewers, leaving about ¼ inch between each shrimp (3 or 4 shrimp per skewer).
4. Arrange 3 skewers in air fryer basket, parallel to each other and spaced evenly apart. Arrange remaining 3 skewers on top, perpendicular to the bottom layer. Air fry until shrimp are opaque throughout, 6 to 8 minutes, flipping and rotating skewers halfway through cooking.
5. Whisk peanut butter, hot tap water, lime juice, cilantro, and fish sauce together in a bowl until smooth. Serve skewers with peanut dipping sauce and lime wedges.

Nutrition Info per Serving:

Calories: 370, Protein: 26g, Fat: 24g, Carbohydrates: 15g, Fiber: 2g, Sugar: 7g, Sodium: 650mg

Spicy Cod

Prep time: 10 minutes, Cook time: 11 minutes, Serves 2

2 (6-ounces) (1½-inch thick) cod fillets
1 tsp. smoked paprika
1 tsp. cayenne pepper
1 tsp. onion powder
1 tsp. garlic powder
Salt and ground black pepper, as required
2 tsps. olive oil

1. Preheat the Air fryer to 390ºF (199ºC) and grease an Air fryer basket.
2. Drizzle the cod fillets with olive oil and rub with the all the spices.
3. Arrange the cod fillets into the Air fryer basket and roast for about 11 minutes.
4. Dish out the cod fillets in the serving plates and serve hot.

Nutrition Info per Serving:

Calories: 277, Fat: 15.4g, Carbohydrates: 2.5g, Sugar: 0.9g, Protein: 33.5g, Sodium: 154mg

Air Fryer Fish Sticks

Prep time: 10 minutes, Cook time: 10 to 12 minutes, Serves 4

Salt and pepper, to taste
1½ pounds (680g) skinless haddock fillets, ¾ inch thick, sliced into 4-inch strips
2 cups panko bread crumbs
1 tbsp. vegetable oil
¼ cup whole wheat flour
¼ cup mayonnaise
2 large eggs
1 tbsp. Old Bay seasoning
Vegetable oil spray

1. Dissolve ¼ cup salt in 2 quarts cold water in a large container. Add the haddock, cover, and let sit for 15 minutes.
2. Toss the panko with the oil in a bowl until evenly coated. Microwave, stirring frequently, until light golden brown, 2 to 4 minutes; transfer to a shallow dish. Whisk the flour, mayonnaise, eggs, Old Bay, ⅛ tsp. salt, and ⅛ tsp. pepper together in a second shallow dish.
3. Set a wire rack in a rimmed baking sheet and spray with vegetable oil spray. Remove the haddock from the brine and thoroughly pat dry with paper towels. Working with 1 piece at a time, dredge the haddock in the egg mixture, letting excess drip off, then coat with the panko mixture, pressing gently to adhere. Transfer the fish sticks to the prepared rack and freeze until firm, about 1 hour.
4. Preheat the air fryer to 400°F (204°C). Lightly spray the air fryer basket with vegetable oil spray. Arrange up to 5 fish sticks in the prepared basket, spaced evenly apart. Air fry until fish sticks are golden and register 140°F (60°C), 10 to 12 minutes, flipping and rotating fish sticks halfway through cooking.
5. Serve warm.

Nutrition Info per Serving:

Calories: 381, Protein: 28g, Fat: 15g, Carbohydrates: 32g, Fiber: 2g, Sugar: 2g, Sodium: 644mg

Breaded Flounder

Prep time: 15 minutes, Cook time: 12 minutes, Serves 3

1 egg
1 cup dry breadcrumbs
3 (6-ounces) flounder fillets
1 lemon, sliced
¼ cup vegetable oil

1. Preheat the Air fryer to 360°F (182°C) and grease an Air fryer basket.
2. Whisk the egg in a shallow bowl and mix breadcrumbs and oil in another bowl.
3. Dip flounder fillets into the whisked egg and coat with the breadcrumb mixture.
4. Arrange flounder fillets into the Air fryer basket and air fry for about 12 minutes.
5. Dish out the flounder fillets onto serving plates and garnish with the lemon slices to serve.

Nutrition Info per Serving:

Calories: 524, Fat: 24.4g, Carbohydrates: 26.5g, Sugar: 2.5g, Protein: 47.8g, Sodium: 463mg

Air Fried Spring Rolls

Prep time: 10 minutes, Cook time: 17 to 22 minutes, Serves 4

2 tsps. minced garlic
2 cups finely sliced cabbage
1 cup matchstick cut carrots
2 (4-ounce / 113-g) cans tiny shrimp, drained
4 tsps. soy sauce
Salt and freshly ground black pepper, to taste
16 square spring roll wrappers
Cooking spray

1. Preheat the air fryer to 370°F (188°C).
2. Spray the air fryer basket lightly with cooking spray. Spray a medium sauté pan with cooking spray.
3. Add the garlic to the sauté pan and cook over medium heat until fragrant, 30 to 45 seconds. Add the cabbage and carrots and sauté until the vegetables are slightly tender, about 5 minutes.
4. Add the shrimp and soy sauce and season with salt and pepper, then stir to combine. Sauté until the moisture has evaporated, 2 more minutes. Set aside to cool.
5. Place a spring roll wrapper on a work surface so it looks like a diamond. Place 1 tbsp. of the shrimp mixture on the lower end of the wrapper.
6. Roll the wrapper away from you halfway, then fold in the right and left sides, like an envelope. Continue to roll to the very end, using a little water to seal the edge. Repeat with the remaining wrappers and filling.
7. Place the spring rolls in the air fryer basket in a single layer, leaving room between each roll. Lightly spray with cooking spray. You may need to cook them in batches.
8. Air fry for 5 minutes. Turn the rolls over, lightly spray with cooking spray, and air fry until heated through and the rolls start to brown, 5 to 10 more minutes. Cool for 5 minutes before serving.

Nutrition Info per Serving:

Calories: 190, Protein: 14g, Fat: 8g, Carbohydrates: 18g, Fiber: 3g, Sugar: 0.1g, Sodium: 160mg

Amazing Salmon Fillets

Prep time: 5 minutes, Cook time: 7 minutes, Serves 2

2 (7-ounce) (¾-inch thick) salmon fillets
1 tbsp. Italian seasoning
1 tbsp. fresh lemon juice

1. Preheat the Air fryer to 355°F (179°C) and grease an Air fryer grill pan.
2. Rub the salmon evenly with Italian seasoning and transfer into the Air fryer grill pan, skin-side up.
3. Grill for about 7 minutes and squeeze lemon juice on it to serve.

Nutrition Info per Serving:

Calories: 88, Fat: 4.1g, Carbohydrates: 0.1g, Sugar: 0g, Protein: 12.9g, Sodium: 55mg

Shrimp Green Casserole

Prep time: 15 minutes, Cook time: 22 minutes, Serves 4

1 pound (454 g) shrimp, cleaned and deveined
2 cups cauliflower, cut into florets
2 green bell pepper, sliced
1 shallot, sliced
2 tbsps. sesame oil
1 cup tomato paste
Cooking spray

1. Preheat the air fryer to 360°F (182°C). Spritz a baking pan with cooking spray.
2. Arrange the shrimp and vegetables in the baking pan. Then, drizzle the sesame oil over the vegetables. Pour the tomato paste over the vegetables.
3. Bake for 10 minutes in the preheated air fryer. Stir with a large spoon and bake for a further 12 minutes.
4. Serve warm.

Nutrition Info per Serving:

Calories: 223, Protein: 24g, Fat: 8g, Carbohydrates: 18g, Fiber: 5g, Sugar: 9g, Sodium: 527mg

Roasted Salmon Fillets

Prep time: 5 minutes, Cook time: 10 minutes, Serves 2

2 (8-ounce / 227 -g) skin-on salmon fillets, 1½ inches thick
1 tsp. vegetable oil
Salt and pepper, to taste
olive oil spray

1. Preheat the air fryer to 400°F (204°C).
2. Make foil sling for air fryer basket by folding 1 long sheet of aluminum foil so it is 4 inches wide. Lay sheet of foil widthwise across basket, pressing foil into and up sides of basket. Fold excess foil as needed so that edges of foil are flush with top of basket. Lightly spray foil and basket with olive oil spray.
3. Pat salmon dry with paper towels, rub with oil, and season with salt and pepper. Arrange fillets skin side down on sling in prepared basket, spaced evenly apart. Air fry salmon until center is still translucent when checked with the tip of a paring knife and registers 125°F (52°C) (for medium-rare), 10 to 14 minutes, using sling to rotate fillets halfway through cooking.
4. Using the sling, carefully remove salmon from air fryer. Slide fish spatula along underside of fillets and transfer to individual serving plates, leaving skin behind. Serve.

Nutrition Info per Serving:

Calories: 366, Protein: 38g, Fat: 23g, Carbohydrates: 0g, Fiber: 0g, Sugar: 0g, Sodium: 120mg

Lime-Chili Shrimp Bowl

Prep time: 10 minutes, Cook time: 10 to 15 minutes, Serves 4

2 tsps. lime juice
1 tsp. olive oil
1 tsp. honey
1 tsp. minced garlic
1 tsp. chili powder
Salt, to taste
12 ounces (340 g) medium shrimp, peeled and deveined
2 cups cooked brown rice
1 (15-ounce / 425-g) can seasoned black beans, warmed
1 large avocado, chopped
1 cup sliced cherry tomatoes
Cooking spray

1. Preheat the air fryer to 400°F (204°C). Spray the air fryer basket lightly with cooking spray.
2. In a medium bowl, mix together the lime juice, olive oil, honey, garlic, chili powder, and salt to make a marinade.
3. Add the shrimp and toss to coat evenly in the marinade.
4. Place the shrimp in the air fryer basket. Air fry for 5 minutes. Shake the basket and air fry until the shrimp are cooked through and starting to brown, an additional 5 to 10 minutes.
5. To assemble the bowls, spoon ¼ of the rice, black beans, avocado, and cherry tomatoes into each of four bowls. Top with the shrimp and serve.

Nutrition Info per Serving:

Calories: 368, Protein: 22g, Fat: 11g, Carbohydrates: 49g, Fiber: 12g, Sugar: 5g, Sodium: 417mg

Garlic Parmesan Shrimp

Prep time: 20 minutes, Cook time: 10 minutes, Serves 2

1 pound shrimp, deveined and peeled
½ cup low-fat parmesan cheese, grated
¼ cup cilantro, diced
1 tbsp. olive oil
1 tsp. salt
1 tsp. fresh cracked pepper
1 tbsp. lemon juice
6 garlic cloves, diced

1. Preheat the Air fryer to 350°F (177°C) and grease an Air fryer basket.
2. Drizzle shrimp with olive oil and lemon juice and season with garlic, salt and cracked pepper.
3. Cover the bowl with plastic wrap and refrigerate for about 3 hours.
4. Stir in the parmesan cheese and cilantro to the bowl and transfer to the Air fryer basket.
5. Air fry for about 10 minutes and serve immediately.

Nutrition Info per Serving:

Calories: 602, Fat: 23.9g, Carbohydrates: 46.5g, Sugar: 2.9g, Protein: 11.3g, Sodium: 886mg

Crab Cakes

Prep time: 20 minutes, Cook time: 20 minutes, Serves 4

1 pound lump crab meat
⅓ cup panko breadcrumbs
¼ cup scallion, finely chopped
2 large eggs
2 tbsps. mayonnaise
1 tsp. Dijon mustard
1 tsp. Worcestershire sauce
1½ tsps. Old Bay seasoning
Ground black pepper, as required

1. Preheat the Air fryer to 375°F (191°C) and grease an Air fryer basket.
2. Mix all the ingredients in a large bowl and cover to refrigerate for about 1 hour.
3. Make 8 equal-sized patties from the mixture and transfer 4 patties into the Air fryer.
4. Bake for about 10 minutes, flipping once in between and repeat with the remaining patties.
5. Dish out and serve warm.

Nutrition Info per Serving:
Calories: 183, Fat: 14.8g, Carbohydrates: 5.9g, Sugar: 1.1g, Protein: 20.1g, Sodium: 996mg

Cajun-Style Salmon Burgers

Prep time: 10 minutes, Cook time: 10 to 15 minutes, Serves 4

4 (5-ounce / 142-g) cans pink salmon in water, any skin and bones removed, drained
2 eggs, beaten
1 cup whole-wheat bread crumbs
4 tbsps. light mayonnaise
2 tsps. Cajun seasoning
2 tsps. dry mustard
4 whole-wheat buns
Cooking spray

1. In a medium bowl, mix the salmon, egg, bread crumbs, mayonnaise, Cajun seasoning, and dry mustard. Cover with plastic wrap and refrigerate for 30 minutes.
2. Preheat the air fryer to 360°F (182°C). Spray the air fryer basket lightly with cooking spray.
3. Shape the mixture into four ½-inch-thick patties about the same size as the buns.
4. Place the salmon patties in the air fryer basket in a single layer and lightly spray the tops with cooking spray. You may need to cook them in batches.
5. Air fry for 6 to 8 minutes. Turn the patties over and lightly spray with cooking spray. Air fry until crispy on the outside, 4 to 7 more minutes.
6. Serve on whole-wheat buns.

Nutrition Info per Serving:
Calories: 276, Protein: 30g, Fat: 14g, Carbohydrates: 10g, Fiber: 2g, Sugar: 1g, Sodium: 537mg

Spicy Orange Shrimp

Prep time: 20 minutes, Cook time: 10 to 15 minutes, Serves 4

⅓ cup orange juice
3 tsps. minced garlic
1 tsp. Old Bay seasoning
¼ to ½ tsp. cayenne pepper
1 pound (454 g) medium shrimp, peeled and deveined, with tails off
Cooking spray

1. In a medium bowl, combine the orange juice, garlic, Old Bay seasoning, and cayenne pepper.
2. Dry the shrimp with paper towels to remove excess water.
3. Add the shrimp to the marinade and stir to evenly coat. Cover with plastic wrap and place in the refrigerator for 30 minutes so the shrimp can soak up the marinade.
4. Preheat the air fryer to 400°F (204°C). Spray the air fryer basket lightly with cooking spray.
5. Place the shrimp into the air fryer basket. Air fry for 5 minutes. Shake the basket and lightly spray with olive oil. Air fry until the shrimp are opaque and crisp, 5 to 10 more minutes.
6. Serve immediately.

Nutrition Info per Serving:
Calories: 131, Protein: 23g, Fat: 1g, Carbohydrates: 7g, Fiber: 0g, Sugar: 4g, Sodium: 216mg

Cod with Asparagus

Prep time: 15 minutes, Cook time: 11 minutes, Serves 2

2 (6-ounces) boneless cod fillets
2 tbsps. fresh parsley, roughly chopped
2 tbsps. fresh dill, roughly chopped
1 bunch asparagus
1 tsp. dried basil
1½ tbsps. fresh lemon juice
1 tbsp. olive oil
Salt and black pepper, to taste

1. Preheat the Air fryer to 400°F (204°C) and grease an Air fryer basket.
2. Mix lemon juice, oil, basil, salt, and black pepper in a small bowl.
3. Combine the cod and ¾ of the oil mixture in another bowl.
4. Coat asparagus with remaining oil mixture and transfer to the Air fryer basket.
5. Roast for about 3 minutes and arrange cod fillets on top of asparagus.
6. Roast for about 8 minutes and dish out in serving plates.

Nutrition Info per Serving:
Calories: 331, Fat: 18g, Carbohydrates: 8.8g, Sugar: 3.5g, Protein: 37.6g, Sodium: 167mg

Salmon Patties

Prep time: 10 minutes, Cook time: 8 minutes, Serves 4

2 (5-ounce / 142 g) cans salmon, flaked
2 large eggs, beaten
⅓ cup minced onion
⅔ cup panko bread crumbs
1½ tsps. Italian-Style seasoning
1 tsp. garlic powder
Cooking spray

1. In a medium bowl, stir together the salmon, eggs, and onion.
2. In a small bowl, whisk the bread crumbs, Italian-Style seasoning, and garlic powder until blended. Add the bread crumb mixture to the salmon mixture and stir until blended. Shape the mixture into 8 patties.
3. Preheat the air fryer to 350ºF (177ºC). Line the air fryer basket with parchment paper.
4. Working in batches as needed, place the patties on the parchment and spritz with oil.
5. Bake for 4 minutes. Flip, spritz the patties with oil, and bake for 4 to 8 minutes more, until browned and firm. Serve.

Nutrition Info per Serving:

Calories: 190, Protein: 21g, Fat: 8g, Carbohydrates: 11g, Fiber: 1g, Sugar: 1g, Sodium: 526mg

Garlic-Lemon Tilapia

Prep time: 5 minutes, Cook time: 10 to 15 minutes, Serves 4

1 tbsp. lemon juice
1 tbsp. olive oil
1 tsp. minced garlic
½ tsp. chili powder
4 (6-ounce / 170-g) tilapia fillets

1. Preheat the air fryer to 380ºF (193ºC). Line the air fryer basket with parchment paper.
2. In a large, shallow bowl, mix together the lemon juice, olive oil, garlic, and chili powder to make a marinade. Place the tilapia fillets in the bowl and coat evenly.
3. Place the fillets in the basket in a single layer, leaving space between each fillet. You may need to cook in more than one batch.
4. Air fry until the fish is cooked and flakes easily with a fork, 10 to 15 minutes.
5. Serve hot.

Nutrition Info per Serving:

Calories: 177, Protein: 33g, Fat: 4g, Carbohydrates: 1g, Fiber: 0g, Sugar: 0g, Sodium: 162mg

Remoulade Crab Cakes

Prep time: 15 minutes, Cook time: 10 minutes, Serves 4

For the Remoulade:
¾ cup mayonnaise
2 tsps. Dijon mustard
1½ tsps. yellow mustard
1 tsp. vinegar
¼ tsp. hot sauce
1 tsp. tiny capers, drained and chopped
¼ tsp. salt
⅛ tsp. ground black pepper
For the Crab Cakes:
1 cup bread crumbs, divided
2 tbsps. mayonnaise
1 scallion, finely chopped
6 ounces (170 g) crab meat
2 tbsps. pasteurized egg product (liquid eggs in a carton)
2 tsps. lemon juice
½ tsp. red pepper flakes
½ tsp. Old Bay seasoning
Cooking spray

1. Preheat the air fryer to 400ºF (204ºC).
2. In a small bowl, whisk to combine the mayonnaise, Dijon mustard, yellow mustard, vinegar, hot sauce, capers, salt, and pepper.
3. Refrigerate for at least 1 hour before serving.
4. Place a parchment liner in the air fryer basket.
5. In a large bowl, mix to combine ½ cup of bread crumbs with the mayonnaise and scallion. Set the other ½ cup of bread crumbs aside in a small bowl.
6. Add the crab meat, egg product, lemon juice, red pepper flakes, and Old Bay seasoning to the large bowl, and stir to combine.
7. Divide the crab mixture into 4 portions, and form into patties.
8. Dredge each patty in the remaining bread crumbs to coat.
9. Place the prepared patties on the liner in the air fryer in a single layer.
10. Spray lightly with cooking spray and air fry for 5 minutes. Flip the crab cakes over, air fry for another 5 minutes, until golden, and serve.

Nutrition Info per Serving:

Calories: 299, Protein: 12g, Fat: 25g, Carbohydrates: 10g, Fiber: 1g, Sugar: 2g, Sodium: 656mg

Seasoned Breaded Shrimp

2 tsps. Old Bay seasoning, divided
½ tsp. garlic powder
½ tsp. onion powder
1 pound (454 g) large shrimp, deveined, with tails on
2 large eggs
½ cup whole-wheat panko bread crumbs
Cooking spray

1. Preheat the air fryer to 380°F.
2. Spray the air fryer basket lightly with cooking spray.
3. In a medium bowl, mix together 1 tsp. of Old Bay seasoning, garlic powder, and onion powder. Add the shrimp and toss with the seasoning mix to lightly coat.
4. In a separate small bowl, whisk the eggs with 1 tsp. water.
5. In a shallow bowl, mix together the remaining 1 tsp. Old Bay seasoning and the panko bread crumbs.
6. Dip each shrimp in the egg mixture and dredge in the bread crumb mixture to evenly coat.
7. Place the shrimp in the air fryer basket, in a single layer. Lightly spray the shrimp with cooking spray. You many need to cook the shrimp in batches.
8. Air fry for 10 to 15 minutes, or until the shrimp is cooked through and crispy, shaking the basket at 5-minute intervals to redistribute and evenly cook.
9. Serve immediately.

Nutrition Info per Serving:

Calories: 168, Protein: 23g, Fat: 4g, Carbohydrates: 9g, Fiber: 1g, Sugar: 1g, Sodium: 581mg

Mahi Mahi with Green Beans

5 cups green beans
2 tbsps. fresh dill, chopped
4 (6-ounces) Mahi Mahi fillets
1 tbsp. avocado oil
Salt, as required
2 garlic cloves, minced
2 tbsps. fresh lemon juice
1 tbsp. olive oil

1. Preheat the Air fryer to 375°F (191°C) and grease an Air fryer basket.
2. Mix the green beans, avocado oil and salt in a large bowl.
3. Arrange green beans into the Air fryer basket and air fry for about 6 minutes.
4. Combine garlic, dill, lemon juice, salt and olive oil in a bowl.
5. Coat Mahi Mahi in this garlic mixture and place on the top of green beans.
6. Air fry for 6 more minutes and dish out to serve warm.

Nutrition Info per Serving:

Calories: 310, Fat: 14.8g, Carbohydrates: 11.5g, Sugar: 2.1g, Protein: 32.6g, Sodium: 127mg

Breaded Shrimp with Lemon

½ cup plain flour
2 egg whites
1 cup breadcrumbs
1 pound large shrimp, peeled and deveined
Salt and ground black pepper, as required
¼ tsp. lemon zest
¼ tsp. cayenne pepper
¼ tsp. red pepper flakes, crushed
2 tbsps. vegetable oil

1. Preheat the Air fryer to 400°F (204°C) and grease an Air fryer basket.
2. Mix flour, salt, and black pepper in a shallow bowl.
3. Whisk the egg whites in a second bowl and mix the breadcrumbs, lime zest and spices in a third bowl.
4. Coat each shrimp with the flour, dip into egg whites and finally, dredge in the breadcrumbs.
5. Drizzle the shrimp evenly with olive oil and arrange half of the coated shrimps into the Air fryer basket.
6. Air fry for about 7 minutes and dish out the coated shrimps onto serving plates.
7. Repeat with the remaining mixture and serve hot.

Nutrition Info per Serving:

Calories: 432, Fat: 11.3g, Carbohydrates: 44.8g, Sugar: 2.5g, Protein: 37.7g, Sodium: 526mg

Spanish Garlic Shrimp

2 tsps. minced garlic
2 tsps. lemon juice
2 tsps. olive oil
½ to 1 tsp. crushed red pepper
12 ounces (340 g) medium shrimp, deveined, with tails on
Cooking spray

1. In a medium bowl, mix together the garlic, lemon juice, olive oil, and crushed red pepper to make a marinade.
2. Add the shrimp and toss to coat in the marinade. Cover with plastic wrap and place the bowl in the refrigerator for 30 minutes.
3. Preheat the air fryer to 400°F (204°C). Spray the air fryer basket lightly with cooking spray.
4. Place the shrimp in the air fryer basket. Air fry for 5 minutes. Shake the basket and air fry until the shrimp are cooked through and nicely browned, an additional 5 to 10 minutes. Cool for 5 minutes before serving.

Nutrition Info per Serving:

Calories: 113, Protein: 16g, Fat: 4g, Carbohydrates: 2g, Fiber: 0g, Sugar: 0.1g, Sodium: 162mg

Simple Salmon Patty Bites

Prep time: 15 minutes, Cook time: 10 to 15 minutes, Serves 4

4 (5-ounce / 142-g) cans pink salmon, skinless, boneless in water, drained
2 eggs, beaten
1 cup whole-wheat panko bread crumbs
4 tbsps. finely minced red bell pepper
2 tbsps. parsley flakes
2 tsps. Old Bay seasoning
Cooking spray

1. Preheat the air fryer to 360°F (182°C).
2. Spray the air fryer basket lightly with cooking spray.
3. In a medium bowl, mix the salmon, eggs, panko bread crumbs, red bell pepper, parsley flakes, and Old Bay seasoning.
4. Using a small cookie scoop, form the mixture into 20 balls.
5. Place the salmon bites in the air fryer basket in a single layer and spray lightly with cooking spray. You may need to cook them in batches.
6. Air fry until crispy for 10 to 15 minutes, shaking the basket a couple of times for even cooking.
7. Serve immediately.

Nutrition Info per Serving:

Calories: 283, Protein: 33g, Fat: 7g, Carbohydrates: 22g, Fiber: 3g, Sugar: 2g, Sodium: 613mg

Crispy Cod Cakes with Salad Greens

Prep time: 15 minutes, Cook time: 12 minutes, Serves 4

1 pound (454 g) cod fillets, cut into chunks
⅓ cup packed fresh basil leaves
3 cloves garlic, crushed
½ tsp. smoked paprika
¼ tsp. salt
¼ tsp. pepper
1 large egg, beaten
1 cup panko bread crumbs
Cooking spray
Salad greens, for serving

1. In a food processor, pulse cod, basil, garlic, smoked paprika, salt, and pepper until cod is finely chopped, stirring occasionally. Form into 8 patties, about 2 inches in diameter. Dip each first into the egg, then into the panko, patting to adhere. Spray with oil on one side.
2. Preheat the air fryer to 400°F (204°C).
3. Working in batches, place half the cakes in the basket, oil-side down; spray with oil. Air fry for 12 minutes, until golden brown and cooked through.
4. Serve cod cakes with salad greens.

Nutrition Info per Serving:

Calories: 235, Protein: 27g, Fat: 6g, Carbohydrates: 16g, Fiber: 1g, Sugar: 1g, Sodium: 434mg

Lemony and Spicy Coconut Crusted Salmon

Prep time: 10 minutes, Cook time: 6 minutes, Serves 4

1 pound salmon
½ cup whole wheat flour
2 egg whites
½ cup breadcrumbs
½ cup unsweetened coconut, shredded
¼ tsp. lemon zest
Salt and freshly ground black pepper, to taste
¼ tsp. cayenne pepper
¼ tsp. red pepper flakes, crushed
Vegetable oil, as required

1. Preheat the Air fryer to 400°F (204°C) and grease an Air fryer basket.
2. Mix the whole wheat flour, salt and black pepper in a shallow dish.
3. Whisk the egg whites in a second shallow dish.
4. Mix the breadcrumbs, coconut, lime zest, salt and cayenne pepper in a third shallow dish.
5. Coat salmon in the flour, then dip in the egg whites and then into the breadcrumb mixture evenly.
6. Place the salmon in the Air fryer basket and drizzle with vegetable oil.
7. Air fry for about 6 minutes and dish out to serve warm.

Nutrition Info per Serving:

Calories: 558, Fat: 22.2g, Carbohydrates: 18.6g, Sugar: 8.7g, Protein: 43g, Sodium: 3456mg

Garlic Scallops

Prep time: 10 minutes, Cook time: 10 to 15 minutes, Serves 4

2 tsps. olive oil
1 packet dry zesty Italian dressing mix
1 tsp. minced garlic
16 ounces (454 g) small scallops, patted dry
Cooking spray

1. Preheat the air fryer to 400°F (204°C).
2. Spray the air fryer basket lightly with cooking spray.
3. In a large zip-top plastic bag, combine the olive oil, Italian dressing mix, and garlic.
4. Add the scallops, seal the zip-top bag, and coat the scallops in the seasoning mixture.
5. Place the scallops in the air fryer basket and lightly spray with cooking spray.
6. Air fry for 5 minutes, shake the basket, and air fry for 5 to 10 more minutes, or until the scallops reach an internal temperature of 120°F (49°C).
7. Serve immediately.

Nutrition Info per Serving:

Calories: 137, Protein: 20g, Fat: 4g, Carbohydrates: 3g, Fiber: 0g, Sugar: 0g, Sodium: 523mg

Oyster Po'Boy

Prep time: 20 minutes, Cook time: 5 minutes, Serves 4

¾ cup whole wheat flour
¼ cup yellow cornmeal
1 tbsp. Cajun seasoning
1 tsp. salt
2 large eggs, beaten
1 tsp. hot sauce
1 pound (454 g) pre-shucked oysters
1 (12-inch) French baguette, quartered and sliced horizontally
Tartar Sauce, as needed
2 cups shredded lettuce, divided
2 tomatoes, cut into slices
Cooking spray

1. In a shallow bowl, whisk the flour, cornmeal, Cajun seasoning, and salt until blended. In a second shallow bowl, whisk together the eggs and hot sauce.
2. One at a time, dip the oysters in the cornmeal mixture, the eggs, and again in the cornmeal, coating thoroughly.
3. Preheat the air fryer to 400°F (204°C). Line the air fryer basket with parchment paper.
4. Place the oysters on the parchment and spritz with oil.
5. Air fry for 2 minutes. Shake the basket, spritz the oysters with oil, and air fry for 3 minutes more until lightly browned and crispy.
6. Spread each sandwich half with Tartar Sauce. Assemble the po'boys by layering each sandwich with fried oysters, ½ cup shredded lettuce, and 2 tomato slices.
7. Serve immediately.

Nutrition Info per Serving:

Calories: 410, Protein: 24g, Fat: 16g, Carbohydrates: 44g, Fiber: 8g, Sugar: 5g, Sodium: 799mg

Shrimp Magic

Prep time: 20 minutes, Cook time: 5 minutes, Serves 3

1½ pounds shrimps, peeled and deveined
Lemongrass stalks
4 garlic cloves, minced
1 red chili pepper, seeded and chopped
2 tbsps. olive oil
½ tsp. smoked paprika

1. Preheat the Air fryer to 390°F (199°C) and grease an Air fryer basket.
2. Mix all the ingredients in a large bowl and refrigerate to marinate for about 2 hours.
3. Thread the shrimps onto lemongrass stalks and transfer into the Air fryer basket.
4. Air fry for about 5 minutes and dish out to serve warm.

Nutrition Info per Serving:

Calories: 367, Fat: 13.3g, Carbohydrates: 7.5g, Sugar: 0.2g, Protein: 52.2g, Sodium: 555mg

Haddock with Cheese Sauce

Prep time: 15 minutes, Cook time: 8 minutes, Serves 4

4 (6-ounce) haddock fillets
6 tbsps. fresh basil, chopped
4 tbsps. pine nuts
2 tbsps. low-fat Parmesan cheese, grated
2 tbsps. olive oil
Salt and black pepper, to taste

1. Preheat the Air fryer to 360°F (182°C) and grease an Air fryer basket.
2. Season the haddock fillets with salt and black pepper and coat evenly with olive oil.
3. Transfer the haddock fillets in the Air fryer basket and air fry for about 8 minutes.
4. Meanwhile, put rest of the ingredients in a food processor and pulse until smooth to make cheese sauce.
5. Dish out the haddock fillets in the bowl and top with cheese sauce to serve.

Nutrition Info per Serving:

Calories: 354, Fat: 17.5g, Carbohydrates: 1.7g, Sugar: 0.3g, Protein: 47g, Sodium: 278mg

Crispy Halibut Strips

Prep time: 20 minutes, Cook time: 14 minutes, Serves 2

2 eggs
1 tbsp. water
¾ cup plain panko breadcrumbs
¾ pound skinless halibut fillets, cut into 1-inch strips
4 tbsps. taco seasoning mix

1. Preheat the Air fryer to 350°F (177°C) and grease an Air fryer basket.
2. Put the taco seasoning mix in a shallow bowl and whisk together eggs and water in a second bowl.
3. Place the breadcrumbs in a third bowl.
4. Dredge the halibut with taco seasoning mix, then dip into the egg mixture and finally, coat evenly with the breadcrumbs.
5. Arrange halibut strips into the Air fryer basket and air fry for about 14 minutes, flipping once in between.
6. Dish out the halibut strips onto serving plates and serve warm.

Nutrition Info per Serving:

Calories: 443, Fat: 11.2g, Carbohydrates: 15.5g, Sugar: 0.4g, Protein: 42.4g, Sodium: 961mg

(Note: Taco seasoning mix - Mix chili powder, garlic powder, onion powder, red pepper flakes, oregano, paprika, cumin, salt and pepper in a small bowl. Store in an airtight container.)

Roasted Cod with Sesame Seeds

Prep time: 5 minutes, Cook time: 7 to 9 minutes, Makes 1 fillet

1 tbsp. reduced-sodium soy sauce
2 tsps. honey
Cooking spray
6 ounces (170 g) fresh cod fillet
1 tsp. sesame seeds

1. Preheat the air fryer to 360°F (182°C).
2. In a small bowl, combine the soy sauce and honey.
3. Spray the air fryer basket with cooking spray, then place the cod in the basket, brush with the soy mixture, and sprinkle sesame seeds on top. Roast for 7 to 9 minutes or until opaque.
4. Remove the fish and allow to cool on a wire rack for 5 minutes before serving.

Nutrition Info per Serving:

Calories: 228, Protein: 29g, Fat: 7g, Carbohydrates: 10g, Fiber: 0g, Sugar: 9g, Sodium: 608mg

Spicy Shrimps

Prep time: 15 minutes, Cook time: 5 minutes, Serves 3

1 pound shrimps, peeled and deveined	½ tsp. red chili flakes
2 tbsps. olive oil	½ tsp. smoked paprika
1 tsp. old bay seasoning	½ tsp. cayenne pepper
	Salt, as required

1. Preheat the Air fryer to 390°F (199°C) and grease an Air fryer basket.
2. Mix shrimp with olive oil and other seasonings in a large bowl.
3. Arrange the shrimp into the Air fryer basket in a single layer and roast for about 5 minutes.
4. Dish out the shrimp onto serving plates and serve hot.

Nutrition Info per Serving:

Calories: 262, Fat: 12g, Carbohydrates: 2.7g, Sugar: 0.1g, Protein: 34.5g, Sodium: 633mg

Zesty Mahi Mahi

Prep time: 10 minutes, Cook time: 8 minutes, Serves 3

1½ pounds Mahi Mahi fillets	½ tsp. red chili powder
1 lemon, cut into slices	Salt and ground black pepper, as required
1 tbsp. fresh dill, chopped	

1. Preheat the Air fryer to 375°F (191°C) and grease an Air fryer basket.
2. Season the Mahi Mahi fillets evenly with chili powder, salt, and black pepper.
3. Arrange the Mahi Mahi fillets into the Air fryer basket and top with the lemon slices.
4. Roast for about 8 minutes and dish out
5. Place the lemon slices over the Mahi Mahi fillets in the serving plates.
6. Garnish with fresh dill and serve warm.

Nutrition Info per Serving:

Calories: 206, Fat: 9.5g, Carbohydrates: 1.3g, Sugar: 0.2g, Protein: 29.7g, Sodium: 124mg

Prawn Burgers

Prep time: 20 minutes, Cook time: 6 minutes, Serves 2

½ cup prawns, peeled, deveined and finely chopped
½ cup breadcrumbs
2-3 tbsps. onion, finely chopped
3 cups fresh baby greens
½ tsp. ginger, minced
½ tsp. garlic, minced
½ tsp. spices powder
½ tsp. ground cumin
¼ tsp. ground turmeric
Salt and ground black pepper, as required

1. Preheat the Air fryer to 390°F (199°C) and grease an Air fryer basket.
2. Mix the prawns, breadcrumbs, onion, ginger, garlic, and spices in a bowl.
3. Make small-sized patties from the mixture and transfer to the Air fryer basket.
4. Bake for about 6 minutes and dish out in a platter.
5. Serve immediately warm alongside the baby greens.

Nutrition Info per Serving:

Calories: 240, Fat: 2.7g, Carbohydrates: 37.4g, Sugar: 4g, Protein: 18g, Sodium: 371mg

Lemony Shrimp and Zucchini

Prep time: 15 minutes, Cook time: 7 to 8 minutes, Serves 4

1¼ pounds (567 g) extra-large raw shrimp, peeled and deveined
2 medium zucchini (about 8 ounces / 227 g each), halved lengthwise and cut into ½-inch-thick slices
1½ tbsps. olive oil
½ tsp. garlic salt
1½ tsps. dried oregano
⅛ tsp. crushed red pepper flakes (optional)
Juice of ½ lemon
1 tbsp. chopped fresh mint
1 tbsp. chopped fresh dill

1. Preheat the air fryer to 350°F (177°C).
2. In a large bowl, combine the shrimp, zucchini, oil, garlic salt, oregano, and pepper flakes (if using) and toss to coat.
3. Working in batches, arrange a single layer of the shrimp and zucchini in the air fryer basket. Air fry for 7 to 8 minutes, shaking the basket halfway, until the zucchini is golden and the shrimp are cooked through.
4. Transfer to a serving dish and tent with foil while you air fry the remaining shrimp and zucchini.
5. Top with the lemon juice, mint, and dill and serve.

Nutrition Info per Serving:

Calories: 199, Protein: 31g, Fat: 6g, Carbohydrates: 8g, Fiber: 2g, Sugar: 4g, Sodium: 568mg

CHAPTER 5
VEGETABLES

Lemony Green Beans

Prep time: 15 minutes, Cook time: 12 minutes, Serves 3

1 pound green beans, trimmed and halved
1 tsp. almond butter, melted
1 tbsp. fresh lemon juice
¼ tsp. garlic powder

1. Preheat the Air fryer to 400ºF (204ºC) and grease an Air fryer basket.
2. Mix all the ingredients in a bowl and toss to coat well.
3. Arrange the green beans into the Air fryer basket and air fry for about 12 minutes.
4. Dish out in a serving plate and serve hot.

Nutrition Info per Serving:

Calories: 60, Fat: 1.5g, Carbohydrates: 11.1g, Sugar: 2.3g, Protein: 2.8g, Sodium: 70mg

Sriracha Golden Cauliflower

Prep time: 5 minutes, Cook time: 17 minutes, Serves 4

¼ cup vegan butter, melted   1 cup bread crumbs
¼ cup sriracha sauce   1 tsp. salt
4 cups cauliflower florets

1. Preheat the air fryer to 375ºF (191ºC).
2. Mix the sriracha and vegan butter in a bowl and pour this mixture over the cauliflower, taking care to cover each floret entirely.
3. In a separate bowl, combine the bread crumbs and salt.
4. Dip the cauliflower florets in the bread crumbs, coating each one well. Air fry in the air fryer for 17 minutes.
5. Serve hot.

Nutrition Info per Serving:

Calories: 238, Protein: 5g, Fat: 12g, Carbohydrates: 28g, Fiber: 5g, Sugar: 3g, Sodium: 786mg

Curried Eggplant

Prep time: 15 minutes, Cook time: 10 minutes, Serves 2

1 large eggplant, cut into   1 tbsp. vegetable oil
½-inch thick slices   ¼ tsp. curry powder
1 garlic clove, minced   Salt, to taste
½ fresh red chili, chopped

1. Preheat the Air fryer to 300ºF (149ºC) and grease an Air fryer basket.
2. Mix all the ingredients in a bowl and toss to coat well.
3. Arrange the eggplant slices in the Air fryer basket and air fry for about 10 minutes, tossing once in between.
4. Dish out onto serving plates and serve hot.

Nutrition Info per Serving:

Calories: 121, Fat: 7.3g, Carbohydrates: 14.2g, Sugar: 7g, Protein: 2.4g, Sodium: 83mg

Mediterranean Air Fried Veggies

Prep time: 10 minutes, Cook time: 6 minutes, Serves 4

1 large zucchini, sliced
1 cup cherry tomatoes, halved
1 parsnip, sliced
1 green pepper, sliced
1 carrot, sliced
1 tsp. mixed herbs
1 tsp. mustard
1 tsp. garlic purée
6 tbsps. olive oil
Salt and ground black pepper, to taste

1. Preheat the air fryer to 400ºF (204ºC).
2. Combine all the ingredients in a bowl, making sure to coat the vegetables well.
3. Transfer to the air fryer and air fry for 6 minutes, ensuring the vegetables are tender and browned.
4. Serve immediately.

Nutrition Info per Serving:

Calories: 202, Protein: 2g, Fat: 18g, Carbohydrates: 11g, Fiber: 3g, Sugar: 5g, Sodium: 109mg

Ratatouille

Prep time: 20 minutes, Cook time: 25 minutes, Serves 4

1 sprig basil
1 sprig flat-leaf parsley
1 sprig mint
1 tbsp. coriander powder
1 tsp. capers
½ lemon, juiced
Salt and ground black pepper, to taste
2 eggplants, sliced crosswise
2 red onions, chopped
4 cloves garlic, minced
2 red peppers, sliced crosswise
1 fennel bulb, sliced crosswise
3 large zucchinis, sliced crosswise
5 tbsps. olive oil
4 large tomatoes, chopped
2 tsps. herbs de Provence

1. Blend the basil, parsley, coriander, mint, lemon juice and capers, with a little salt and pepper. Make sure all ingredients are well-incorporated.
2. Preheat the air fryer to 400ºF (204ºC).
3. Coat the eggplant, onions, garlic, peppers, fennel, and zucchini with olive oil.
4. Transfer the vegetables into a baking dish and top with the tomatoes and herb purée. Sprinkle with more salt and pepper, and the herbs de Provence.
5. Air fry for 25 minutes.
6. Serve immediately.

Nutrition Info per Serving:

Calories: 234, Protein: 5g, Fat: 14g, Carbohydrates: 27g, Fiber: 10g, Sugar: 15g, Sodium: 378mg

Almond Asparagus

Prep time: 15 minutes, Cook time: 6 minutes, Serves 3

1 pound asparagus	2 tbsps. balsamic vinegar
⅓ cup almonds, sliced	Salt and black pepper, to taste
2 tbsps. olive oil	

1. Preheat the Air fryer to 400°F (204°C) and grease an Air fryer basket.
2. Mix asparagus, oil, vinegar, salt, and black pepper in a bowl and toss to coat well.
3. Arrange asparagus into the Air fryer basket and sprinkle with the almond slices.
4. Roast for about 6 minutes and dish out to serve hot.

Nutrition Info per Serving:

Calories: 173, Fat: 14.8g, Carbohydrates: 8.2g, Sugar: 3.3g, Protein: 5.6g, Sodium: 54mg

Crispy Jicama Fries

Prep time: 5 minutes, Cook time: 20 minutes, Serves 1

1 small jicama, peeled	¼ tsp. garlic powder
¼ tsp. onion powder	¼ tsp. ground black pepper
¾ tsp. chili powder	

1. Preheat the air fryer to 350°F (177°C).
2. To make the fries, cut the jicama into matchsticks of the desired thickness.
3. In a bowl, toss them with the onion powder, chili powder, garlic powder, and black pepper to coat. Transfer the fries into the air fryer basket.
4. Air fry for 20 minutes, giving the basket an occasional shake throughout the cooking process. The fries are ready when they are hot and golden.
5. Serve immediately.

Nutrition Info per Serving:

Calories: 110, Protein: 1g, Fat: 0g, Carbohydrates: 26g, Fiber: 15g, Sugar: 8g, Sodium: 12mg

Herb-Roasted Veggies

Prep time: 10 minutes, Cook time: 14 to 18 minutes, Serves 4

1 red bell pepper, sliced	⅓ cup diced red onion
1 (8-ounce / 227-g) package sliced mushrooms	3 garlic cloves, sliced
	1 tsp. olive oil
1 cup green beans, cut into 2-inch pieces	½ tsp. dried basil
	½ tsp. dried tarragon

1. Preheat the air fryer to 350°F (177°C).
2. In a medium bowl, mix the red bell pepper, mushrooms, green beans, red onion, and garlic. Drizzle with the olive oil. Toss to coat.
3. Add the herbs and toss again.
4. Place the vegetables in the air fryer basket. Roast for 14 to 18 minutes, or until tender. Serve immediately.

Nutrition Info per Serving:

Calories: 31, Protein: 2g, Fat: 1g, Carbohydrates: 6g, Fiber: 2g, Sugar: 3g, Sodium: 6mg

Spicy Cauliflower Roast

Prep time: 15 minutes, Cook time: 20 minutes, Serves 4

For the Cauliflower:	For the Sauce:
5 cups cauliflower florets	½ cup nonfat Greek yogurt
3 tbsps. vegetable oil	¼ cup chopped fresh cilantro
½ tsp. ground cumin	1 jalapeño, coarsely chopped
½ tsp. ground coriander	4 cloves garlic, peeled
½ tsp. kosher salt	½ tsp. kosher salt
	2 tbsps. water

1. Preheat the air fryer to 400°F (204°C).
2. In a large bowl, combine the cauliflower, oil, cumin, coriander, and salt. Toss to coat.
3. Put the cauliflower in the air fryer basket. Roast for 20 minutes, stirring halfway through the roasting time.
4. Meanwhile, in a blender, combine the yogurt, cilantro, jalapeño, garlic, and salt. Blend, adding the water as needed to keep the blades moving and to thin the sauce.
5. At the end of roasting time, transfer the cauliflower to a large serving bowl. Pour the sauce over and toss gently to coat. Serve immediately.

Nutrition Info per Serving:

Calories: 170, Protein: 5g, Fat: 10g, Carbohydrates: 18g, Fiber: 6g, Sugar: 7g, Sodium: 360mg

Gold Ravioli

Prep time: 10 minutes, Cook time: 6 minutes, Serves 4

½ cup panko bread crumbs
2 tsps. nutritional yeast
1 tsp. dried basil
1 tsp. dried oregano
1 tsp. garlic powder
Salt and ground black pepper, to taste
¼ cup aquafaba
8 ounces (227 g) ravioli
Cooking spray

1. Cover the air fryer basket with aluminum foil and coat with a light brushing of oil.
2. Preheat the air fryer to 400°F (204°C). Combine the panko bread crumbs, nutritional yeast, basil, oregano, and garlic powder. Sprinkle with salt and pepper to taste.
3. Put the aquafaba in a separate bowl. Dip the ravioli in the aquafaba before coating it in the panko mixture. Spritz with cooking spray and transfer to the air fryer.
4. Air fry for 6 minutes. Shake the air fryer basket halfway.
5. Serve hot.

Nutrition Info per Serving:

Calories: 235, Protein: 8g, Fat: 4g, Carbohydrates: 42g, Fiber: 3g, Sugar: 1g, Sodium: 425mg

Golden Garlicky Mushrooms

Prep time: 10 minutes, Cook time: 10 minutes, Serves 4

6 small mushrooms
1 tbsp. bread crumbs
1 tbsp. olive oil
1 ounce (28 g) onion, peeled and diced
1 tsp. parsley
1 tsp. garlic purée
Salt and ground black pepper, to taste

1. Preheat the air fryer to 350ºF (177ºC).
2. Combine the bread crumbs, oil, onion, parsley, salt, pepper and garlic in a bowl. Cut out the mushrooms' stalks and stuff each cap with the crumb mixture.
3. Air fry in the air fryer for 10 minutes.
4. Serve hot.

Nutrition Info per Serving:

Calories: 43, Protein: 1g, Fat: 4g, Carbohydrates: 2g, Fiber: 0g, Sugar: 0g, Sodium: 28mg

Carrot and Celery Croquettes

Prep time: 10 minutes, Cook time: 6 minutes, Serves 4

2 medium-sized carrots, trimmed and grated
2 medium-sized celery stalks, trimmed and grated
½ cup finely chopped leek
1 tbsp. garlic paste
¼ tsp. freshly cracked black pepper
1 tsp. fine sea salt
1 tbsp. finely chopped fresh dill
1 egg, lightly whisked
¼ cup whole wheat flour
¼ tsp. baking powder
½ cup bread crumbs
Cooking spray
Chive mayo, for serving

1. Preheat the air fryer to 360ºF (182ºC).
2. Drain any excess liquid from the carrots and celery by placing them on a paper towel.
3. Stir together the vegetables with all of the other ingredients, save for the bread crumbs and chive mayo.
4. Use your hands to mold 1 tbsp. of the vegetable mixture into a ball and repeat until all of the mixture has been used up. Press down on each ball with your hand or a palette knife. Cover completely with bread crumbs. Spritz the croquettes with cooking spray.
5. Arrange the croquettes in a single layer in the air fryer basket and air fry for 6 minutes.
6. Serve warm with the chive mayo on the side.

Nutrition Info per Serving:

Calories: 144, Protein: 5g, Fat: 3g, Carbohydrates: 26g, Fiber: 4g, Sugar: 3g, Sodium: 610mg

Air Fried Asparagus

Prep time: 5 minutes, Cook time: 5 minutes, Serves 4

1 pound (454 g) fresh asparagus spears, trimmed
1 tbsp. olive oil
Salt and ground black pepper, to taste

1. Preheat the air fryer to 375ºF (191ºC).
2. Combine all the ingredients and transfer to the air fryer basket.
3. Air fry for 5 minutes or until soft.
4. Serve hot.

Nutrition Info per Serving:

Calories: 32, Protein: 2g, Fat: 2g, Carbohydrates: 3g, Fiber: 2g, Sugar: 1g, Sodium: 0mg

Chermoula Beet Roast

Prep time: 15 minutes, Cook time: 12 minutes, Serves 3

For the Chermoula:
1 cup packed fresh cilantro leaves
½ cup packed fresh parsley leaves
6 cloves garlic, peeled
2 tsps. smoked paprika
2 tsps. ground cumin
1 tsp. ground coriander
½ to 1 tsp. cayenne pepper
Pinch of crushed saffron (optional)
½ cup extra-virgin olive oil
Kosher salt, to taste
For the Beets:
3 medium beets, trimmed, peeled, and cut into 1-inch chunks
2 tbsps. chopped fresh cilantro
2 tbsps. chopped fresh parsley

1. In a food processor, combine the cilantro, parsley, garlic, paprika, cumin, coriander, and cayenne. Pulse until coarsely chopped. Add the saffron, if using, and process until combined. With the food processor running, slowly add the olive oil in a steady stream; process until the sauce is uniform. Season with salt.
2. Preheat the air fryer to 375ºF (191ºC).
3. In a large bowl, drizzle the beets with ½ cup of the chermoula to coat. Arrange the beets in the air fryer basket. Roast for 25 to minutes, or until the beets are tender.
4. Transfer the beets to a serving platter. Sprinkle with the chopped cilantro and parsley and serve.

Nutrition Info per Serving:

Calories: 263, Protein: 3g, Fat: 23g, Carbohydrates: 13g, Fiber: 4g, Sugar: 6g, Sodium: 119mg

Delightful Mushrooms

Prep time: 20 minutes, Cook time: 22 minutes, Serves 4

2 cups mushrooms, sliced
2 tbsps. low-fat cheddar cheese, shredded
1 tbsp. fresh chives, chopped
2 tbsps. olive oil

1. Preheat the Air fryer to 355°F (179°C) and grease an Air fryer basket.
2. Coat the mushrooms with olive oil and arrange into the Air fryer basket.
3. Air fry for about 20 minutes and dish out in a platter.
4. Top with chives and cheddar cheese and air fry for 2 more minutes.
5. Dish out and serve warm.

Nutrition Info per Serving:
Calories: 218, Fat: 7.9g, Carbohydrates: 33.6g, Sugar: 2.5g, Protein: 4.6g, Sodium: 55mg

Broccoli with Cauliflower

Prep time: 15 minutes, Cook time: 20 minutes, Serves 4

1½ cups broccoli, cut into 1-inch pieces
1½ cups cauliflower, cut into 1-inch pieces
1 tbsp. olive oil
Salt, as required

1. Preheat the Air fryer to 375°F (191°C) and grease an Air fryer basket.
2. Mix the vegetables, olive oil, and salt in a bowl and toss to coat well.
3. Arrange the veggie mixture in the Air fryer basket and roast for about 20 minutes, tossing once in between.
4. Dish out in a bowl and serve hot.

Nutrition Info per Serving:
Calories: 51, Fat: 3.7g, Carbohydrates: 4.3g, Sugar: 1.5g, Protein: 1.7g, Sodium: 61mg

Sautéed Green Beans

Prep time: 10 minutes, Cook time: 10 minutes, Serves 2

8 ounces fresh green beans, trimmed and cut in half
1 tsp. sesame oil
1 tbsp. soy sauce

1. Preheat the Air fryer to 390°F (199°C) and grease an Air fryer basket.
2. Mix green beans, soy sauce, and sesame oil in a bowl and toss to coat well.
3. Arrange green beans into the Air fryer basket and air fry for about 10 minutes, tossing once in between.
4. Dish out onto serving plates and serve hot.

Nutrition Info per Serving:
Calories: 59, Fats: 2.4g, Carbohydrates: 59g, Sugar: 1.7g, Proteins: 2.6g, Sodium: 458mg

Sesame Seeds Bok Choy

Prep time: 10 minutes, Cook time: 6 minutes, Serves 4

4 bunches baby bok choy, bottoms removed and leaves separated
1 tsp. sesame seeds
Olive oil cooking spray
1 tsp. garlic powder

1. Preheat the Air fryer to 325°F (163°C) and grease an Air fryer basket.
2. Arrange the bok choy leaves into the Air fryer basket and spray with the cooking spray.
3. Sprinkle with garlic powder and air fry for about 6 minutes, shaking twice in between.
4. Dish out in the bok choy onto serving plates and serve garnished with sesame seeds.

Nutrition Info per Serving:
Calories: 26, Fat: 0.7g, Carbohydrates: 4g, Sugar: 1.9g, Protein: 2.5g, Sodium: 98mg

Cauliflower Faux Rice

Prep time: 15 minutes, Cook time: 42 minutes, Serves 8

1 large head cauliflower, rinsed and drained, cut into florets
½ lemon, juiced
2 garlic cloves, minced
2 (8-ounce / 227-g) cans mushrooms
1 (8-ounce / 227-g) can water chestnuts
¾ cup peas
1 egg, beaten
4 tbsps. soy sauce
1 tbsp. peanut oil
1 tbsp. sesame oil
1 tbsp. minced fresh ginger
Cooking spray

1. Preheat the air fryer to 350°F (177°C).
2. Mix the cauliflower, peanut oil, soy sauce, sesame oil, minced ginger, lemon juice, and minced garlic until combine well.
3. In a food processor, pulse the florets in small batches to break them down to resemble rice grains. Pour into the air fryer basket.
4. Drain the chestnuts and roughly chop them. Pour into the basket. Air fry for 20 minutes.
5. In the meantime, drain the mushrooms. Add the mushrooms and the peas to the air fryer and continue to air fry for another 15 minutes.
6. Lightly spritz a frying pan with cooking spray. Add the beaten egg and cook for 2 minutes, ensuring it is firm. Lay the omelet on a cutting board and slice it up.
7. When the cauliflower mixture is ready, add the sliced omelet to the cauliflower mixture, then bake for an additional 5 minutes. Serve hot.

Nutrition Info per Serving:
Calories: 131, Fat: 6.7 g, Protein: 4 g, Carbohydrates: 15 g, Fiber: 3.6 g, Sugar: 1.7 g, Sodium: 147 mg

Green Beans and Mushroom Casserole

Prep time: 15 minutes, Cook time: 12 minutes, Serves 6

24 ounces fresh green beans, trimmed
2 cups fresh button mushrooms, sliced
⅓ cup French fried onions
3 tbsps. olive oil
2 tbsps. fresh lemon juice
1 tsp. ground sage
1 tsp. garlic powder
1 tsp. onion powder
Salt and black pepper, to taste

1. Preheat the Air fryer to 400ºF (204ºC) and grease an Air fryer basket.
2. Mix the green beans, mushrooms, oil, lemon juice, sage, and spices in a bowl and toss to coat well.
3. Arrange the green beans mixture into the Air fryer basket and air fry for about 12 minutes.
4. Dish out in a serving dish and top with fried onions to serve.

Nutrition Info per Serving:

Calories: 65, Fat: 1.6g, Carbohydrates: 11g, Sugar: 2.4g, Protein: 3g, Sodium: 52mg

Peppery Brown Rice Fritters

Prep time: 10 minutes, Cook time: 8 to 10 minutes, Serves 4

1 (10-ounce / 284-g) bag frozen cooked brown rice, thawed
1 egg
3 tbsps. brown rice flour
⅓ cup finely grated carrots
⅓ cup minced red bell pepper
2 tbsps. minced fresh basil
3 tbsps. grated low-fat Parmesan cheese
2 tsps. olive oil

1. Preheat the air fryer to 380ºF (193ºC).
2. In a small bowl, combine the thawed rice, egg, and flour and mix to blend.
3. Stir in the carrots, bell pepper, basil, and Parmesan cheese.
4. Form the mixture into 8 fritters and drizzle with the olive oil.
5. Put the fritters carefully into the air fryer basket. Air fry for 8 to 10 minutes, or until the fritters are golden brown and cooked through.
6. Serve immediately.

Nutrition Info per Serving:

Calories: 166, Protein: 6g, Fat: 5g, Carbohydrates: 25g, Fiber: 2g, Sugar: 1g, Sodium: 121mg

Cheesy Mushrooms

Prep time: 10 minutes, Cook time: 8 minutes, Serves 4

6-ounce button mushrooms, stemmed
2 tbsps. low-fat mozzarella cheese, grated
2 tbsps. low-fat cheddar cheese, grated
2 tbsps. olive oil
2 tbsps. Italian dried mixed herbs
Salt and freshly ground black pepper, to taste
1 tsp. dried dill

1. Preheat the Air fryer to 355ºF (179ºC) and grease an Air fryer basket.
2. Mix mushrooms, Italian dried mixed herbs, oil, salt and black pepper in a bowl and toss to coat well.
3. Arrange the mushrooms in the Air fryer basket and top with mozzarella cheese and cheddar cheese.
4. Air fry for about 8 minutes and sprinkle with dried dill to serve.

Nutrition Info per Serving:

Calories: 94, Fat: 8.9g, Carbohydrates: 1.7g, Sugar: 0.8g, Protein: 3.3g, Sodium: 46mg

Crunchy Fried Okra

Prep time: 5 minutes, Cook time: 8 to 10 minutes, Serves 4

1 cup self-rising yellow cornmeal
1 tsp. Italian-style seasoning
1 tsp. paprika
1 tsp. salt
½ tsp. freshly ground black pepper
2 large eggs, beaten
2 cups okra slices
Cooking spray

1. Preheat the air fryer to 400ºF (204ºC). Line the air fryer basket with parchment paper.
2. In a shallow bowl, whisk the cornmeal, Italian-style seasoning, paprika, salt, and pepper until blended. Place the beaten eggs in a second shallow bowl.
3. Add the okra to the beaten egg and stir to coat. Add the egg and okra mixture to the cornmeal mixture and stir until coated.
4. Place the okra on the parchment and spritz it with oil.
5. Air fry for 4 minutes. Shake the basket, spritz the okra with oil, and air fry for 4 to 6 minutes more until lightly browned and crispy.
6. Serve immediately.

Nutrition Info per Serving:

Calories: 190, Protein: 7g, Fat: 6g, Carbohydrates: 30g, Fiber: 6g, Sugar: 2g, Sodium: 750mg

Herbed Eggplant

Prep time: 15 minutes, Cook time: 15 minutes, Serves 2

1 large eggplant, cubed
½ tsp. dried marjoram, crushed
½ tsp. dried oregano, crushed
½ tsp. dried thyme, crushed
½ tsp. garlic powder
Salt and black pepper, to taste
Olive oil cooking spray

1. Preheat the Air fryer to 390ºF (199ºC) and grease an Air fryer basket.
2. Mix herbs, garlic powder, salt, and black pepper in a bowl.
3. Spray the eggplant cubes with cooking spray and rub with the herb mixture.
4. Arrange the eggplant cubes in the Air fryer basket and air fry for about 15 minutes, flipping twice in between.
5. Dish out onto serving plates and serve hot.

Nutrition Info per Serving:

Calories: 62, Fat: 0.5g, Carbohydrates: 14.5g, Sugar: 7.1g, Protein: 2.4g, Sodium: 83mg

Beef Stuffed Bell Peppers

Prep time: 10 minutes, Cook time: 30 minutes, Serves 4

1 pound (454 g) ground beef
1 tbsp. taco seasoning mix
1 can diced tomatoes and green chilis
4 green bell peppers
1 cup shredded Monterey jack cheese, divided

1. Preheat the air fryer to 350ºF (177ºC).
2. Set a skillet over a high heat and cook the ground beef for 8 minutes. Make sure it is cooked through and browned all over. Drain the fat.
3. Stir in the taco seasoning mix, and the diced tomatoes and green chilis. Allow the mixture to cook for a further 4 minutes.
4. In the meantime, slice the tops off the green peppers and remove the seeds and membranes.
5. When the meat mixture is fully cooked, spoon equal amounts of it into the peppers and top with the Monterey jack cheese. Then place the peppers into the air fryer. Air fry for 15 minutes.
6. The peppers are ready when they are soft, and the cheese is bubbling and brown. Serve warm.

Nutrition Info per Serving:

Calories: 438, Protein: 24g, Fat: 24g, Carbohydrates: 10g, Fiber: 2g, Sugar: 5g, Sodium: 517mg

Cashew Stuffed Mushrooms

Prep time: 10 minutes, Cook time: 15 minutes, Serves 6

1 cup basil
½ cup cashew, soaked overnight
½ cup nutritional yeast
1 tbsp. lemon juice
2 cloves garlic
1 tbsp. olive oil
Salt, to taste
1 pound (454 g) baby Bella mushroom, stems removed

1. Preheat the air fryer to 400ºF (204ºC).
2. Prepare the pesto. In a food processor, blend the basil, cashew nuts, nutritional yeast, lemon juice, garlic and olive oil to combine well. Sprinkle with salt as desired.
3. Turn the mushrooms cap-side down and spread the pesto on the underside of each cap.
4. Transfer to the air fryer and air fry for 15 minutes.
5. Serve warm.

Nutrition Info per Serving:

Calories: 137, Protein: 6g, Fat: 10g, Carbohydrates: 9g, Fiber: 2g, Sugar: 2g, Sodium: 56mg

Glazed Veggies

Prep time: 20 minutes, Cook time: 20 minutes, Serves 4

2 ounces cherry tomatoes
1 large parsnip, peeled and chopped
1 large carrot, peeled and chopped
1 large zucchini, chopped
1 green bell pepper, seeded and chopped
6 tbsps. olive oil, divided
3 tbsps. honey
1 tsp. Dijon mustard
1 tsp. mixed dried herbs
1 tsp. garlic paste
Salt and black pepper, to taste

1. Preheat the Air fryer to 350ºF (177ºC) and grease an Air fryer pan.
2. Arrange cherry tomatoes, parsnip, carrot, zucchini and bell pepper in the Air fryer pan and drizzle with 3 tbsps. of olive oil.
3. Air fry for about 15 minutes and remove from the Air fryer.
4. Mix remaining olive oil, honey, mustard, herbs, garlic, salt, and black pepper in a bowl.
5. Pour this mixture over the vegetables in the Air fryer pan and set the Air fryer to 390ºF (199ºC).
6. Air fry for about 5 minutes and dish out to serve hot.

Nutrition Info per Serving:

Calories: 288, Fat: 21.4g, Carbohydrates: 26.7g, Sugar: 18.7g, Protein: 2.1g, Sodium: 79mg

Mushrooms with Peas

Prep time: 15 minutes, Cook time: 15 minutes, Serves 4

16 ounces cremini mushrooms, halved
½ cup frozen peas
½ cup soy sauce
4 tbsps. maple syrup
4 tbsps. rice vinegar
4 garlic cloves, finely chopped
2 tsps. Chinese five spice powder
½ tsp. ground ginger

1. Preheat the Air fryer to 350ºF (177ºC) and grease an Air fryer pan.
2. Mix soy sauce, maple syrup, vinegar, garlic, five spice powder, and ground ginger in a bowl.
3. Arrange the mushrooms in the Air fryer pan and air fry for about 10 minutes.
4. Stir in the soy sauce mixture and peas and air fry for about 5 more minutes.
5. Dish out the mushroom mixture in plates and serve hot.

Nutrition Info per Serving:

Calories: 132, Fats: 0.3g, Carbohydrates: 25g, Sugar: 15.4g, Proteins: 6.1g, Sodium: 6.1mg

Cauliflower Tater Tots

Prep time: 15 minutes, Cook time: 16 minutes, Serves 12

1 pound (454 g) cauliflower, steamed and chopped
½ cup nutritional yeast
1 tbsp. oats
1 tbsp. desiccated coconuts
3 tbsps. flaxseed meal
3 tbsps. water
1 onion, chopped
1 tsp. minced garlic
1 tsp. chopped parsley
1 tsp. chopped oregano
1 tsp. chopped chives
Salt and ground black pepper, to taste
½ cup bread crumbs

1. Preheat the air fryer to 390ºF (199ºC).
2. Drain any excess water out of the cauliflower by wringing it with a paper towel.
3. In a bowl, combine the cauliflower with the remaining ingredients, save the bread crumbs. Using the hands, shape the mixture into several small balls.
4. Coat the balls in the bread crumbs and transfer to the air fryer basket. Air fry for 6 minutes, then raise the temperature to 400ºF (204ºC) and then air fry for an additional 10 minutes.
5. Serve immediately.

Nutrition Info per Serving:

Calories: 48, Protein: 2g, Fat: 1g, Carbohydrates: 9g, Fiber: 3g, Sugar: 1g, Sodium: 67mg

Couscous Stuffed Tomatoes

Prep time: 10 minutes, Cook time: 25 minutes, Serves 4

4 tomatoes, tops and seeds removed
1 parsnip, peeled and finely chopped
1 cup mushrooms, chopped
1½ cups couscous
1 tsp. olive oil
1 garlic clove, minced
1 tbsp. mirin sauce

1. Preheat the Air fryer to 355ºF (179ºC) and grease an Air fryer basket.
2. Heat olive oil in a skillet on low heat and add parsnips, mushrooms and garlic.
3. Cook for about 5 minutes and stir in the mirin sauce and couscous.
4. Stuff the couscous mixture into the tomatoes and arrange into the Air fryer basket.
5. Bake for about 20 minutes and dish out to serve warm.

Nutrition Info per Serving:

Calories: 361, Fat: 2g, Carbohydrates: 75.5g, Sugar: 5.1g, Protein: 10.4g, Sodium: 37mg

Tofu with Veggies

Prep time: 25 minutes, Cook time: 22 minutes, Serves 3

½ (14-ounces) block firm tofu, pressed and crumbled
1 cup carrot, peeled and chopped
3 cups cauliflower rice
½ cup broccoli, finely chopped
½ cup frozen peas
4 tbsps. low-sodium soy sauce, divided
1 tsp. ground turmeric
1 tbsp. fresh ginger, minced
2 garlic cloves, minced
1 tbsp. rice vinegar
1½ tsps. sesame oil, toasted

1. Preheat the Air fryer to 370ºF (188ºC) and grease an Air fryer basket.
2. Mix the tofu, carrot, onion, 2 tbsps. of soy sauce, and turmeric in a bowl.
3. Transfer the tofu mixture into the Air fryer basket and air fry for about 10 minutes.
4. Meanwhile, mix the cauliflower rice, broccoli, peas, ginger, garlic, vinegar, sesame oil, and remaining soy sauce in a bowl.
5. Stir in the cauliflower rice into the Air fryer basket and air fry for about 12 minutes.
6. Dish out the tofu mixture onto serving plates and serve hot.

Nutrition Info per Serving:

Calories: 162, Fat: 5.5g, Carbohydrates: 20.4g, Sugar: 8.3g, Protein: 11.4g, Sodium: 1263mg

Golden Pickles

Prep time: 10 minutes, Cook time: 15 minutes, Serves 4

14 dill pickles, sliced
¼ cup whole wheat flour
⅛ tsp. baking powder
Pinch of salt
2 tbsps. cornstarch plus 3 tbsps. water
6 tbsps. panko bread crumbs
½ tsp. paprika
Cooking spray

1. Preheat the air fryer to 400ºF (204ºC).
2. Drain any excess moisture out of the dill pickles on a paper towel.
3. In a bowl, combine the whole wheat flour, baking powder and salt.
4. Throw in the cornstarch and water mixture and combine well with a whisk.
5. Put the panko bread crumbs in a shallow dish along with the paprika. Mix thoroughly.
6. Dip the pickles in the flour batter, before coating in the bread crumbs. Spritz all the pickles with the cooking spray.
7. Transfer to the air fryer basket and air fry for 15 minutes, or until golden brown.
8. Serve immediately.

Nutrition Info per Serving:
Calories: 64, Protein: 1g, Fat: 1g, Carbohydrates: 14g, Fiber: 1g, Sugar: 1g, Sodium: 384mg

Herbed Veggies Combo

Prep time: 15 minutes, Cook time: 35 minutes, Serves 4

½ pound carrots, peeled and sliced
1 pound yellow squash, sliced
1 pound zucchini, sliced
½ tbsp. fresh basil, chopped
½ tbsp. tarragon leaves, chopped
6 tsps. olive oil, divided
Salt and ground white pepper, to taste

1. Preheat the Air fryer to 400ºF (204ºC) and grease an Air fryer basket.
2. Mix two tsps. of oil and carrot slices in a bowl.
3. Arrange the carrot slices in the Air fryer basket and air fry for about 5 minutes.
4. Mix the remaining oil, yellow squash, zucchini, salt, and white pepper in a large bowl and toss to coat well.
5. Transfer the zucchini mixture into air fryer basket with carrots and air fry for about 30 minutes, tossing twice in between.
6. Dish out in a bowl and sprinkle with the herbs to serve.

Nutrition Info per Serving:
Calories: 120, Fat: 7.4g, Carbohydrates: 13.3g, Sugar: 6.7g, Protein: 3.3g, Sodium: 101mg

Cheesy Brussels Sprouts

Prep time: 15 minutes, Cook time: 10 minutes, Serves 3

1 pound Brussels sprouts, trimmed and halved
¼ cup whole wheat breadcrumbs
¼ cup low-fat Parmesan cheese, shredded
1 tbsp. balsamic vinegar
1 tbsp. extra-virgin olive oil
Salt and black pepper, to taste

1. Preheat the Air fryer to 400ºF (204ºC) and grease an Air fryer basket.
2. Mix Brussels sprouts, vinegar, oil, salt, and black pepper in a bowl and toss to coat well.
3. Arrange the Brussels sprouts in the Air fryer basket and air fry for about 5 minutes.
4. Sprinkle with breadcrumbs and cheese and air fry for about 5 more minutes.
5. Dish out and serve hot.

Nutrition Info per Serving:
Calories: 240, Fats: 12.6g, Carbohydrates: 19.4g, Sugar: 3.4g, Proteins: 16.3g, Sodium: 548mg

Veggies Stuffed Eggplants

Prep time: 20 minutes, Cook time: 14 minutes, Serves 5

10 small eggplants, halved lengthwise
1 onion, chopped
1 tomato, chopped
¼ cup low-fat cottage cheese, chopped
½ green bell pepper, seeded and chopped
1 tbsp. fresh lime juice
1 tbsp. vegetable oil
½ tsp. garlic, chopped
Salt and ground black pepper, as required
2 tbsps. tomato paste

1. Preheat the Air fryer to 320ºF (160ºC) and grease an Air fryer basket.
2. Cut a slice from one side of each eggplant lengthwise and scoop out the flesh in a bowl.
3. Drizzle the eggplants with lime juice and arrange in the Air fryer basket.
4. Air fry for about 4 minutes and remove from the Air fryer.
5. Heat vegetable oil in a skillet over medium heat and add garlic and onion.
6. Sauté for about 2 minutes and stir in the eggplant flesh, tomato, salt, and black pepper.
7. Sauté for about 3 minutes and add cheese, bell pepper, tomato paste, and cilantro.
8. Cook for about 1 minute and stuff this mixture into the eggplants.
9. Close each eggplant with its cut part and set the Air fryer to 360ºF (182ºC).
10. Arrange in the Air fryer basket and air fry for about 5 minutes.
11. Dish out in a serving plate and serve hot.

Nutrition Info per Serving:
Calories: 83, Fat: 3.2g, Carbohydrates: 11.9g, Sugar: 6.1g, Protein: 3.4g, Sodium: 87mg

Herb-Roasted Veggies

Prep time: 10 minutes, Cook time: 14 to 18 minutes, Serves 4

1 red bell pepper, sliced
1 (8-ounce / 227-g) package sliced mushrooms
1 cup green beans, cut into 2-inch pieces
⅓ cup diced red onion
3 garlic cloves, sliced
1 tsp. olive oil
½ tsp. dried basil
½ tsp. dried tarragon

1. Preheat the air fryer to 350°F (177°C).
2. In a medium bowl, mix the red bell pepper, mushrooms, green beans, red onion, and garlic. Drizzle with the olive oil. Toss to coat.
3. Add the herbs and toss again.
4. Place the vegetables in the air fryer basket. Roast for 14 to 18 minutes, or until tender. Serve immediately.

Nutrition Info per Serving:

Calories: 31, Protein: 2g, Fat: 1g, Carbohydrates: 6g, Fiber: 2g, Sugar: 3g, Sodium: 6mg

Perfectly Roasted Mushrooms

Prep time: 10 minutes, Cook time: 32 minutes, Serves 4

1 tbsp. vegan butter
2 pounds mushrooms, quartered
2 tbsps. white vermouth
2 tsps. herbs de Provence
½ tsp. garlic powder

1. Preheat the Air fryer to 320°F (160°C) and grease an Air fryer pan.
2. Mix herbs de Provence, garlic powder and butter in the Air fryer pan and transfer into the Air fryer basket.
3. Air fry for about 2 minutes and stir in the mushrooms.
4. Air fry for about 25 minutes and add white vermouth.
5. Cook for 5 more minutes and dish out to serve warm.

Nutrition Info per Serving:

Calories: 83, Fat: 3.5g, Carbohydrates: 7.9g, Sugar: 4g, Protein: 7.2g, Sodium: 34mg

Parmesan Broccoli

Prep time: 10 minutes, Cook time: 20 minutes, Serves 2

10 ounces frozen broccoli
2 tbsps. low-fat Parmesan cheese, grated
3 tbsps. balsamic vinegar
1 tbsp. olive oil
⅛ tsp. cayenne pepper
Salt and black pepper, as required

1. Preheat the Air fryer to 400°F (204°C) and grease an Air fryer basket.
2. Mix broccoli, vinegar, oil, cayenne, salt, and black pepper in a bowl and toss to coat well.
3. Arrange broccoli into the Air fryer basket and roast for about 20 minutes.
4. Dish out in a bowl and top with Parmesan cheese to serve.

Nutrition Info per Serving:

Calories: 173, Fat: 11.5g, Carbohydrates: 10.7g, Sugar: 2.5g, Protein: 10g, Sodium: 505mg

Saltine Wax Beans

Prep time: 10 minutes, Cook time: 7 minutes, Serves 4

½ cup whole wheat flour
1 tsp. smoky chipotle powder
½ tsp. ground black pepper
1 tsp. sea salt flakes
2 eggs, beaten
½ cup crushed saltines
10 ounces (283 g) wax beans
Cooking spray

1. Preheat the air fryer to 360°F (182°C).
2. Combine the whole wheat flour, chipotle powder, black pepper, and salt in a bowl. Put the eggs in a second bowl. Put the crushed saltines in a third bowl.
3. Wash the beans with cold water and discard any tough strings.
4. Coat the beans with the flour mixture, before dipping them into the beaten egg. Cover them with the crushed saltines.
5. Spritz the beans with cooking spray.
6. Air fry for 4 minutes. Give the air fryer basket a good shake and continue to air fry for 3 minutes. Serve hot.

Nutrition Info per Serving:

Calories: 121, Protein: 6g, Fat: 4g, Carbohydrates: 17g, Fiber: 3g, Sugar: 1g, Sodium: 597mg

Sweet and Spicy Cauliflower

Prep time: 15 minutes, Cook time: 25 minutes, Serves 4

1 head cauliflower, cut into florets
¾ cup onion, thinly sliced
2 scallions, chopped
5 garlic cloves, finely sliced
1½ tbsps. soy sauce
1 tbsp. hot sauce
1 tbsp. rice vinegar
1 tsp. coconut sugar
Pinch of red pepper flakes
Ground black pepper, as required

1. Preheat the Air fryer to 350°F (177°C) and grease an Air fryer basket.
2. Arrange the cauliflower florets into the Air fryer basket and roast for about 10 minutes.
3. Add the onions and garlic and roast for 10 more minutes.
4. Meanwhile, mix soy sauce, hot sauce, vinegar, coconut sugar, red pepper flakes, and black pepper in a bowl.
5. Pour the soy sauce mixture into the cauliflower mixture.
6. Air fry for about 5 minutes and dish out onto serving plates.
7. Garnish with scallions and serve warm.

Nutrition Info per Serving:

Calories: 72, Fat: 0.2g, Carbohydrates: 13.8g, Sugar: 3.1g, Protein: 3.6g, Sodium: 1300mg

Kidney Beans Oatmeal in Peppers

Prep time: 15 minutes, Cook time: 6 minutes, Serves 2 to 4

2 large bell peppers, halved lengthwise, deseeded
2 tbsps. cooked kidney beans
2 tbsps. cooked chickpeas
2 cups cooked oatmeal
1 tsp. ground cumin
½ tsp. paprika
½ tsp. salt or to taste
¼ tsp. black pepper powder
¼ cup nonfat yogurt

1. Preheat the air fryer to 355ºF (179ºC).
2. Put the bell peppers, cut-side down, in the air fryer basket. Air fry for 2 minutes.
3. Take the peppers out of the air fryer and let cool.
4. In a bowl, combine the rest of the ingredients.
5. Divide the mixture evenly and use each portion to stuff a pepper.
6. Return the stuffed peppers to the air fryer and continue to air fry for 4 minutes.
7. Serve hot.

Nutrition Info per Serving:
Calories: 235, Protein: 9g, Fat: 2g, Carbohydrates: 40g, Fiber: 8g, Sugar: 2g, Sodium: 322mg

Breadcrumbs Stuffed Mushrooms

Prep time: 15 minutes, Cook time: 10 minutes, Serves 4

1½ spelt bread slices
1 tbsp. flat-leaf parsley, finely chopped
16 small button mushrooms, stemmed and gills removed
1½ tbsps. olive oil
1 garlic clove, crushed
Salt and black pepper, to taste

1. Preheat the Air fryer to 390ºF (199ºC) and grease an Air fryer basket.
2. Put the bread slices in a food processor and pulse until fine crumbs form.
3. Transfer the crumbs into a bowl and stir in the olive oil, garlic, parsley, salt, and black pepper.
4. Stuff the breadcrumbs mixture in each mushroom cap and arrange the mushrooms in the Air fryer basket.
5. Air fry for about 10 minutes and dish out in a bowl to serve warm.

Nutrition Info per Serving:
Calories: 64, Fat: 5.5g, Carbohydrates: 3.3g, Sugar: 0.5g, Protein: 1.6g, Sodium: 65mg

Tofu Bites

Prep time: 15 minutes, Cook time: 30 minutes, Serves 4

1 packaged firm tofu, cubed and pressed to remove excess water
1 tbsp. soy sauce
1 tbsp. ketchup
1 tbsp. maple syrup
½ tsp. vinegar
1 tsp. liquid smoke
1 tsp. hot sauce
2 tbsps. sesame seeds
1 tsp. garlic powder
Salt and ground black pepper, to taste
Cooking spray

1. Preheat the air fryer to 375ºF (191ºC).
2. Spritz a baking dish with cooking spray.
3. Combine all the ingredients to coat the tofu completely and allow the marinade to absorb for half an hour.
4. Transfer the tofu to the baking dish, then air fry for 15 minutes. Flip the tofu over and air fry for another 15 minutes on the other side.
5. Serve immediately.

Nutrition Info per Serving:
Calories: 124, Protein: 8g, Fat: 7g, Carbohydrates: 10g, Fiber: 2g, Sugar: 5g, Sodium: 482mg

Garden Fresh Veggie Medley

Prep time: 10 minutes, Cook time: 15 minutes, Serves 4

2 yellow bell peppers, seeded and chopped
1 eggplant, chopped
1 zucchini, chopped
3 tomatoes, chopped
2 small onions, chopped
2 garlic cloves, minced
2 tbsps. herbs de Provence
1 tbsp. olive oil
1 tbsp. balsamic vinegar
Salt and black pepper, to taste

1. Preheat the Air fryer to 355ºF (179ºC) and grease an Air fryer basket.
2. Mix all the ingredients in a bowl and toss to coat well.
3. Transfer into the Air fryer basket and air fry for about 15 minutes.
4. Keep in the Air fryer for about 5 minutes and dish out to serve hot.

Nutrition Info per Serving:
Calories: 119, Fat: 4.2g, Carbohydrates: 19.3g, Sugar: 10.7g, Protein: 3.6g, Sodium: 16mg

Green Beans with Shallot

Prep time: 10 minutes, Cook time: 10 minutes, Serves 4

1½ pounds (680 g) French green beans, stems removed and blanched
1 tbsp. salt
½ pound (227 g) shallots, peeled and cut into quarters
½ tsp. ground white pepper
2 tbsps. olive oil

1. Preheat the air fryer to 400ºF (204ºC).
2. Coat the vegetables with the rest of the ingredients in a bowl.
3. Transfer to the air fryer basket and air fry for 10 minutes, making sure the green beans achieve a light brown color.
4. Serve hot.

Nutrition Info per Serving:
Calories: 111, Protein: 2g, Fat: 6g, Carbohydrates: 14g, Fiber: 3g, Sugar: 5g, Sodium: 690mg

Okra with Green Beans

Prep time: 10 minutes, Cook time: 20 minutes, Serves 2

½ (10-ounces) bag frozen cut okra
½ (10-ounces) bag frozen cut green beans
¼ cup nutritional yeast
3 tbsps. balsamic vinegar
Salt and black pepper, to taste

1. Preheat the Air fryer to 400ºF (204ºC) and grease an Air fryer basket.
2. Mix the okra, green beans, nutritional yeast, vinegar, salt, and black pepper in a bowl and toss to coat well.
3. Arrange the okra mixture into the Air fryer basket and air fry for about 20 minutes.
4. Dish out in a serving dish and serve hot.

Nutrition Info per Serving:

Calories: 126, Fat: 1.3g, Carbohydrates: 19.7g, Sugar: 2.1g, Protein: 11.9g, Sodium: 100mg

Basil Tomatoes

Prep time: 10 minutes, Cook time: 10 minutes, Serves 2

2 tomatoes, halved
1 tbsp. fresh basil, chopped
Olive oil cooking spray
Salt and black pepper, as required

1. Preheat the Air fryer to 320ºF (160ºC) and grease an Air fryer basket.
2. Spray the tomato halves evenly with olive oil cooking spray and season with salt, black pepper and basil.
3. Arrange the tomato halves into the Air fryer basket, cut sides up.
4. Air fry for about 10 minutes and dish out onto serving plates.

Nutrition Info per Serving:

Calories: 22, Fat: 4.8g, Carbohydrates: 4.8g, Sugar: 3.2g, Protein: 1.1g, Sodium: 84mg

Sesame Taj Tofu

Prep time: 5 minutes, Cook time: 25 minutes, Serves 4

1 block firm tofu, pressed and cut into 1-inch thick cubes
2 tbsps. soy sauce
2 tsps. toasted sesame seeds
1 tsp. rice vinegar
1 tbsp. cornstarch

1. Preheat the air fryer to 400ºF (204ºC).
2. Add the tofu, soy sauce, sesame seeds, and rice vinegar in a bowl together and mix well to coat the tofu cubes. Then cover the tofu in cornstarch and put it in the air fryer basket.
3. Air fry for 25 minutes, giving the basket a shake at five-minute intervals to ensure the tofu cooks evenly.
4. Serve immediately.

Nutrition Info per Serving:

Calories: 109, Protein: 9g, Fat: 6g, Carbohydrates: 6g, Fiber: 1g, Sugar: 1g, Sodium: 332mg

Stuffed Okra

Prep time: 15 minutes, Cook time: 12 minutes, Serves 2

8 ounces large okra
¼ cup chickpea flour
¼ of onion, chopped
2 tbsps. coconut, grated freshly
1 tsp. garam masala powder
½ tsp. ground turmeric
½ tsp. red chili powder
½ tsp. ground cumin
Salt, to taste

1. Preheat the Air fryer to 390ºF (199ºC) and grease an Air fryer basket.
2. Mix the flour, onion, grated coconut, and spices in a bowl and toss to coat well.
3. Stuff the flour mixture into okra and arrange into the Air fryer basket.
4. Air fry for about 12 minutes and dish out in a serving plate.

Nutrition Info per Serving:

Calories: 166, Fat: 3.7g, Carbohydrates: 26.6g, Sugar: 5.3g, Protein: 7.6g, Sodium: 103mg

Balsamic Brussels Sprouts

Prep time: 5 minutes, Cook time: 13 minutes, Serves 2

2 cups Brussels sprouts, halved
1 tbsp. olive oil
1 tbsp. balsamic vinegar
1 tbsp. maple syrup
¼ tsp. sea salt

1. Preheat the air fryer to 375ºF (191ºC).
2. Evenly coat the Brussels sprouts with the olive oil, balsamic vinegar, maple syrup, and salt.
3. Transfer to the air fryer basket and air fry for 5 minutes. Give the basket a good shake, turn the heat to 400ºF (204ºC) and continue to air fry for another 8 minutes.
4. Serve hot.

Nutrition Info per Serving:

Calories: 142, Protein: 3g, Fat: 6g, Carbohydrates: 23g, Fiber: 5g, Sugar: 11g, Sodium: 327mg

Spicy Tofu

Prep time: 10 minutes, Cook time: 13 minutes, Serves 3

1 (14-ounces) block extra-firm tofu, pressed and cut into ¾-inch cubes
3 tsps. cornstarch
1½ tbsps. avocado oil
1½ tsps. paprika
1 tsp. onion powder
1 tsp. garlic powder
Salt and black pepper, to taste

1. Preheat the Air fryer to 390ºF (199ºC) and grease an Air fryer basket.
2. Mix the tofu, oil, cornstarch, and spices in a bowl and toss to coat well.
3. Arrange the tofu pieces in the Air fryer basket and air fry for about 13 minutes, tossing twice in between.
4. Dish out the tofu onto serving plates and serve hot.

Nutrition Info per Serving:

Calories: 121, Fat: 6.6g, Carbohydrates: 7g, Sugar: 1.4g, Protein: 11.3g, Sodium: 68mg

Roasted Lemony Broccoli

Prep time: 5 minutes, Cook time: 15 minutes, Serves 6

2 heads broccoli, cut into florets
2 tsps. extra-virgin olive oil, plus more for coating
1 tsp. salt
½ tsp. black pepper
1 clove garlic, minced
½ tsp. lemon juice

1. Cover the air fryer basket with aluminum foil and coat with a light brushing of oil.
2. Preheat the air fryer to 375°F (191°C).
3. In a bowl, combine all ingredients, save for the lemon juice, and transfer to the air fryer basket. Roast for 15 minutes.
4. Serve with the lemon juice.

Nutrition Info per Serving:

Calories: 47, Protein: 2g, Fat: 2g, Carbohydrates: 7g, Fiber: 3g, Sugar: 2g, Sodium: 394mg

Bell Peppers Cups

Prep time: 10 minutes, Cook time: 8 minutes, Serves 4

8 mini red bell peppers, tops and seeds removed
1 tsp. fresh parsley, chopped
¾ cup low-fat Ricotta cheese, crumbled
½ tbsp. olive oil
Freshly ground black pepper, to taste

1. Preheat the Air fryer to 390°F (199°C) and grease an Air fryer basket.
2. Mix Ricotta cheese, parsley, olive oil and black pepper in a bowl.
3. Stuff the bell peppers with Ricotta cheese mixture and arrange in the Air fryer basket.
4. Air fry for about 8 minutes and dish out to serve hot.

Nutrition Info per Serving:

Calories: 163, Fat: 8.4g, Carbohydrates: 15.5g, Sugar: 11.2 g, Protein: 6.4g, Sodium: 324mg

Easy Glazed Carrots

Prep time: 10 minutes, Cook time: 12 minutes, Serves 4

3 cups carrots, peeled and cut into large chunks
1 tbsp. olive oil
1 tbsp. honey
Salt and black pepper, to taste

1. Preheat the Air fryer to 390°F (199°C) and grease an Air fryer basket.
2. Mix all the ingredients in a bowl and toss to coat well.
3. Transfer into the Air fryer basket and air fry for about 12 minutes.
4. Dish out and serve hot.

Nutrition Info per Serving:

Calories: 80, Fat: 3.5g, Carbohydrates: 12.4g, Sugar: 8.4g, Protein: 0.7g, Sodium: 57mg

Rosemary and Orange Roasted Chickpeas

Prep time: 5 minutes, Cook time: 10 to 12 minutes, Makes 4 cups

4 cups cooked chickpeas
2 tbsps. vegetable oil
1 tsp. kosher salt
1 tsp. cumin
1 tsp. cumin
1 tsp. paprika
Zest of 1 orange
1 tbsp. chopped fresh rosemary

1. Preheat the air fryer to 400°F (204°C).
2. Make sure the chickpeas are completely dry prior to roasting. In a medium bowl, toss the chickpeas with oil, salt, cumin, and paprika.
3. Working in batches, spread the chickpeas in a single layer in the air fryer basket. Air fry for 10 to 12 minutes until crisp, shaking once halfway through.
4. Return the warm chickpeas to the bowl and toss with the orange zest and rosemary. Allow to cool completely.
5. Serve.

Nutrition Info per Serving:

Calories: 120, Protein: 4g, Fat: 5g, Carbohydrates: 15g, Fiber: 4g, Sugar: 2g, Sodium: 235mg

Gorgonzola Mushrooms with Horseradish Mayo

Prep time: 15 minutes, Cook time: 10 minutes, Serves 5

½ cup bread crumbs
2 cloves garlic, pressed
2 tbsps. chopped fresh coriander
⅓ tsp. kosher salt
½ tsp. crushed red pepper flakes
1½ tbsps. olive oil
20 medium mushrooms, stems removed
½ cup grated low-fat Gorgonzola cheese
¼ cup low-fat mayonnaise
1 tsp. prepared horseradish, well-drained
1 tbsp. finely chopped fresh parsley

1. Preheat the air fryer to 380°F (193°C).
2. Combine the bread crumbs together with the garlic, coriander, salt, red pepper, and olive oil.
3. Take equal-sized amounts of the breadcrumb mixture and use them to stuff the mushroom caps. Add the grated Gorgonzola on top of each.
4. Put the mushrooms in the air fryer baking pan and transfer to the air fryer.
5. Air fry for 10 minutes, ensuring the stuffing is warm throughout.
6. In the meantime, prepare the horseradish mayo. Mix the mayonnaise, horseradish and parsley.
7. When the mushrooms are ready, serve with the mayo.

Nutrition Info per Serving:

Calories: 160, Protein: 7g, Fat: 11g, Carbohydrates: 10g, Fiber: 1g, Sugar: 1g, Sodium: 480mg

Air Fried Green Tomatoes

Prep time: 5 minutes, Cook time: 6 to 8 minutes, Serves 4

4 medium green tomatoes
⅓ cup whole wheat flour
2 egg whites
¼ cup nonfat almond milk
1 cup ground almonds
½ cup panko bread crumbs
2 tsps. olive oil
1 tsp. paprika
1 clove garlic, minced

1. Preheat the air fryer to 400ºF (204ºC).
2. Rinse the tomatoes and pat dry. Cut the tomatoes into ½-inch slices, discarding the thinner ends.
3. Put the flour on a plate. In a shallow bowl, beat the egg whites with the almond milk until frothy. And in another plate, combine the almonds, bread crumbs, olive oil, paprika, and garlic and mix well.
4. Dip the tomato slices into the flour, then into the egg white mixture, then into the almond mixture to coat.
5. Place four of the coated tomato slices in the air fryer basket. Air fry for 6 to 8 minutes, or until the tomato coating is crisp and golden brown. Repeat with remaining tomato slices and serve immediately.

Nutrition Info per Serving:
Calories: 224, Protein: 10g, Fat: 13g, Carbohydrates: 21g, Fiber: 5g, Sugar: 6g, Sodium: 279mg

Spices Stuffed Eggplants

Prep time: 15 minutes, Cook time: 12 minutes, Serves 4

8 baby eggplants
4 tsps. olive oil, divided
¾ tbsp. dry mango powder
¾ tbsp. ground coriander
½ tsp. ground cumin
½ tsp. ground turmeric
½ tsp. garlic powder
Salt, to taste

1. Preheat the Air fryer to 370ºF (188ºC) and grease an Air fryer basket.
2. Make 2 slits from the bottom of each eggplant leaving the stems intact.
3. Add 1 tsp. of oil, mango powder, coriander, cumin, turmeric and garlic powder in a bowl, mix well.
4. Fill each slit of eggplants with this spices mixture.
5. Brush the outer side of each eggplant with remaining oil and arrange in the Air fryer basket.
6. Air fry for about 12 minutes and dish out in a serving plate to serve hot.

Nutrition Info per Serving:
Calories: 317, Fats: 6.7g, Carbohydrates: 65g, Sugar: 33g, Proteins: 10.9g, Sodium: 61mg

Sesame Seeds Spinach

Prep time: 10 minutes, Cook time: 6 minutes, Serves 4

4 bunches spinach leaves
2 tsps. sesame seeds
1 tsp. garlic powder
1 tsp. ginger powder
Salt, to taste

1. Preheat the Air fryer to 325ºF (163ºC) and grease an Air fryer basket.
2. Arrange the spinach leaves into the Air fryer basket and season with salt, garlic powder and ginger powder.
3. Air fry for about 6 minutes, shaking once in between and dish out onto serving plates.
4. Top with sesame seeds and serve hot.

Nutrition Info per Serving:
Calories: 26, Fat: 0.7g, Carbohydrates: 4g, Sugar: 1.9g, Protein: 2.5g, Sodium: 98mg

Roasted Eggplant Slices

Prep time: 5 minutes, Cook time: 15 minutes, Serves 1

1 large eggplant, sliced
2 tbsps. olive oil
¼ tsp. salt
½ tsp. garlic powder

1. Preheat the air fryer to 390ºF (199ºC).
2. Apply the olive oil to the slices with a brush, coating both sides. Season each side with sprinklings of salt and garlic powder.
3. Put the slices in the air fryer and roast for 15 minutes.
4. Serve immediately.

Nutrition Info per Serving:
Calories: 240, Protein: 2g, Fat: 22g, Carbohydrates: 10g, Fiber: 5g, Sugar: 6g, Sodium: 300mg

Broccoli with Olives

Prep time: 15 minutes, Cook time: 19 minutes, Serves 4

2 pounds broccoli, stemmed and cut into 1-inch florets
⅓ cup Kalamata olives, halved and pitted
¼ cup low-fat Parmesan cheese, grated
2 tbsps. olive oil
Salt and ground black pepper, as required
2 tsps. fresh lemon zest, grated

1. Preheat the Air fryer to 400ºF (204ºC) and grease an Air fryer basket.
2. Boil the broccoli for about 4 minutes and drain well.
3. Mix broccoli, oil, salt, and black pepper in a bowl and toss to coat well.
4. Arrange broccoli into the Air fryer basket and air fry for about 15 minutes.
5. Stir in the olives, lemon zest and cheese and dish out to serve.

Nutrition Info per Serving:
Calories: 169, Fat: 10.2g, Carbohydrates: 16g, Sugar: 3.9g, Protein: 8.5g, Sodium: 254mg

CHAPTER 6
SALADS

Pork Neck Salad

Prep time: 20 minutes, Cook time: 12 minutes, Serves 2

½ pound pork neck
1 ripe tomato, thickly sliced
1 red onion, sliced
1 scallion, chopped
1 bunch fresh basil leaves
1 tbsp. soy sauce
1 tbsp. fish sauce
½ tbsp. oyster sauce

1. Preheat the Air fryer to 340ºF (171ºC) and grease an Air fryer basket.
2. Mix all the sauces in a bowl and coat the pork neck in it.
3. Refrigerate for about 3 hours and then transfer into the Air fryer basket.
4. Air fry for about 12 minutes and dish out in a platter.
5. Cut into desired size slices and keep aside.
6. Mix rest of the ingredients in a bowl and top with the pork slices to serve.

Nutrition Info per Serving:

Calories: 448, Fat: 39.7g, Carbohydrates: 15.2g, Sugar: 8.5g, Protein: 20.5g, Sodium: 2000mg

Mixed Veggie Salad

Prep time: 25 minutes, Cook time: 1 hour 20 minutes, Serves 8

3 medium carrots, cut into ½-inch thick rounds
3 small radishes, sliced into ½-inch thick rounds
8 cherry tomatoes, cut in eighths
2 red bell peppers, seeded and chopped
½ cup low-fat Parmesan cheese, grated
2 tbsps. olive oil, divided
½ cup Italian dressing
Salt, as required

1. Preheat the Air fryer to 365ºF (185ºC) and grease an Air fryer basket.
2. Mix carrots and 1 tbsp. of olive oil in a bowl and toss to coat well.
3. Arrange the carrots in the Air fryer basket and air fry for about 25 minutes.
4. Mix radishes and 1 tbsp. of olive oil in another bowl and toss to coat well.
5. Arrange the radishes in the Air fryer basket and air fry for about 40 minutes.
6. Set the Air fryer to 330ºF (166ºC) and place the cherry tomatoes into the Air fryer basket.
7. Air fry for about 15 minutes and combine all the Air fried vegetables.
8. Stir in the remaining ingredients except Parmesan cheese and refrigerate covered for at least 2 hours to serve.
9. Garnish with Parmesan cheese and serve.

Nutrition Info per Serving:

Calories: 137, Fat: 9.5g, Carbohydrates: 15.4g, Sugar: 1.8g, Protein: 26.2g, Sodium: 249mg

Zucchini Salad

Prep time: 15 minutes, Cook time: 30 minutes, Serves 4

1 pound zucchini, cut into rounds
5 cups fresh spinach, chopped
¼ cup low-fat Ricotta cheese, crumbled
2 tbsps. olive oil
1 tsp. garlic powder
Salt and black pepper, as required
2 tbsps. fresh lemon juice

1. Preheat the Air fryer to 400ºF (204ºC) and grease an Air fryer basket.
2. Mix the zucchini, oil, garlic powder, salt, and black pepper in a bowl and toss to coat well.
3. Arrange the zucchini slices in the Air fryer basket and air fry for about 30 minutes, flipping thrice in between.
4. Dish out the zucchini slices in a serving bowl and keep aside to cool.
5. Add spinach, Ricotta cheese, lemon juice, a little bit of salt and black pepper and mix well.
6. Toss to coat well and serve immediately.

Nutrition Info per Serving:

Calories: 116, Fat: 9.4g, Carbohydrates: 6.2g, Sugar: 2.8g, Protein: 4g, Sodium: 186mg

Lemon Chicken and Spinach Salad

Prep time: 10 minutes, Cook time: 16 to 20 minutes, Serves 4

3 (5-ounce / 142-g) low-sodium boneless, skinless chicken breasts, cut into 1-inch cubes
5 tsps. olive oil
½ tsp. dried thyme
1 medium red onion, sliced
1 red bell pepper, sliced
1 small zucchini, cut into strips
3 tbsps. freshly squeezed lemon juice
6 cups fresh baby spinach

1. Preheat the air fryer to 400ºF (204ºC).
2. In a large bowl, mix the chicken with the olive oil and thyme. Toss to coat. Transfer to a medium metal bowl and roast for 8 minutes in the air fryer.
3. Add the red onion, red bell pepper, and zucchini. Roast for 8 to 12 minutes more, stirring once during cooking, or until the chicken reaches an internal temperature of 165ºF (74ºC) on a meat thermometer.
4. Remove the bowl from the air fryer and stir in the lemon juice.
5. Put the spinach in a serving bowl and top with the chicken mixture. Toss to combine and serve immediately.

Nutrition Info per Serving:

Calories: 252, Protein: 26g, Fat: 10g, Carbohydrates: 16g, Fiber: 4g, Sugar: 7g, Sodium: 169mg

Cauliflower Salad

Prep time: 20 minutes, Cook time: 10 minutes, Serves 4

¼ cup golden raisins
1 cup boiling water
1 head cauliflower, cut into small florets
¼ cup pecans, toasted and chopped
2 tbsps. fresh mint leaves, chopped

¼ cup olive oil
1 tbsp. curry powder
Salt, to taste
For Dressing:
1 cup mayonnaise
2 tbsps. coconut sugar
1 tbsp. fresh lemon juice

1. Preheat the Air fryer to 390°F (199°C) and grease an Air fryer basket.
2. Mix the cauliflower, pecans, curry powder, salt, and olive oil in a bowl and toss to coat well.
3. Arrange the cauliflower florets in the Air fryer basket and roast for about 10 minutes.
4. Dish out the cauliflower florets in a serving bowl and keep aside to cool.
5. Meanwhile, add the raisins in boiling water in a bowl for about 20 minutes.
6. Drain the raisins well and mix with the cauliflower florets.
7. Mix all the ingredients for dressing in a bowl and pour over the salad.
8. Toss to coat well and serve immediately.

Nutrition Info per Serving:

Calories: 162, Fat: 3.1g, Carbohydrates: 25.3g, Sugar: 1.6g, Protein: 11.3g, Sodium: 160mg

Beet Salad with Lemon Vinaigrette

Prep time: 10 minutes, Cook time: 12 to 15 minutes, Serves 4

6 medium red and golden beets, peeled and sliced
1 tsp. olive oil
¼ tsp. kosher salt
½ cup crumbled low-fat Ricotta cheese
8 cups mixed greens

Cooking spray
For the Vinaigrette:
2 tsps. olive oil
2 tbsps. chopped fresh chives
Juice of 1 lemon

1. Preheat the air fryer to 360°F (182°C).
2. In a large bowl, toss the beets, olive oil, and kosher salt.
3. Spray the air fryer basket with cooking spray, then place the beets in the basket and air fry for 12 to 15 minutes or until tender.
4. While the beets cook, make the vinaigrette in a large bowl by whisking together the olive oil, lemon juice, and chives.
5. Remove the beets from the air fryer, toss in the vinaigrette, and allow to cool for 5 minutes. Add the Ricotta and serve on top of the mixed greens.

Nutrition Info per Serving:

Calories: 153, Protein: 5g, Fat: 7g, Carbohydrates: 20g, Fiber: 5g, Sugar: 12g, Sodium: 314mg

Eggplant Salad

Prep time: 15 minutes, Cook time: 15 minutes, Serves 2

1 eggplant, cut into ½-inch-thick slices crosswise
1 avocado, peeled, pitted and chopped
2 tbsps. canola oil
Salt and ground black pepper, as required
1 tsp. fresh lemon juice
For Dressing:
1 tbsp. extra-virgin olive oil
1 tbsp. red wine vinegar
1 tbsp. honey
1 tbsp. fresh oregano leaves, chopped
1 tsp. fresh lemon zest, grated
1 tsp. Dijon mustard
Salt and ground black pepper, as required

1. Preheat the Air fryer to 400°F (204°C) and grease an Air fryer basket.
2. Mix eggplant, oil, salt, and black pepper in a bowl and toss to coat well.
3. Arrange the eggplants pieces in the Air fryer basket and air fry for about 15 minutes, flipping twice in between.
4. Dish out the eggplants pieces in a serving bowl and keep aside to cool.
5. Add avocado and lemon juice and mix well.
6. Mix all the ingredients for dressing in a bowl and pour over the salad.
7. Toss to coat well and serve immediately.

Nutrition Info per Serving:

Calories: 489, Fat: 41.4g, Carbohydrates: 32.7g, Sugar: 16.2g, Protein: 4.6g, Sodium: 118mg

Lush Vegetable Salad

Prep time: 15 minutes, Cook time: 10 minutes, Serves 4

6 plum tomatoes, halved
2 large red onions, sliced
4 long red pepper, sliced
2 yellow pepper, sliced
6 cloves garlic, crushed
1 tbsp. extra-virgin olive oil

1 tsp. paprika
½ lemon, juiced
Salt and ground black pepper, to taste
1 tbsp. baby capers

1. Preheat the air fryer to 420°F (216°C).
2. Put the tomatoes, onions, peppers, and garlic in a large bowl and cover with the extra-virgin olive oil, paprika, and lemon juice. Sprinkle with salt and pepper as desired.
3. Line the inside of the air fryer basket with aluminum foil. Put the vegetables inside and air fry for 10 minutes, ensuring the edges turn brown.
4. Serve in a salad bowl with the baby capers.

Nutrition Info per Serving:

Calories: 96, Protein: 2g, Fat: 3g, Carbohydrates: 17g, Fiber: 5g, Sugar: 8g, Sodium: 18mg

Fig, Chickpea, and Arugula Salad

Prep time: 15 minutes, Cook time: 20 minutes, Serves 4

8 fresh figs, halved
1½ cups cooked chickpeas
1 tsp. crushed roasted cumin seeds
4 tbsps. balsamic vinegar
2 tbsps. extra-virgin olive oil, plus more for greasing
Salt and ground black pepper, to taste
3 cups arugula rocket, washed and dried

1. Preheat the air fryer to 375°F (191°C).
2. Cover the air fryer basket with aluminum foil and grease lightly with oil. Put the figs in the air fryer basket and air fry for 10 minutes.
3. In a bowl, combine the chickpeas and cumin seeds.
4. Remove the air fried figs from the air fryer and replace with the chickpeas. Air fry for 10 minutes. Leave to cool.
5. In the meantime, prepare the dressing. Mix the balsamic vinegar, olive oil, salt and pepper.
6. In a salad bowl, combine the arugula rocket with the cooled figs and chickpeas.
7. Toss with the sauce and serve.

Nutrition Info per Serving:

Calories: 264, Protein: 7g, Fat: 11g, Carbohydrates: 40g, Fiber: 8g, Sugar: 13g, Sodium: 60mg

Roasted Chicken and Vegetable Salad

Prep time: 10 minutes, Cook time: 10 to 13 minutes, Serves 4

3 (4-ounce / 113-g) low-sodium boneless, skinless chicken breasts, cut into 1-inch cubes
1 small red onion, sliced
1 red bell pepper, sliced
1 cup green beans, cut into 1-inch pieces
2 tbsps. low-fat ranch salad dressing
2 tbsps. freshly squeezed lemon juice
½ tsp. dried basil
4 cups mixed lettuce

1. Preheat the air fryer to 400°F (204°C).
2. In the air fryer basket, roast the chicken, red onion, red bell pepper, and green beans for 10 to 13 minutes, or until the chicken reaches an internal temperature of 165°F (74°C) on a meat thermometer, tossing the food in the basket once during cooking.
3. While the chicken cooks, in a serving bowl, mix the ranch dressing, lemon juice, and basil.
4. Transfer the chicken and vegetables to a serving bowl and toss with the dressing to coat. Serve immediately on lettuce leaves.

Nutrition Info per Serving:

Calories: 184, Protein: 21g, Fat: 4g, Carbohydrates: 16g, Fiber: 4g, Sugar: 5g, Sodium: 256mg

Brussels Sprouts Salad

Prep time: 20 minutes, Cook time: 15 minutes, Serves 4

1 pound fresh medium Brussels sprouts, trimmed and halved vertically
2 apples, cored and chopped
1 red onion, sliced
4 cups lettuce, torn
3 tsps. olive oil
Salt and ground black pepper, as required
For Dressing:
2 tbsps. extra-virgin olive oil
2 tbsps. fresh lemon juice
1 tbsp. apple cider vinegar
1 tbsp. honey
1 tsp. Dijon mustard
Salt and ground black pepper, as required

1. Preheat the Air fryer to 360°F (182°C) and grease an Air fryer basket.
2. Mix Brussels sprouts, oil, salt, and black pepper in a bowl and toss to coat well.
3. Arrange the Brussels sprouts in the Air fryer basket and air fry for about 15 minutes, flipping once in between.
4. Dish out the Brussels sprouts in a serving bowl and keep aside to cool.
5. Add apples, onion, and lettuce and mix well.
6. Mix all the ingredients for dressing in a bowl and pour over the salad.
7. Toss to coat well and serve immediately.

Nutrition Info per Serving:

Calories: 235, Fat: 11.3g, Carbohydrates: 34.5g, Sugar: 20.3g, Protein: 4.9g, Sodium: 88mg

Radish Salad

Prep time: 15 minutes, Cook time: 30 minutes, Serves 4

1½ pounds radishes, trimmed and halved
½ pound fresh mozzarella, sliced
6 cups fresh salad greens
3 tbsps. olive oil
1 tsp. honey
1 tbsp. balsamic vinegar
Salt and black pepper, to taste

1. Preheat the Air fryer to 350°F (177°C) and grease an Air fryer basket.
2. Mix the radishes, salt, black pepper, and olive oil in a bowl and toss to coat well.
3. Arrange the radishes in the Air fryer basket and roast for about 30 minutes, flipping twice in between.
4. Dish out the radishes in a serving bowl and keep aside to cool.
5. Add mozzarella cheese and greens and mix well.
6. Mix honey, oil, vinegar, salt, and black pepper in a bowl and pour over the salad.
7. Toss to coat well and serve immediately.

Nutrition Info per Serving:

Calories: 468, Fat: 38.5g, Carbohydrates: 33.1g, Sugar: 17.1g, Protein: 3.3g, Sodium: 127mg

Crab Cakes with Lettuce and Apple Salad

Prep time: 10 minutes, Cook time: 13 minutes, Serves 2

8 ounces (227 g) lump crab meat, picked over for shells
2 tbsps. panko bread crumbs
1 scallion, minced
1 large egg
1 tbsp. mayonnaise
1½ tsps. Dijon mustard
Pinch of cayenne pepper
2 shallots, sliced thin
1 tbsp. extra-virgin olive oil, divided
1 tsp. lemon juice, plus lemon wedges for serving
⅛ tsp. salt
Pinch of pepper
½ (3-ounce / 85-g) small head Bibb lettuce, torn into bite-size pieces
½ apple, cored and sliced thin

1. Preheat the air fryer to 400ºF (204ºC).
2. Line large plate with triple layer of paper towels. Transfer crab meat to prepared plate and pat dry with additional paper towels. Combine panko, scallion, egg, mayonnaise, mustard, and cayenne in a bowl. Using a rubber spatula, gently fold in crab meat until combined; discard paper towels. Divide crab mixture into 4 tightly packed balls, then flatten each into 1-inch-thick cake (cakes will be delicate). Transfer cakes to plate and refrigerate until firm, about 10 minutes.
3. Toss shallots with ½ tsp. oil in separate bowl; transfer to air fryer basket. Air fry until shallots are browned, 5 to 7 minutes, tossing once halfway through cooking. Return shallots to now-empty bowl and set aside.
4. Arrange crab cakes in air fryer basket, spaced evenly apart. Return basket to air fryer and air fry until crab cakes are light golden brown on both sides, 8 to 10 minutes, flipping and rotating cakes halfway through cooking.
5. Meanwhile, whisk remaining 2½ tsps. oil, lemon juice, salt, and pepper together in large bowl. Add lettuce, apple, and shallots and toss to coat. Serve crab cakes with salad, passing lemon wedges separately.

Nutrition Info per Serving:

Calories: 394, Protein: 20g, Fat: 23g, Carbohydrates: 29g, Fiber: 4g, Sugar: 13g, Sodium: 711mg

Radish and Mozzarella Salad

Prep time: 15 minutes, Cook time: 30 minutes, Serves 4

1½ pounds radishes, trimmed and halved
½ pound fresh mozzarella, sliced
Salt and freshly ground black pepper, to taste
3 tbsps. olive oil
1 tsp. honey

1. Preheat the Air fryer to 350ºF (177ºC) and grease an Air fryer basket with olive oil.
2. Mix radishes, mozzarella, salt, black pepper and 2 tbsps. of olive oil in a bowl and toss to coat well.
3. Arrange the radishes mixture in the Air fryer basket and air fry for about 30 minutes, flipping twice in between.
4. Dish out in a bowl and top with the remaining ingredients to serve.

Nutrition Info per Serving:

Calories: 265, Fat: 18.5g, Carbohydrates: 9.3g, Sugar: 4.6g, Protein: 17.4g, Sodium: 411mg

Moroccan Spiced Halibut with Chickpea Salad

Prep time: 15 minutes, Cook time: 12 minutes, Serves 2

¾ tsp. ground coriander
½ tsp. ground cumin
¼ tsp. ground ginger
⅛ tsp. ground cinnamon
Salt and pepper, to taste
2 (8-ounce / 227-g) skinless halibut fillets, 1¼ inches thick
4 tsps. extra-virgin olive oil, divided, plus extra for drizzling
1 (15-ounce / 425-g) can chickpeas, rinsed
1 tbsp. lemon juice, plus lemon wedges for serving
1 tsp. harissa
½ tsp. honey
2 carrots, peeled and shredded
2 tbsps. chopped fresh mint, divided
Vegetable oil spray

1. Preheat the air fryer to 300ºF (149ºC).
2. Make foil sling for air fryer basket by folding 1 long sheet of aluminum foil so it is 4 inches wide. Lay sheet of foil widthwise across basket, pressing foil into and up sides of basket. Fold excess foil as needed so that edges of foil are flush with top of basket. Lightly spray foil and basket with vegetable oil spray.
3. Combine coriander, cumin, ginger, cinnamon, ⅛ tsp. salt, and ⅛ tsp. pepper in a small bowl. Pat halibut dry with paper towels, rub with 1 tsp. oil, and sprinkle all over with spice mixture. Arrange fillets skinned side down on sling in prepared basket, spaced evenly apart. Bake until halibut flakes apart when gently prodded with a paring knife and registers 140ºF (60ºC), 12 to 16 minutes, using the sling to rotate fillets halfway through cooking.
4. Meanwhile, microwave chickpeas in medium bowl until heated through, about 2 minutes. Stir in remaining 1 tbsp. oil, lemon juice, harissa, honey, ⅛ tsp. salt, and ⅛ tsp. pepper. Add carrots and 1 tbsp. mint and toss to combine. Season with salt and pepper, to taste.
5. Using sling, carefully remove halibut from air fryer and transfer to individual plates. Sprinkle with remaining 1 tbsp. mint and drizzle with extra oil to taste. Serve with salad and lemon wedges.

Nutrition Info per Serving:

Calories: 467, Protein: 49g, Fat: 17g, Carbohydrates: 31g, Fiber: 9g, Sugar: 7g, Sodium: 514mg

CHAPTER 7
APPETIZER AND SIDES

Tofu with Peanut Butter Sauce

Prep time: 20 minutes, Cook time: 15 minutes, Serves 3

For the Tofu:
6 bamboo skewers, presoaked and halved
1 (14-ounces) block tofu, pressed and cut into strips
2 tbsps. fresh lime juice
2 tbsps. soy sauce
1 tbsp. maple syrup
1 tsp. Sriracha sauce
2 tsps. fresh ginger, peeled
2 garlic cloves, peeled
For the Sauce:
1 (2-inches) piece fresh ginger, peeled
2 garlic cloves, peeled
½ cup creamy peanut butter
1 tbsp. soy sauce
1 tbsp. fresh lime juice
1-2 tsps. Sriracha sauce
6 tbsps. of water

1. Preheat the Air fryer to 370ºF (188ºC) and grease an Air fryer basket.
2. Put all the ingredients except tofu in a food processor and pulse until smooth.
3. Transfer the mixture into a bowl and marinate tofu in it.
4. Thread one tofu strip onto each little bamboo stick and arrange them in the Air fryer basket.
5. Air fry for about 15 minutes and dish out onto serving plates.
6. Mix all the ingredients for the sauce in a food processor and pulse until smooth.
7. Drizzle the sauce over tofu and serve warm.

Nutrition Info per Serving:
Calories: 385, Fats: 27.3g, Carbohydrates: 9.3g, Sugar: 9.1g, Proteins: 23g, Sodium: 1141mg

Sweet and Sour Brussels Sprouts

Prep time: 10 minutes, Cook time: 10 minutes, Serves 2

2 cups Brussels sprouts, trimmed and halved lengthwise
1 tbsp. balsamic vinegar
1 tbsp. maple syrup
Salt, as required

1. Preheat the Air fryer to 400ºF (204ºC) and grease an Air fryer basket.
2. Mix all the ingredients in a bowl and toss to coat well.
3. Arrange the Brussels sprouts in the Air fryer basket and air fry for about 10 minutes, shaking once halfway through.
4. Dish out in a bowl and serve hot.

Nutrition Info per Serving:
Calories: 66, Fat: 0.3g, Carbohydrates: 14.8g, Sugar: 7.9g, Protein: 3g, Sodium: 101mg

Shishito Peppers with Herb Dressing

Prep time: 10 minutes, Cook time: 6 minutes, Serves 2 to 4

6 ounces (170 g) shishito peppers
1 tbsp. olive oil
Kosher salt and freshly ground black pepper, to taste
½ cup mayonnaise
2 tbsps. finely chopped fresh basil leaves
2 tbsps. finely chopped fresh flat-leaf parsley
1 tbsp. finely chopped fresh tarragon
1 tbsp. finely chopped fresh chives
Finely grated zest of ½ lemon
1 tbsp. fresh lemon juice
Flaky sea salt, for serving

1. Preheat the air fryer to 400ºF (204ºC).
2. In a bowl, toss together the shishitos and oil to evenly coat and season with kosher salt and black pepper. Transfer to the air fryer and air fry for 6 minutes, shaking the basket halfway through, or until the shishitos are blistered and lightly charred.
3. Meanwhile, in a small bowl, whisk together the mayonnaise, basil, parsley, tarragon, chives, lemon zest, and lemon juice.
4. Pile the peppers on a plate, sprinkle with flaky sea salt, and serve hot with the dressing.

Nutrition Info per Serving:
Calories: 165, Protein: 1g, Fat: 18g, Carbohydrates: 1g, Fiber: 0g, Sugar: 0g, Sodium: 192mg

Air Fried Olives

Prep time: 5 minutes, Cook time: 8 minutes, Serves 4

1 (5½-ounce / 156-g) jar pitted green olives
½ cup whole wheat flour
Salt and pepper, to taste
½ cup whole wheat bread crumbs
1 egg
Cooking spray

1. Preheat the air fryer to 400ºF (204ºC).
2. Remove the olives from the jar and dry thoroughly with paper towels.
3. In a small bowl, combine the flour with salt and pepper to taste. Place the bread crumbs in another small bowl. In a third small bowl, beat the egg.
4. Spritz the air fryer basket with cooking spray.
5. Dip the olives in the flour, then the egg, and then the bread crumbs.
6. Place the breaded olives in the air fryer. It is okay to stack them. Spray the olives with cooking spray. Air fry for 6 minutes. Flip the olives and air fry for an additional 2 minutes, or until brown and crisp.
7. Cool before serving.

Nutrition Info per Serving:
Calories: 90, Protein: 3g, Fat: 3g, Carbohydrates: 13g, Fiber: 2g, Sugar: 0g, Sodium: 540mg

Zucchini Balls

Prep time: 5 minutes, Cook time: 10 minutes, Serves 4

4 zucchinis
1 egg

½ cup grated low-fat Parmesan cheese
1 tbsp. Italian herbs
1 cup grated coconut

1. Thinly grate the zucchinis and dry with a cheesecloth, ensuring to remove all the moisture.
2. In a bowl, combine the zucchinis with the egg, Parmesan, Italian herbs, and grated coconut, mixing well to incorporate everything. Using the hands, mold the mixture into balls.
3. Preheat the air fryer to 400ºF (204ºC).
4. Lay the zucchini balls in the air fryer basket and air fry for 10 minutes.
5. Serve hot.

Nutrition Info per Serving:

Calories: 132, Protein: 9g, Fat: 8g, Carbohydrates: 10g, Fiber: 3g, Sugar: 4g, Sodium: 340mg

Air Fryer Plantains

Prep time: 10 minutes, Cook time: 10 minutes, Serves 4

2 ripe plantains
2 tsps. avocado oil
⅛ tsp. salt

1. Preheat the Air fryer to 400ºF (204ºC) and grease an Air fryer basket.
2. Mix the plantains with avocado oil and salt in a bowl.
3. Arrange the coated plantains in the Air fryer basket and air fry for about 10 minutes.
4. Dish out in a bowl and serve immediately.

Nutrition Info per Serving:

Calories: 112, Fat: 0.6g, Carbohydrates: 28.7g, Sugar: 13.4g, Protein: 1.2g, Sodium: 77mg

Easy Roasted Asparagus

Prep time: 5 minutes, Cook time: 6 minutes, Serves 4

1 pound (454 g) asparagus, trimmed and halved crosswise
1 tsp. extra-virgin olive oil
Salt and pepper, to taste
Lemon wedges, for serving

1. Preheat the air fryer to 400ºF (204ºC).
2. Toss the asparagus with the oil, ⅛ tsp. salt, and ⅛ tsp. pepper in bowl. Transfer to air fryer basket.
3. Place the basket in air fryer and roast for 6 to 8 minutes, or until tender and bright green, tossing halfway through cooking.
4. Season with salt and pepper and serve with lemon wedges.

Nutrition Info per Serving:

Calories: 25, Protein: 2g, Fat: 1g, Carbohydrates: 4g, Fiber: 2g, Sugar: 2g, Sodium: 75mg

Spicy Chicken Bites

Prep time: 10 minutes, Cook time: 10 to 12 minutes, Makes 30 bites

8 ounces boneless and skinless chicken thighs, cut into 30 pieces
¼ tsp. kosher salt

2 tbsps. hot sauce
Cooking spray

1. Preheat the air fryer to 390ºF (199ºC).
2. Spray the air fryer basket with cooking spray and season the chicken bites with the kosher salt, then place in the basket and air fry for 10 to 12 minutes or until crispy.
3. While the chicken bites cook, pour the hot sauce into a large bowl.
4. Remove the bites and add to the sauce bowl, tossing to coat. Serve warm.

Nutrition Info per Serving:

Calories: 80, Protein: 10g, Fat: 4g, Carbohydrates: 1g, Fiber: 0g, Sugar: 0g, Sodium: 350mg

Air Fried Zucchini Gratin

Prep time: 10 minutes, Cook time: 15 minutes, Serves 4

2 zucchinis, cut into 8 equal sized pieces
1 tbsp. fresh parsley, chopped
2 tbsps. bread crumbs
4 tbsps. low-fat Parmesan cheese, grated
1 tbsp. olive oil
Salt and black pepper, to taste

1. Preheat the Air fryer to 360ºF (182ºC) and grease an Air fryer basket.
2. Arrange the zucchini pieces in the Air fryer basket with their skin side down.
3. Top with the remaining ingredients and air fry for about 15 minutes.
4. Dish out and serve warm.

Nutrition Info per Serving:

Calories: 481, Fat: 11.1g, Carbohydrates: 9.1g, Sugar: 3g, Protein: 7g, Sodium: 203mg

Sautéed Spinach

Prep time: 15 minutes, Cook time: 9 minutes, Serves 2

1 small onion, chopped
6 ounces fresh spinach
2 tbsps. olive oil

1 tsp. ginger, minced
Salt and black pepper, to taste

1. Preheat the Air fryer to 360ºF (182ºC) and grease an Air fryer pan.
2. Put olive oil, onions and ginger in the Air fryer pan and place in the Air fryer basket.
3. Air fry for about 4 minutes and add spinach, salt, and black pepper.
4. Air fry for about 4 more minutes and dish out in a bowl to serve.

Nutrition Info per Serving:

Calories: 156, Fat: 14.4g, Carbohydrates: 6.9g, Sugar: 1.9g, Protein: 2.9g, Sodium: 146mg

Tuna Patty Sliders

Prep time: 15 minutes, Cook time: 10 to 15 minutes, Serves 4

3 (5-ounce / 142-g) cans tuna, packed in water
⅔ cup whole-wheat panko bread crumbs
⅓ cup shredded low-fat Parmesan cheese
1 tbsp. sriracha
¾ tsp. black pepper
10 whole-wheat slider buns
Cooking spray

1. Preheat the air fryer to 350ºF (177ºC).
2. Spray the air fryer basket lightly with cooking spray.
3. In a medium bowl combine the tuna, bread crumbs, Parmesan cheese, sriracha, and black pepper and stir to combine.
4. Form the mixture into 10 patties.
5. Place the patties in the air fryer basket in a single layer. Spray the patties lightly with cooking spray. You may need to cook them in batches.
6. Air fry for 6 to 8 minutes. Turn the patties over and lightly spray with cooking spray. Air fry until golden brown and crisp, another 4 to 7 more minutes. Serve the patties on buns.

Nutrition Info per Serving:

Calories: 250, Protein: 28g, Fat: 6g, Carbohydrates: 21g, Fiber: 4g, Sugar: 3g, Sodium: 660mg

Cheesy Stuffed Mushrooms

Prep time: 10 minutes, Cook time: 8 to 12 minutes, Serves 4

16 medium button mushrooms, rinsed and patted dry
⅓ cup low-sodium salsa
3 garlic cloves, minced
1 medium onion, finely chopped
1 jalapeño pepper, minced
⅛ tsp. cayenne pepper
3 tbsps. shredded Pepper Jack cheese
2 tsps. olive oil

1. Preheat the air fryer to 350ºF (177ºC).
2. Remove the stems from the mushrooms and finely chop them, reserving the whole caps.
3. In a medium bowl, mix the salsa, garlic, onion, jalapeño, cayenne, and Pepper Jack cheese. Stir in the chopped mushroom stems.
4. Stuff this mixture into the mushroom caps, mounding the filling. Drizzle the olive oil on the mushrooms. Air fry the mushrooms in the air fryer basket for 8 to 12 minutes, or until the filling is hot and the mushrooms are tender.
5. Serve immediately.

Nutrition Info per Serving:

Calories: 75, Protein: 4g, Fat: 3g, Carbohydrates: 9g, Fiber: 2g, Sugar: 4g, Sodium: 180mg

Buffalo Cauliflower with Sour Dip

Prep time: 10 minutes, Cook time: 10 to 14 minutes, Serves 6

1 large head cauliflower, separated into small florets
1 tbsp. olive oil
½ tsp. garlic powder
⅓ cup low-sodium hot wing sauce, divided
⅔ cup nonfat Greek yogurt
½ tsp. Tabasco sauce
1 celery stalk, chopped
1 tbsp. crumbled blue cheese

1. Preheat the air fryer to 380ºF (193ºC).
2. In a large bowl, toss the cauliflower florets with the olive oil. Sprinkle with the garlic powder and toss again to coat. Put half of the cauliflower in the air fryer basket. Air fry for 5 to 7 minutes, or until the cauliflower is browned, shaking the basket once during cooking.
3. Transfer to a serving bowl and toss with half of the wing sauce. Repeat with the remaining cauliflower and wing sauce.
4. In a small bowl, stir together the yogurt, Tabasco sauce, celery, and blue cheese. Serve the cauliflower with the dip.

Nutrition Info per Serving:

Calories: 80, Protein: 5g, Fat: 3g, Carbohydrates: 10g, Fiber: 3g, Sugar: 4g, Sodium: 270mg

Merguez Meatballs

Prep time: 10 minutes, Cook time: 10 minutes, Serves 4

1 pound (454 g) ground chicken
2 garlic cloves, finely minced
1 tbsp. sweet Hungarian paprika
1 tsp. kosher salt
1 tsp. coconut sugar
1 tsp. ground cumin
½ tsp. black pepper
½ tsp. ground fennel
½ tsp. ground coriander
½ tsp. cayenne pepper
¼ tsp. ground allspice

1. In a large bowl, gently mix the chicken, garlic, paprika, salt, sugar, cumin, black pepper, fennel, coriander, cayenne, and allspice until all the ingredients are incorporated. Let stand for 30 minutes at room temperature, or cover and refrigerate for up to 24 hours.
2. Preheat the air fryer to 400ºF (204ºC).
3. Form the mixture into 16 meatballs. Arrange them in a single layer in the air fryer basket. Air fry for 10 minutes, turning the meatballs halfway through the cooking time. Use a meat thermometer to ensure the meatballs have reached an internal temperature of 165ºF (74ºC).
4. Serve warm.

Nutrition Info per Serving:

Calories: 190, Protein: 22g, Fat: 10g, Carbohydrates: 4g, Fiber: 1g, Sugar: 1g, Sodium: 640mg

Shrimp Kebabs

Prep time: 15 minutes, Cook time: 10 minutes, Serves 2

¾ pound shrimp, peeled and deveined
1 tbsp. fresh cilantro, chopped
Wooden skewers, presoaked
2 tbsps. fresh lemon juice
1 tsp. garlic, minced
½ tsp. paprika
½ tsp. ground cumin
Salt and ground black pepper, as required

1. Preheat the Air fryer to 350ºF (177ºC) and grease an Air fryer basket.
2. Mix lemon juice, cumin, garlic, and paprika in a bowl.
3. Stir in the shrimp and mix to coat well. Season with salt and pepper to taste.
4. Thread the shrimp onto presoaked wooden skewers and transfer to the Air fryer basket.
5. Roast for about 10 minutes, flipping once in between.
6. Dish out the mixture onto serving plates and serve garnished with fresh cilantro.

Nutrition Info per Serving:

Calories: 212, Fat: 3.2g, Carbohydrates: 3.9g, Sugar: 0.4g, Protein: 39.1g, Sodium: 497mg

Salsa Stuffed Eggplants

Prep time: 15 minutes, Cook time: 25 minutes, Serves 2

1 large eggplant
8 cherry tomatoes, quartered
½ tbsp. fresh parsley
2 tsps. olive oil, divided
2 tsps. fresh lemon juice, divided
2 tbsps. tomato salsa
Salt and black pepper, as required

1. Preheat the Air fryer to 390ºF (199ºC) and grease an Air fryer basket.
2. Arrange the eggplant into the Air fryer basket and air fry for about 15 minutes.
3. Cut the eggplant in half lengthwise and drizzle evenly with one tsp. of oil.
4. Set the Air fryer to 355ºF (179ºC) and arrange the eggplant into the Air fryer basket, cut-side up.
5. Air fry for another 10 minutes and dish out in a bowl.
6. Scoop out the flesh from the eggplant and transfer into a bowl.
7. Stir in the tomatoes, salsa, parsley, salt, black pepper, remaining oil, and lemon juice.
8. Squeeze lemon juice on the eggplant halves and stuff with the salsa mixture to serve.

Nutrition Info per Serving:

Calories: 192, Fat: 6.1g, Carbohydrates: 33.8g, Sugar: 20.4g, Protein: 6.9g, Sodium: 204mg

Hummus Mushroom Pizza

Prep time: 15 minutes, Cook time: 25 minutes, Serves 2

4 Portobello mushroom caps, stemmed and gills removed
3 ounces zucchini, shredded
2 tbsps. sweet red pepper, seeded and chopped
4 Kalamata olives, sliced
½ cup hummus
1 tbsp. balsamic vinegar
Salt and black pepper, to taste
4 tbsps. pasta sauce
1 garlic clove, minced
1 tsp. dried basil

1. Preheat the Air fryer to 330ºF (166ºC) and grease an Air fryer basket.
2. Coat both sides of all Portobello mushroom cap with vinegar.
3. Season the inside of each mushroom cap with salt and black pepper.
4. Divide pasta sauce and garlic inside each mushroom.
5. Arrange mushroom caps into the Air fryer basket and air fry for about 3 minutes.
6. Remove from the Air fryer and top zucchini, red peppers and olives on each mushroom cap.
7. Season with basil, salt, and black pepper and transfer into the Air fryer basket.
8. Air fry for about 3 more minutes and dish out in a serving platter.
9. Spread hummus on each mushroom pizza and serve.

Nutrition Info per Serving:

Calories: 115, Fat: 4.1g, Carbohydrates: 15.4g, Sugar: 4.8g, Protein: 6.7g, Sodium: 264mg

Spiced Butternut Squash

Prep time: 15 minutes, Cook time: 20 minutes, Serves 4

1 medium butternut squash, peeled, seeded and cut into chunk
2 tsps. cumin seeds
2 tbsps. pine nuts
2 tbsps. fresh cilantro, chopped
⅛ tsp. garlic powder
⅛ tsp. chili flakes, crushed
Salt and ground black pepper, as required
1 tbsp. olive oil

1. Preheat the Air fryer to 375ºF (191ºC) and grease an Air fryer basket.
2. Mix the squash, spices and olive oil in a bowl.
3. Arrange the butternut squash chunks into the Air fryer basket and air fry for about 20 minutes.
4. Dish out the butternut squash chunks onto serving plates and serve garnished with pine nuts and cilantro.

Nutrition Info per Serving:

Calories: 165, Fat: 6.9g, Carbohydrates: 27.6g, Sugar: 5.2g, Protein: 3.1g, Sodium: 50mg

Air Fryer Naked Chicken Tenders

Prep time: 5 minutes, Cook time: 7 minutes, Serves 4

For the Seasoning:
1 tsp. kosher salt
½ tsp. garlic powder
½ tsp. onion powder
½ tsp. chili powder
¼ tsp. sweet paprika
¼ tsp. freshly ground black pepper
For the Chicken:
8 chicken breast tenders (1 pound / 454 g total)
2 tbsps. mayonnaise

1. Preheat the air fryer to 375ºF (191ºC).
2. For the seasoning: In a small bowl, combine the salt, garlic powder, onion powder, chili powder, paprika, and pepper.
3. For the chicken: Place the chicken in a medium bowl and add the mayonnaise. Mix well to coat all over, then sprinkle with the seasoning mix.
4. Working in batches, arrange a single layer of the chicken in the air fryer basket. Air fry for 6 to 7 minutes, flipping halfway, until cooked through in the center. Serve immediately.

Nutrition Info per Serving:

Calories: 220, Protein: 26g, Fat: 12g, Carbohydrates: 1g, Fiber: 0g, Sugar: 0g, Sodium: 692mg

Black Bean and Tomato Chili

Prep time: 15 minutes, Cook time: 23 minutes, Serves 6

1 tbsp. olive oil
1 medium onion, diced
3 garlic cloves, minced
1 cup vegetable broth
3 cans black beans, drained and rinsed
2 cans diced tomatoes
2 chipotle peppers, chopped
2 tsps. cumin
2 tsps. chili powder
1 tsp. dried oregano
½ tsp. salt

1. Over a medium heat, fry the garlic and onions in the olive oil for 3 minutes.
2. Add the remaining ingredients, stirring constantly and scraping the bottom to prevent sticking.
3. Preheat the air fryer to 400ºF (204ºC).
4. Take a dish and place the mixture inside. Put a sheet of aluminum foil on top.
5. Transfer to the air fryer and bake for 20 minutes.
6. When ready, plate up and serve immediately.

Nutrition Info per Serving:

Calories: 243, Protein: 11g, Fat: 4g, Carbohydrates: 41g, Fiber: 13g, Sugar: 5g, Sodium: 683mg

Radish Sticks

Prep time: 10 minutes, Cook time: 12 minutes, Serves 2

1 large radish, peeled and cut into sticks
1 tbsp. fresh rosemary, finely chopped
1 tbsp. olive oil
2 tsps. coconut sugar
¼ tsp. cayenne pepper
Salt and black pepper, as needed

1. Preheat the Air fryer to 390ºF (199ºC) and grease an Air fryer basket.
2. Mix radish with all other ingredients in a bowl until well combined.
3. Arrange the radish sticks in the Air fryer basket and air fry for about 12 minutes.
4. Dish out and serve warm.

Nutrition Info per Serving:

Calories: 96, Fat: 7.3g, Carbohydrates: 8.7g, Sugar: 5.8g, Protein: 0.4g, Sodium: 26mg

Crispy Chickpeas

Prep time: 5 minutes, Cook time: 15 minutes, Serves 4

1 (15-ounces / 425-g) can chickpeas, drained but not rinsed
2 tbsps. olive oil
1 tsp. salt
2 tbsps. lemon juice

1. Preheat the air fryer to 400ºF (204ºC).
2. Add all the ingredients together in a bowl and mix. Transfer this mixture to the air fryer basket.
3. Air fry for 15 minutes, ensuring the chickpeas become nice and crispy.
4. Serve immediately.

Nutrition Info per Serving:

Calories: 174, Protein: 6g, Fat: 8g, Carbohydrates: 19g, Fiber: 5g, Sugar: 3g, Sodium: 594mg

Classic Shrimp Empanadas

Prep time: 10 minutes, Cook time: 8 minutes, Serves 5

½ pound (227g) raw shrimp, peeled, deveined and chopped
¼ cup chopped red onion
1 scallion, chopped
2 garlic cloves, minced
2 tbsps. minced red bell pepper
2 tbsps. chopped fresh cilantro
½ tbsp. fresh lime juice
¼ tsp. sweet paprika
⅛ tsp. kosher salt
⅛ tsp. crushed red pepper flakes (optional)
1 large egg, beaten
10 frozen Goya Empanada Discos, thawed
Cooking spray

1. In a medium bowl, combine the shrimp, red onion, scallion, garlic, bell pepper, cilantro, lime juice, paprika, salt, and pepper flakes (if using).
2. In a small bowl, beat the egg with 1 tsp. water until smooth.
3. Place an empanada disc on a work surface and put 2 tbsps. of the shrimp mixture in the center. Brush the outer edges of the disc with the egg wash. Fold the disc over and gently press the edges to seal. Use a fork and press around the edges to crimp and seal completely. Brush the tops of the empanadas with the egg wash.
4. Preheat the air fryer to 380ºF (193ºC).
5. Spray the bottom of the air fryer basket with cooking spray to prevent sticking. Working in batches, arrange a single layer of the empanadas in the air fryer basket and air fry for about 8 minutes, flipping halfway, until golden brown and crispy.
6. Serve hot.

Nutrition Info per Serving:

Calories: 227, Protein: 10g, Fat: 6g, Carbohydrates: 33g, Fiber: 2g, Sugar: 1g, Sodium: 400mg

Beet Chips

Prep time: 10 minutes, Cook time: 15 minutes, Serves 6

4 medium beets, peeled and thinly sliced
¼ tsp. smoked paprika
½ tsp. salt
2 tbsps. olive oil

1. Preheat the Air fryer to 325ºF (163ºC) and grease an Air fryer basket.
2. Mix together all the ingredients in a bowl until well combined.
3. Arrange the beet slices in the Air fryer basket and air fry for about 15 minutes.
4. Dish out and serve warm.

Nutrition Info per Serving:

Calories: 60, Fat: 4.8g, Carbohydrates: 5.3g, Sugar: 3.7g, Protein: 0.9g, Sodium: 236mg

Cauliflower, Chickpea, and Avocado Mash

1 medium head cauliflower, cut into florets
1 can chickpeas, drained and rinsed
1 tbsp. extra-virgin olive oil
2 tbsps. lemon juice
Salt and ground black pepper, to taste
4 flatbreads, toasted
2 ripe avocados, mashed

1. Preheat the air fryer to 425°F (218°C).
2. In a bowl, mix the chickpeas, cauliflower, lemon juice and olive oil. Sprinkle salt and pepper as desired.
3. Put inside the air fryer basket and air fry for 25 minutes.
4. Spread on top of the flatbread along with the mashed avocado. Sprinkle with more pepper and salt and serve.

Nutrition Info per Serving:

Calories: 420, Protein: 12g, Fat: 22g, Carbohydrates: 38g, Fiber: 14g, Sugar: 3g, Sodium: 440mg

Turkey Hoisin Burgers

1 pound (454 g) lean ground turkey
¼ cup whole-wheat bread crumbs
¼ cup hoisin sauce
2 tbsps. soy sauce
4 whole-wheat buns
Olive oil spray

1. In a large bowl, mix together the turkey, bread crumbs, hoisin sauce, and soy sauce.
2. Form the mixture into 4 equal patties. Cover with plastic wrap and refrigerate the patties for 30 minutes.
3. Preheat the air fryer to 370°F (188°C). Spray the air fryer basket lightly with olive oil spray.
4. Place the patties in the air fryer basket in a single layer. Spray the patties lightly with olive oil spray.
5. Air fry for 10 minutes. Flip the patties over, lightly spray with olive oil spray, and air fry for an additional 5 to 10 minutes, until golden brown.
6. Place the patties on buns and top with your choice of low-calorie burger toppings like sliced tomatoes, onions, and cabbage slaw. Serve immediately.

Nutrition Info per Serving:

Calories: 180, Protein: 20g, Fat: 6g, Carbohydrates: 11g, Fiber: 1g, Sugar: 5g, Sodium: 590mg

Herbed Carrots

cooking spray
6 large carrots, peeled and sliced lengthwise
4 tbsps. olive oil
½ tbsp. fresh oregano, chopped
½ tbsp. fresh parsley, chopped
Salt and black pepper, to taste
½ cup fat-free Italian dressing

1. Preheat the Air fryer to 360°F (182°C) and grease an Air fryer basket with cooking spray.
2. Mix the carrot slices and 4 tbsps. olive oil in a bowl and toss to coat well.
3. Arrange the carrot slices in the Air fryer basket and air fry for about 12 minutes.
4. Dish out the carrot slices onto serving plates and sprinkle with herbs, salt and black pepper.
5. Transfer into the Air fryer basket and air fry for 2 more minutes.
6. Dish out and serve hot.

Nutrition Info per Serving:

Calories: 93, Fat: 7.2g, Carbohydrates: 7.3g, Sugar: 3.8g, Protein: 0.7g, Sodium: 252mg

Artichoke-Spinach Dip

1 (14-ounce / 397-g) can artichoke hearts packed in water, drained and chopped
1 (10-ounce / 284-g) package frozen spinach, thawed and drained
1 tsp. minced garlic
2 tbsps. mayonnaise
¼ cup nonfat plain Greek yogurt
¼ cup shredded part-skim Mozzarella cheese
¼ cup grated low-fat Parmesan cheese
¼ tsp. freshly ground black pepper
Cooking spray

1. Preheat the air fryer to 360°F (182°C).
2. Wrap the artichoke hearts and spinach in a paper towel and squeeze out any excess liquid, then transfer the vegetables to a large bowl.
3. Add the minced garlic, mayonnaise, plain Greek yogurt, Mozzarella, Parmesan, and black pepper to the large bowl, stirring well to combine.
4. Spray a baking pan with cooking spray, then transfer the dip mixture to the pan and air fry for 10 minutes.
5. Remove the dip from the air fryer and allow to cool in the pan on a wire rack for 10 minutes before serving.

Nutrition Info per Serving:

Calories: 60, Protein: 3g, Fat: 3.5g, Carbohydrates: 4g, Fiber: 1g, Sugar: 1g, Sodium: 180mg

Tofu with Orange Sauce

1 pound extra-firm tofu, pressed and cubed
½ cup water
4 tsps. cornstarch, divided
2 scallions (green part), chopped
1 tbsp. tamari
⅓ cup fresh orange juice
1 tbsp. honey
1 tsp. orange zest, grated
1 tsp. garlic, minced
1 tsp. fresh ginger, minced
¼ tsp. red pepper flakes, crushed

1. Preheat the Air fryer to 390°F (199°C) and grease an Air fryer basket.
2. Mix the tofu, cornstarch, and tamari in a bowl and toss to coat well.
3. Arrange half of the tofu pieces in the Air fryer basket and air fry for about 10 minutes.
4. Repeat with the remaining tofu and dish out in a bowl.
5. Put all the ingredients except scallions in a small pan over medium-high heat and bring to a boil.
6. Pour this sauce over the tofu and garnish with scallions to serve.

Nutrition Info per Serving:

Calories: 148, Fat: 6.7g, Carbohydrates: 13g, Sugar: 6.9g, Protein: 12.1g, Sodium: 263mg

CHAPTER 8
POULTRY

Lemon Parmesan Chicken

Prep time: 10 minutes, Cook time: 20 minutes, Serves 4

1 egg
2 tbsps. lemon juice
2 tsps. minced garlic
½ tsp. salt
½ tsp. freshly ground black pepper
4 boneless, skinless chicken breasts, thin cut
Olive oil spray
½ cup whole-wheat bread crumbs
¼ cup grated low-fat Parmesan cheese

1. In a medium bowl, whisk together the egg, lemon juice, garlic, salt, and pepper. Add the chicken breasts, cover, and refrigerate for up to 1 hour.
2. In a shallow bowl, combine the bread crumbs and Parmesan cheese.
3. Preheat the air fryer to 360°F (182°C). Spray the air fryer basket lightly with olive oil spray.
4. Remove the chicken breasts from the egg mixture, then dredge them in the bread crumb mixture, and place in the air fryer basket in a single layer. Lightly spray the chicken breasts with olive oil spray. You may need to cook the chicken in batches.
5. Air fry for 8 minutes. Flip the chicken over, lightly spray with olive oil spray, and air fry until the chicken reaches an internal temperature of 165°F (74°C), for an additional 7 to 12 minutes.
6. Serve warm.

Nutrition Info per Serving:

Calories: 259, Protein: 34g, Fat: 6g, Carbohydrates: 15g, Fiber: 2g, Sugar: 1g, Sodium: 620mg

Mini Turkey Meatloaves with Carrot

Prep time: 6 minutes, Cook time: 20 to 24 minutes, Serves 4

⅓ cup minced onion
¼ cup grated carrot
2 garlic cloves, minced
2 tbsps. ground almonds
2 tsps. olive oil
1 tsp. dried marjoram
1 egg white
¾ pound (340 g) ground turkey breast

1. Preheat the air fryer to 400°F (204°C).
2. In a medium bowl, stir together the onion, carrot, garlic, almonds, olive oil, marjoram, and egg white.
3. Add the ground turkey. With your hands, gently but thoroughly mix until combined.
4. Double 16 foil muffin cup liners to make 8 cups. Divide the turkey mixture evenly among the liners.
5. Bake for 20 to 24 minutes, or until the meatloaves reach an internal temperature of 165°F (74°C) on a meat thermometer. Serve immediately.

Nutrition Info per Serving:

Calories: 141, Protein: 15g, Fat: 7g, Carbohydrates: 5g, Fiber: 1g, Sugar: 2g, Sodium: 80mg

Tempero Baiano Brazilian Chicken

Prep time: 5 minutes, Cook time: 20 minutes, Serves 4

1 tsp. cumin seeds
1 tsp. dried oregano
1 tsp. dried parsley
1 tsp. ground turmeric
½ tsp. coriander seeds
1 tsp. kosher salt
½ tsp. black peppercorns
½ tsp. cayenne pepper
¼ cup fresh lime juice
2 tbsps. olive oil
1½ pounds (680 g) chicken drumsticks

1. In a clean coffee grinder or spice mill, combine the cumin, oregano, parsley, turmeric, coriander seeds, salt, peppercorns, and cayenne. Process until finely ground.
2. In a small bowl, combine the ground spices with the lime juice and oil. Place the chicken in a resealable plastic bag. Add the marinade, seal, and massage until the chicken is well coated. Marinate at room temperature for 30 minutes or in the refrigerator for up to 24 hours.
3. Preheat the air fryer to 400°F (204°C).
4. Place the drumsticks skin-side up in the air fryer basket and air fry for 20 to 25 minutes, turning the drumsticks halfway through the cooking time. Use a meat thermometer to ensure that the chicken has reached an internal temperature of 165°F (74°C). Serve immediately.

Nutrition Info per Serving:

Calories: 322, Protein: 26g, Fat: 22g, Carbohydrates: 3g, Fiber: 1g, Sugar: 0g, Sodium: 644mg

Jerk Chicken, Pineapple and Veggie Kabobs

Prep time: 20 minutes, Cook time: 18 minutes, Serves 8

8 (4-ounces) boneless, skinless chicken thigh fillets, trimmed and cut into cubes
2 large zucchinis, sliced
8 ounces white mushrooms, stems removed
1 (20-ounces) can pineapple chunks, drained
Wooden skewers, presoaked
1 tbsp. jerk seasoning
Salt and black pepper, to taste
1 tbsp. jerk sauce

1. Preheat the Air fryer to 370°F (188°C) and grease an Air fryer basket.
2. Mix the chicken cubes and jerk seasoning in a bowl.
3. Season the zucchini slices and mushrooms evenly with salt and black pepper.
4. Thread chicken, zucchinis, mushrooms and pineapple chunks onto presoaked wooden skewers.
5. Transfer half of the skewers in the Air fryer basket and roast for about 9 minutes.
6. Repeat with the remaining mixture and dish out to serve hot.

Nutrition Info per Serving:

Calories: 274, Fat: 8.7g, Carbohydrates: 14.1g, Sugar: 9.9g, Protein: 35.1g, Sodium: 150mg

Chicken with Veggies

4 small artichoke hearts, quartered
4 fresh large button mushrooms, quartered
½ small onion, cut in large chunks
2 skinless, boneless chicken breasts
2 tbsps. fresh parsley, chopped
2 garlic cloves, minced
2 tbsps. chicken broth
2 tbsps. red wine vinegar
2 tbsps. olive oil
1 tbsp. Dijon mustard
⅛ tsp. dried thyme
⅛ tsp. dried basil
Salt and black pepper, as required

1. Preheat the Air fryer to 350ºF (177ºC) and grease a baking dish lightly.
2. Mix the garlic, broth, vinegar, olive oil, mustard, thyme, and basil in a bowl.
3. Place the artichokes, mushrooms, onions, salt, and black pepper in the baking dish.
4. Layer with the chicken breasts and spread half of the mustard mixture evenly on it.
5. Transfer the baking dish into the Air fryer basket and air fry for about 23 minutes.
6. Coat the chicken breasts with the remaining mustard mixture and flip the side.
7. Air fry for about 22 minutes and serve garnished with parsley.

Nutrition Info per Serving:

Calories: 448, Fat: 19.1g, Carbohydrates: 39.1g, Sugar: 5g, Protein: 38.5g, Sodium: 566mg

Roasted Chicken with Garlic

4 (5-ounce / 142-g) low-sodium bone-in skinless chicken breasts
1 tbsp. olive oil
1 tbsp. freshly squeezed lemon juice
3 tbsps. cornstarch
1 tsp. dried basil leaves
⅛ tsp. freshly ground black pepper
20 garlic cloves, unpeeled

1. Preheat the air fryer to 370ºF (188ºC).
2. Rub the chicken with the olive oil and lemon juice on both sides and sprinkle with the cornstarch, basil, and pepper.
3. Place the seasoned chicken in the air fryer basket and top with the garlic cloves. Roast for about 25 minutes, or until the garlic is soft and the chicken reaches an internal temperature of 165ºF (74ºC) on a meat thermometer. Serve immediately.

Nutrition Info per Serving:

Calories: 262, Protein: 28g, Fat: 10g, Carbohydrates: 16g, Fiber: 1g, Sugar: 0.5g, Sodium: 65mg

Turkey Stuffed Bell Peppers

½ pound (227 g) lean ground turkey
4 medium bell peppers
1 (15-ounce / 425-g) can black beans, drained and rinsed
1 cup shredded reduced-fat Cheddar cheese
1 cup cooked long-grain brown rice
1 cup mild salsa
1¼ tsps. chili powder
1 tsp. salt
½ tsp. ground cumin
½ tsp. freshly ground black pepper
Olive oil spray
Chopped fresh cilantro, for garnish

1. Preheat the air fryer to 360ºF (182ºC).
2. In a large skillet over medium-high heat, cook the turkey, breaking it up with a spoon, until browned, about 5 minutes. Drain off any excess fat.
3. Cut about ½ inch off the tops of the peppers and then cut in half lengthwise. Remove and discard the seeds and set the peppers aside.
4. In a large bowl, combine the browned turkey, black beans, Cheddar cheese, rice, salsa, chili powder, salt, cumin, and black pepper. Spoon the mixture into the bell peppers.
5. Lightly spray the air fryer basket with olive oil spray.
6. Place the stuffed peppers in the air fryer basket. Air fry until heated through, 10 to 15 minutes. Garnish with cilantro and serve.

Nutrition Info per Serving:

Calories: 295, Protein: 22g, Fat: 9g, Carbohydrates: 33g, Fiber: 10g, Sugar: 5g, Sodium: 757mg

Appetizing Chicken

¾ pound chicken pieces
1 tbsp. fresh rosemary, chopped
1 lemon, cut into wedges
1 tsp. ginger, minced
1 tbsp. soy sauce
½ tbsp. olive oil
1 tbsp. oyster sauce
3 tbsps. coconut sugar

1. Preheat the Air fryer to 390ºF (199ºC) and grease an Air fryer basket.
2. Mix chicken, ginger, soy sauce and olive oil in a bowl.
3. Marinate and refrigerate for about 30 minutes and transfer the chicken in the Air fryer basket.
4. Air fry for about 6 minutes and dish out.
5. Meanwhile, mix the remaining ingredients in a small bowl and spread over the chicken.
6. Squeeze juice from lemon wedges over chicken and top with the wedges.
7. Transfer into the Air fryer basket and air fry for about 13 minutes.
8. Dish out and serve warm.

Nutrition Info per Serving:

Calories: 353, Fat: 9g, Carbohydrates: 16.2g, Sugar: 13.4g, Protein: 50g, Sodium: 618mg

Delightful Turkey Wings

Prep time: 10 minutes, Cook time: 26 minutes, Serves 4

2 pounds turkey wings
4 tbsps. chicken rub
3 tbsps. olive oil

1. Preheat the Air fryer to 380ºF (193ºC) and grease an Air fryer basket.
2. Mix the turkey wings, chicken rub, and olive oil in a bowl until well combined.
3. Arrange the turkey wings into the Air fryer basket and roast for about 26 minutes, flipping once in between.
4. Dish out the turkey wings in a platter and serve hot.

Nutrition Info per Serving:
Calories: 204, Fat: 15.5g, Carbohydrates: 3g, Sugar: 0g, Protein: 12g, Sodium: 465mg

Sriracha Turkey Legs

Prep time: 10 minutes, Cook time: 35 minutes, Serves 2

1-pound turkey legs
1 tbsp. vegan butter
1 tbsp. cilantro
1 tbsp. chives
1 tbsp. scallions
4 tbsps. sriracha sauce
1½ tbsps. soy sauce
½ lime, juiced

1. Preheat the Air fryer to 360ºF (182ºC) for 3 minutes and grease an Air fryer basket.
2. Arrange the turkey legs in the Air fryer basket and roast for about 30 minutes, flipping several times in between.
3. Mix butter, scallions, sriracha sauce, soy sauce and lime juice in the saucepan and cook for about 3 minutes until the sauce thickens.
4. Drizzle this sauce over the turkey legs and garnish with cilantro and chives to serve.

Nutrition Info per Serving:
Calories: 361, Fat: 16.3g, Carbohydrates: 9.3g, Sugar: 18.2g, Protein: 33.3g, Sodium: 515mg

Crispy Herbed Turkey Breast

Prep time: 5 minutes, Cook time: 30 minutes, Serves 2

½ tbsp. fresh rosemary, chopped
½ tbsp. fresh parsley, chopped
2 turkey breasts
1 garlic clove, minced
1 tbsp. ginger, minced
1 tsp. five spice powder
Salt and black pepper, to taste

1. Preheat the Air fryer to 340ºF (171ºC) and grease an Air fryer basket.
2. Mix garlic, herbs, five spice powder, salt and black pepper in a bowl.
3. Brush the turkey breasts generously with garlic mixture and transfer into the Air fryer.
4. Air fry for about 25 minutes and set the Air fryer to 390ºF (199ºC).
5. Air fry for about 5 more minutes and dish out to serve warm.

Nutrition Info per Serving:
Calories: 138, Fat: 4.5g, Carbohydrates: 1g, Sugar: 0g, Protein: 22g, Sodium: 82mg

Beer Coated Duck Breast

Prep time: 15 minutes, Cook time: 20 minutes, Serves 2

1 tbsp. fresh thyme, chopped
1 cup beer
1 (10½-ounces) duck breast
6 cherry tomatoes
1 tbsp. olive oil
1 tsp. mustard
Salt and ground black pepper, as required
1 tbsp. balsamic vinegar

1. Preheat the Air fryer to 390ºF (199ºC) and grease an Air fryer basket.
2. Mix the olive oil, mustard, thyme, beer, salt, and black pepper in a bowl.
3. Coat the duck breasts generously with marinade and refrigerate, covered for about 4 hours.
4. Cover the duck breasts and arrange into the Air fryer basket.
5. Roast for about 15 minutes and remove the foil from breast.
6. Set the Air fryer to 355ºF (179ºC) and place the duck breast and tomatoes into the Air Fryer basket.
7. Air fry for about 5 minutes and dish out the duck breasts and cherry tomatoes.
8. Drizzle with vinegar and serve immediately.

Nutrition Info per Serving:
Calories: 332, Fat: 13.7g, Carbohydrates: 9.2g, Sugar: 2.5g, Protein: 34.6g, Sodium: 88mg

Chicken Satay with Peanut Sauce

Prep time: 12 minutes, Cook time: 12 to 18 minutes, Serves 4

½ cup crunchy peanut butter
⅓ cup chicken broth
3 tbsps. low-sodium soy sauce
2 tbsps. lemon juice
2 cloves garlic, minced
2 tbsps. olive oil
1 tsp. curry powder
1 pound (454 g) chicken tenders

1. Preheat the air fryer to 390ºF (199ºC).
2. In a medium bowl, combine the peanut butter, chicken broth, soy sauce, lemon juice, garlic, olive oil, and curry powder, and mix well with a wire whisk until smooth. Remove 2 tbsps. of this mixture to a small bowl. Put remaining sauce into a serving bowl and set aside.
3. Add the chicken tenders to the bowl with the 2 tbsps. sauce and stir to coat. Let stand for a few minutes to marinate, then run a bamboo skewer through each chicken tender lengthwise.
4. Put the chicken in the air fryer basket and air fry in batches for 6 to 9 minutes or until the chicken reaches 165ºF (74ºC) on a meat thermometer. Serve the chicken with the reserved sauce.

Nutrition Info per Serving:
Calories: 446, Protein: 29g, Fat: 32g, Carbohydrates: 10g, Fiber: 2g, Sugar: 3g, Sodium: 571mg

Thai Curry Meatballs

Prep time: 10 minutes, Cook time: 10 minutes, Serves 4

1 pound (454 g) ground chicken
¼ cup chopped fresh cilantro
1 tsp. chopped fresh mint
1 tbsp. fresh lime juice
1 tbsp. Thai red, green, or yellow curry paste
1 tbsp. fish sauce
2 garlic cloves, minced
2 tsps. minced fresh ginger
½ tsp. kosher salt
½ tsp. black pepper
¼ tsp. red pepper flakes

1. Preheat the air fryer to 400ºF (204ºC).
2. In a large bowl, gently mix the ground chicken, cilantro, mint, lime juice, curry paste, fish sauce, garlic, ginger, salt, black pepper, and red pepper flakes until thoroughly combined.
3. Form the mixture into 16 meatballs. Place the meatballs in a single layer in the air fryer basket. Air fry for 10 minutes, turning the meatballs halfway through the cooking time. Use a meat thermometer to ensure the meatballs have reached an internal temperature of 165ºF (74ºC). Serve immediately.

Nutrition Info per Serving:

Calories: 176, Protein: 21g, Fat: 8g, Carbohydrates: 4g, Fiber: 1g, Sugar: 1g, Sodium: 619mg

Turkish Chicken Kebabs

Prep time: 15 minutes, Cook time: 15 minutes, Serves 4

¼ cup nonfat plain Greek yogurt
1 tbsp. minced garlic
1 tbsp. tomato paste
1 tbsp. fresh lemon juice
1 tbsp. vegetable oil
1 tsp. kosher salt
1 tsp. ground cumin
1 tsp. sweet Hungarian paprika
½ tsp. ground cinnamon
½ tsp. black pepper
½ tsp. cayenne pepper
1 pound (454 g) boneless, skinless chicken thighs, quartered crosswise

1. In a large bowl, combine the yogurt, garlic, tomato paste, lemon juice, vegetable oil, salt, cumin, paprika, cinnamon, black pepper, and cayenne. Stir until the spices are blended into the yogurt.
2. Add the chicken to the bowl and toss until well coated. Marinate at room temperature for 30 minutes, or cover and refrigerate for up to 24 hours.
3. Preheat the air fryer to 375ºF (191ºC).
4. Arrange the chicken in a single layer in the air fryer basket. Air fry for 10 minutes. Turn the chicken and air fry for 5 minutes more. Use a meat thermometer to ensure the chicken has reached an internal temperature of 165ºF (74ºC).
5. Serve warm.

Nutrition Info per Serving:

Calories: 184, Protein: 22g, Fat: 7g, Carbohydrates: 6g, Fiber: 1g, Sugar: 2g, Sodium: 698mg

Easy Tandoori Chicken

Prep time: 5 minutes, Cook time: 18 to 23 minutes, Serves 4

⅔ cup coconut yogurt
2 tbsps. freshly squeezed lemon juice
2 tsps. curry powder
½ tsp. ground cinnamon
2 garlic cloves, minced
2 tsps. olive oil
4 (5-ounce / 142-g) low-sodium boneless, skinless chicken breasts

1. In a medium bowl, whisk the yogurt, lemon juice, curry powder, cinnamon, garlic, and olive oil.
2. With a sharp knife, cut thin slashes into the chicken. Add it to the yogurt mixture and turn to coat. Let stand for 10 minutes at room temperature. You can also prepare this ahead of time and marinate the chicken in the refrigerator for up to 24 hours.
3. Preheat the air fryer to 360ºF (182ºC).
4. Remove the chicken from the marinade and shake off any excess liquid. Discard any remaining marinade.
5. Roast the chicken for 10 minutes. With tongs, carefully turn each piece. Roast for 8 to 13 minutes more, or until the chicken reaches an internal temperature of 165ºF (74ºC) on a meat thermometer. Serve immediately.

Nutrition Info per Serving:

Calories: 190, Protein: 30g, Fat: 5g, Carbohydrates: 4g, Fiber: 1g, Sugar: 2g, Sodium: 252mg

Curried Chicken

Prep time: 15 minutes, Cook time: 18 minutes, Serves 3

1 pound boneless chicken, cubed
½ tbsp. cornstarch
1 egg
1 medium yellow onion, thinly sliced
½ cup evaporated milk
1 tbsp. light soy sauce
2 tbsps. olive oil
3 tsps. garlic, minced
1 tsp. fresh ginger, grated
5 curry leaves
1 tsp. curry powder
1 tbsp. chili sauce
1 tsp. coconut sugar
Salt and black pepper, as required

1. Preheat the Air fryer to 390ºF (199ºC) and grease an Air fryer basket.
2. Mix the chicken cubes, soy sauce, cornstarch and egg in a bowl and keep aside for about 1 hour.
3. Arrange the chicken cubes into the Air Fryer basket and air fry for about 10 minutes.
4. Heat olive oil in a medium skillet and add onion, green chili, garlic, ginger, and curry leaves.
5. Sauté for about 4 minutes and stir in the chicken cubes, curry powder, chili sauce, sugar, salt, and black pepper.
6. Mix well and add the evaporated milk.
7. Cook for about 4 minutes and dish out the chicken mixture into a serving bowl to serve.

Nutrition Info per Serving:

Calories: 363, Fat: 19g, Carbohydrates: 10g, Sugar: 0.8g, Protein: 37.1g, Sodium: 789mg

Herbed Turkey Breast

Prep time: 20 minutes, Cook time: 45 minutes, Serves 6

1 tbsp. olive oil
Cooking spray
2 garlic cloves, minced
2 tsps. Dijon mustard
1½ tsps. rosemary
1½ tsps. sage
1½ tsps. thyme
1 tsp. salt
½ tsp. freshly ground black pepper
3 pounds (1.4 kg) turkey breast, thawed if frozen

1. Preheat the air fryer to 370ºF (188ºC). Spray the air fryer basket lightly with cooking spray.
2. In a small bowl, mix together the garlic, olive oil, Dijon mustard, rosemary, sage, thyme, salt, and pepper to make a paste. Smear the paste all over the turkey breast.
3. Place the turkey breast in the air fryer basket. Air fry for 20 minutes. Flip turkey breast over and baste it with any drippings that have collected in the bottom drawer of the air fryer. Air fry until the internal temperature of the meat reaches at least 170ºF (77ºC), 20 more minutes.
4. If desired, increase the temperature to 400ºF (204ºC), flip the turkey breast over one last time, and air fry for 5 minutes to get a crispy exterior.
5. Let the turkey rest for 10 minutes before slicing and serving.

Nutrition Info per Serving:
Calories: 210, Protein: 30g, Fat: 5g, Carbohydrates: 2g, Fiber: 1g, Sugar: 0g, Sodium: 547mg

Almond-Crusted Chicken Nuggets

Prep time: 10 minutes, Cook time: 10 to 13 minutes, Serves 4

1 egg white
1 tbsp. freshly squeezed lemon juice
½ tsp. dried basil
½ tsp. ground paprika
1 pound (454 g) low-sodium boneless, skinless chicken breasts, cut into 1½-inch cubes
½ cup ground almonds
2 slices low-sodium whole-wheat bread, crumbled

1. Preheat the air fryer to 400ºF (204ºC).
2. In a shallow bowl, beat the egg white, lemon juice, basil, and paprika with a fork until foamy.
3. Add the chicken and stir to coat.
4. On a plate, mix the almonds and bread crumbs.
5. Toss the chicken cubes in the almond and bread crumb mixture until coated.
6. Bake the nuggets in the air fryer, in two batches, for 10 to 13 minutes, or until the chicken reaches an internal temperature of 165ºF (74ºC) on a meat thermometer. Serve immediately.

Nutrition Info per Serving:
Calories: 254, Protein: 29g, Fat: 10g, Carbohydrates: 10g, Fiber: 3g, Sugar: 2g, Sodium: 160mg

Roasted Cajun Turkey

Prep time: 10 minutes, Cook time: 30 minutes, Serves 4

2 pounds (907 g) turkey thighs, skinless and boneless
1 red onion, sliced
2 bell peppers, sliced
1 habanero pepper, minced
1 carrot, sliced
1 tbsp. Cajun seasoning mix
1 tbsp. fish sauce
2 cups chicken broth
Nonstick cooking spray

1. Preheat the air fryer to 360ºF (182ºC).
2. Spritz the bottom and sides of a baking dish with nonstick cooking spray.
3. Arrange the turkey thighs in the baking dish. Add the onion, peppers, and carrot. Sprinkle with Cajun seasoning. Add the fish sauce and chicken broth.
4. Roast in the preheated air fryer for 30 minutes until cooked through. Serve warm.

Nutrition Info per Serving:
Calories: 290, Protein: 31g, Fat: 7g, Carbohydrates: 22g, Fiber: 5g, Sugar: 7g, Sodium: 650mg

Coconut Chicken Meatballs

Prep time: 10 minutes, Cook time: 14 minutes, Serves 4

1 pound (454 g) ground chicken
2 scallions, finely chopped
1 cup chopped fresh cilantro leaves
¼ cup unsweetened shredded coconut
1 tbsp. hoisin sauce
1 tbsp. soy sauce
2 tsps. sriracha or other hot sauce
1 tsp. toasted sesame oil
½ tsp. kosher salt
1 tsp. black pepper

1. Preheat the air fryer to 350ºF (177ºC).
2. In a large bowl, gently mix the chicken, scallions, cilantro, coconut, hoisin, soy sauce, sriracha, sesame oil, salt, and pepper until thoroughly combined (the mixture will be wet and sticky).
3. Place a sheet of parchment paper in the air fryer basket. Using a small scoop or teaspoon, drop rounds of the mixture in a single layer onto the parchment paper.
4. Air fry for 10 minutes, turning the meatballs halfway through the cooking time. Increase the temperature to 400ºF (204ºC) and air fry for 4 minutes more to brown the outsides of the meatballs. Use a meat thermometer to ensure the meatballs have reached an internal temperature of 165ºF (74ºC).
5. Transfer the meatballs to a serving platter. Repeat with any remaining chicken mixture. Serve.

Nutrition Info per Serving:
Calories: 272, Protein: 28g, Fat: 16g, Carbohydrates: 6g, Fiber: 2g, Sugar: 2g, Sodium: 589mg

Ginger Chicken Thighs

Prep time: 10 minutes, Cook time: 10 minutes, Serves 4

¼ cup julienned peeled fresh ginger
2 tbsps. vegetable oil
1 tbsp. honey
1 tbsp. soy sauce
1 tbsp. ketchup
1 tsp. garam masala
1 tsp. ground turmeric
¼ tsp. kosher salt
½ tsp. cayenne pepper
Vegetable oil spray
1 pound (454 g) boneless, skinless chicken thighs, cut crosswise into thirds
¼ cup chopped fresh cilantro, for garnish

1. In a small bowl, combine the ginger, oil, honey, soy sauce, ketchup, garam masala, turmeric, salt, and cayenne. Whisk until well combined. Place the chicken in a resealable plastic bag and pour the marinade over. Seal the bag and massage to cover all of the chicken with the marinade. Marinate at room temperature for 30 minutes or in the refrigerator for up to 24 hours.
2. Preheat the air fryer to 350°F (177°C).
3. Spray the air fryer basket with vegetable oil spray and add the chicken and as much of the marinade and julienned ginger as possible. Bake for 10 minutes. Use a meat thermometer to ensure the chicken has reached an internal temperature of 165°F (74°C).
4. To serve, garnish with cilantro.

Nutrition Info per Serving:

Calories: 277, Protein: 21g, Fat: 17g, Carbohydrates: 13g, Fiber: 1g, Sugar: 8g, Sodium: 448mg

Spinach Stuffed Chicken Breasts

Prep time: 15 minutes, Cook time: 29 minutes, Serves 2

1¾ ounces fresh spinach
¼ cup low-fat ricotta cheese, shredded
2 (4-ounces) skinless, boneless chicken breasts
2 tbsps. low-fat cheddar cheese, grated
1 tbsp. olive oil
Salt and ground black pepper, as required
¼ tsp. paprika

1. Preheat the Air fryer to 390°F (199°C) and grease an Air fryer basket.
2. Heat olive oil in a medium skillet over medium heat and cook spinach for about 4 minutes.
3. Add the ricotta and cook for about 1 minute.
4. Cut the slits in each chicken breast horizontally and stuff with the spinach mixture.
5. Season each chicken breast evenly with salt and black pepper and top with cheddar cheese and paprika.
6. Arrange chicken breasts into the Air fryer basket in a single layer and air fry for about 25 minutes.
7. Dish out and serve hot.

Nutrition Info per Serving:

Calories: 279, Fat: 16g, Carbohydrates: 2.7g, Sugar: 0.3g, Protein: 31.4g, Sodium: 220mg

Whole Chicken Roast

Prep time: 10 minutes, Cook time: 1 hour, Serves 6

1 tsp. salt
1 tsp. Italian seasoning
½ tsp. freshly ground black pepper
½ tsp. paprika
½ tsp. garlic powder
½ tsp. onion powder
2 tbsps. olive oil, plus more as needed
1 (4-pound / 1.8-kg) fryer chicken

1. Preheat the air fryer to 360°F (182°C).
2. Grease the air fryer basket lightly with olive oil.
3. In a small bowl, mix the salt, Italian seasoning, pepper, paprika, garlic powder, and onion powder.
4. Remove any giblets from the chicken. Pat the chicken dry thoroughly with paper towels, including the cavity.
5. Brush the chicken all over with the olive oil and rub it with the seasoning mixture.
6. Truss the chicken or tie the legs with butcher's twine. This will make it easier to flip the chicken during cooking.
7. Put the chicken in the air fryer basket, breast-side down. Air fry for 30 minutes. Flip the chicken over and baste it with any drippings collected in the bottom drawer of the air fryer. Lightly brush the chicken with olive oil.
8. Air fry for 20 minutes. Flip the chicken over one last time and air fry until a thermometer inserted into the thickest part of the thigh reaches at least 165°F (74°C) and it's crispy and golden, 10 more minutes. Continue to cook, checking every 5 minutes until the chicken reaches the correct internal temperature.
9. Let the chicken rest for 10 minutes before carving and serving.

Nutrition Info per Serving:

Calories: 200, Protein: 20g, Fat: 12g, Carbohydrates: 1g, Fiber: 0g, Sugar: 0g, Sodium: 400mg

Fried Chicken Thighs

Prep time: 10 minutes, Cook time: 25 minutes, Serves 4

½ cup almond flour
1 egg beaten
4 small chicken thighs
1½ tbsps. Old Bay Cajun Seasoning
1 tsp. seasoning salt

1. Preheat the Air fryer to 400°F (204°C) for 3 minutes and grease an Air fryer basket.
2. Whisk the egg in a shallow bowl and place the old bay, flour and salt in another bowl.
3. Dip the chicken in the egg and coat with the flour mixture.
4. Arrange the chicken thighs in the Air fryer basket and air fry for about 25 minutes.
5. Dish out in a platter and serve warm.

Nutrition Info per Serving:

Calories: 180, Fat: 20g, Carbohydrates: 3g, Sugar: 1.2g, Protein: 21g, Sodium: 686mg

Sweet and Spicy Turkey Meatballs

Prep time: 15 minutes, Cook time: 15 minutes, Serves 6

1 pound (454 g) lean ground turkey
½ cup whole-wheat panko bread crumbs
1 egg, beaten
1 tbsp. soy sauce
¼ cup plus 1 tbsp. hoisin sauce, divided
2 tsps. minced garlic
⅛ tsp. salt
⅛ tsp. freshly ground black pepper
1 tsp. sriracha
Olive oil spray

1. Preheat the air fryer to 350ºF (177ºC). Spray the air fryer basket lightly with olive oil spray.
2. In a large bowl, mix together the turkey, panko bread crumbs, egg, soy sauce, 1 tbsp. of hoisin sauce, garlic, salt, and black pepper.
3. Using a tablespoon, form the mixture into 24 meatballs.
4. In a small bowl, combine the remaining ¼ cup of hoisin sauce and sriracha to make a glaze and set aside.
5. Place the meatballs in the air fryer basket in a single layer. You may need to cook them in batches.
6. Air fry for 8 minutes. Brush the meatballs generously with the glaze and air fry until cooked through, an additional 4 to 7 minutes. Serve warm.

Nutrition Info per Serving:

Calories: 150, Protein: 14g, Fat: 6g, Carbohydrates: 10g, Fiber: 1g, Sugar: 4g, Sodium: 450mg

Apricot-Glazed Chicken

Prep time: 5 minutes, Cook time: 12 minutes, Serves 2

2 tbsps. apricot preserves
½ tsp. minced fresh thyme or ⅛ tsp. dried
2 (8-ounce / 227-g) boneless, skinless chicken breasts, trimmed
1 tsp. olive oil
Salt and pepper, to taste

1. Preheat the air fryer to 400ºF (204ºC).
2. Microwave apricot preserves and thyme in bowl until fluid, about 30 seconds; set aside. Pound chicken to uniform thickness as needed. Pat dry with paper towels, rub with oil, and season with salt and pepper.
3. Arrange breasts skin-side down in air fryer basket, spaced evenly apart, alternating ends. Air fry the chicken for 4 minutes. Flip chicken and brush skin side with apricot-thyme mixture. Air fry until chicken registers 160ºF (71ºC), 8 to 12 minutes more.
4. Transfer chicken to serving platter, tent loosely with aluminum foil, and let rest for 5 minutes. Serve.

Nutrition Info per Serving:

Calories: 309, Protein: 34g, Fat: 9g, Carbohydrates: 25g, Fiber: 0.5g, Sugar: 16g, Sodium: 208mg

Simple Chicken Shawarma

Prep time: 10 minutes, Cook time: 15 minutes, Serves 4

For the Shawarma Spice:
2 tsps. dried oregano
1 tsp. ground cinnamon
1 tsp. ground cumin
1 tsp. ground coriander
1 tsp. kosher salt
½ tsp. ground allspice
½ tsp. cayenne pepper
For the Chicken:
1 pound (454 g) boneless, skinless chicken thighs, cut into large bite-size chunks
2 tbsps. vegetable oil
For Serving:
Tzatziki
Pita bread

1. For the shawarma spice: In a small bowl, combine the oregano, cayenne, cumin, coriander, salt, cinnamon, and allspice.
2. For the chicken: In a large bowl, toss together the chicken, vegetable oil, and shawarma spice to coat. Marinate at room temperature for 30 minutes or cover and refrigerate for up to 24 hours.
3. Preheat the air fryer to 350ºF (177ºC). Place the chicken in the air fryer basket. Air fry for 15 minutes, or until the chicken reaches an internal temperature of 165ºF (74ºC).
4. Transfer the chicken to a serving platter. Serve with tzatziki and pita bread.

Nutrition Info per Serving:

Calories: 260, Protein: 26g, Fat: 14g, Carbohydrates: 8g, Fiber: 2g, Sugar: 1g, Sodium: 651mg

Spicy Green Crusted Chicken

Prep time: 10 minutes, Cook time: 40 minutes, Serves 6

6 eggs, beaten
6 tsps. parsley
4 tsps. thyme
1 pound chicken pieces
6 tsps. oregano
Salt and freshly ground black pepper, to taste
4 tsps. paprika

1. Preheat the Air fryer to 360ºF (182ºC) and grease an Air fryer basket.
2. Whisk eggs in a bowl and mix all the ingredients in another bowl except chicken pieces.
3. Dip the chicken in eggs and then coat generously with the dry mixture.
4. Arrange half of the chicken pieces in the Air fryer basket and air fry for about 20 minutes.
5. Repeat with the remaining mixture and dish out to serve hot.

Nutrition Info per Serving:

Calories: 218, Fat: 10.4g, Carbohydrates: 2.6g, Sugar: 0.6g, Protein: 27.9g, Sodium: 128mg

Crunchy Stuffed Chicken Breast

Prep time: 20 minutes, Cook time: 45 minutes, Serves 2

1 medium eggplant, halved lengthwise
¼ cup pomegranate seeds
2 (4-ounce) chicken breasts, skinless and boneless
2 egg whites
¼ cup breadcrumbs
Salt, to taste
1 tsp. thyme
Freshly ground black pepper, to taste
½ tbsp. olive oil

1. Preheat the Air fryer to 390ºF (199ºC) and grease an Air fryer basket.
2. Season the eggplant halves with some salt and keep aside for about 20 minutes.
3. Arrange the eggplant halves in the Air fryer basket, cut side up and air fry for about 20 minutes.
4. Dish out and scoop out the flesh from each eggplant half.
5. Put the eggplant pulp and a pinch of salt and black pepper in the food processor and pulse until a puree is formed.
6. Dish out the eggplant puree into a bowl and stir in the pomegranate seeds.
7. Cut the chicken breasts lengthwise to make a pocket and stuff in the eggplant mixture.
8. Whisk together egg whites, a pinch of salt and black pepper in a shallow dish.
9. Mix breadcrumbs, thyme and olive oil in another dish.
10. Dip the chicken breasts in the egg white mixture and then coat with flour.
11. Set the Air fryer to 355ºF (179ºC) and transfer the chicken breasts into the Air fryer basket.
12. Air fry for about 25 minutes and dish out to serve warm.

Nutrition Info per Serving:
Calories: 386, Fat: 13.1g, Carbohydrates: 26.5g, Sugar: 9.4g, Protein: 40.6g, Sodium: 312mg

Special Salsa Chicken Steak

Prep time: 10 minutes, Cook time: 30 minutes, Serves 6

2 pounds chicken steak	2 cups salsa
½ cup shredded Monterey Jack cheese	½ tsp. hot pepper sauce
1 cup tomato sauce	Salt and black pepper, to
½ tsp. garlic powder	taste

1. Preheat the Air fryer to 450ºF (232ºC) and grease an Air fryer basket.
2. Season the chicken steak with garlic powder, salt and black pepper and marinate for about 8 hours.
3. Mix salsa, tomato sauce and hot pepper sauce in a bowl.
4. Arrange the steak pieces in the Air fryer basket and drizzle with the salsa mixture.
5. Roast for about 30 minutes and dish out to serve with cheese.

Nutrition Info per Serving:
Calories: 345, Fat: 14.3g, Carbohydrates: 7.6g, Sugar: 4.3g, Protein: 45.1g, Sodium: 828mg

Easy Asian Turkey Meatballs

Prep time: 10 minutes, Cook time: 11 to 14 minutes, Serves 4

2 tbsps. peanut oil, divided
1 small onion, minced
¼ cup water chestnuts, finely chopped
½ tsp. ground ginger
2 tbsps. low-sodium soy sauce
¼ cup panko bread crumbs
1 egg, beaten
1 pound (454 g) ground turkey

1. Preheat the air fryer to 400ºF (204ºC).
2. In a round metal pan, combine 1 tbsp. of peanut oil and onion. Air fry for 1 to 2 minutes or until crisp and tender. Transfer the onion to a medium bowl.
3. Add the water chestnuts, ground ginger, soy sauce, and bread crumbs to the onion and mix well. Add egg and stir well. Mix in the ground turkey until combined.
4. Form the mixture into 1-inch meatballs. Drizzle the remaining 1 tbsp. of oil over the meatballs.
5. Bake the meatballs in the pan in batches for 10 to 12 minutes or until they are 165ºF (74ºC) on a meat thermometer. Rest for 5 minutes before serving.

Nutrition Info per Serving:
Calories: 274, Protein: 21g, Fat: 18g, Carbohydrates: 8g, Fiber: 1g, Sugar: 2g, Sodium: 432mg

Herbed Roasted Chicken

Prep time: 15 minutes, Cook time: 1 hour, Serves 5

1 (5-pounds) whole chicken
3 garlic cloves, minced
1 tsp. fresh lemon zest, finely grated
1 tsp. dried thyme, crushed
1 tsp. dried oregano, crushed
1 tsp. dried rosemary, crushed
1 tsp. smoked paprika
Salt and ground black pepper, as required
2 tbsps. fresh lemon juice
2 tbsps. olive oil

1. Preheat the Air fryer to 360ºF (182ºC) and grease an Air fryer basket.
2. Mix the garlic, lemon zest, herbs and spices in a bowl.
3. Rub the herb mixture over the chicken and drizzle with lemon juice and oil.
4. Keep aside for about 2 hours at room temperature and transfer into the Air fryer basket.
5. Roast for about 50 minutes and carefully flip the chicken.
6. Roast for 10 more minutes and dish out in a plate.
7. Cut into desired size pieces with a knife and serve warm.

Nutrition Info per Serving:
Calories: 860, Fat: 50g, Carbohydrates: 1.3g, Sugar: 0.2g, Protein: 71.1g, Sodium: 299mg

Nutty Chicken Tenders

Prep time: 5 minutes, Cook time: 12 minutes, Serves 4

1 pound (454 g) chicken tenders	¼ cup coarse mustard
1 tsp. kosher salt	2 tbsps. honey
1 tsp. black pepper	1 cup finely crushed pecans
½ tsp. smoked paprika	

1. Preheat the air fryer to 350°F (177°C).
2. Place the chicken in a large bowl. Sprinkle with the salt, pepper, and paprika. Toss until the chicken is coated with the spices. Add the mustard and honey and toss until the chicken is coated.
3. Place the pecans on a plate. Working with one piece of chicken at a time, roll the chicken in the pecans until both sides are coated. Lightly brush off any loose pecans. Place the chicken in the air fryer basket.
4. Bake for 12 minutes, or until the chicken is cooked through and the pecans are golden brown.
5. Serve warm.

Nutrition Info per Serving:

Calories: 399, Protein: 30g, Fat: 25g, Carbohydrates: 18g, Fiber: 3g, Sugar: 13g, Sodium: 716mg

Honey Rosemary Chicken

Prep time: 10 minutes, Cook time: 20 minutes, Serves 4

¼ cup balsamic vinegar	½ tsp. freshly ground black pepper
2 tbsps. honey	2 whole boneless, skinless chicken breasts (about 1 pound / 454 g each), halved
2 tbsps. olive oil	
1 tbsp. dried rosemary leaves	
1 tsp. salt	Cooking spray

1. In a large resealable bag, combine the vinegar, honey, olive oil, rosemary, salt, and pepper. Add the chicken pieces, seal the bag, and refrigerate to marinate for at least 2 hours.
2. Preheat the air fryer to 325°F (163°C). Line the air fryer basket with parchment paper.
3. Remove the chicken from the marinade and place it on the parchment. Spritz with cooking spray.
4. Bake for 10 minutes. Flip the chicken, spritz it with cooking spray, and bake for 10 minutes more until the internal temperature reaches 165°F (74°C) and the chicken is no longer pink inside. Let sit for 5 minutes before serving.

Nutrition Info per Serving:

Calories: 348, Protein: 30g, Fat: 13g, Carbohydrates: 30g, Fiber: 0.1g, Sugar: 10g, Sodium: 625mg

Tex-Mex Chicken Breasts

Prep time: 10 minutes, Cook time: 17 to 20 minutes, Serves 4

1 pound (454 g) low-sodium boneless, skinless chicken breasts, cut into 1-inch cubes	2 tsps. olive oil
	⅔ cup canned low-sodium black beans, rinsed and drained
1 medium onion, chopped	½ cup low-sodium salsa
1 red bell pepper, chopped	2 tsps. chili powder
1 jalapeño pepper, minced	

1. Preheat the air fryer to 400°F (204°C).
2. In a medium metal bowl, mix the chicken, onion, bell pepper, jalapeño, and olive oil. Roast for 10 minutes, stirring once during cooking.
3. Add the black beans, salsa, and chili powder. Roast for 7 to 10 minutes more, stirring once, until the chicken reaches an internal temperature of 165°F (74°C) on a meat thermometer. Serve immediately.

Nutrition Info per Serving:

Calories: 215, Protein: 27g, Fat: 6g, Carbohydrates: 15g, Fiber: 4g, Sugar: 5g, Sodium: 251mg

Paprika Indian Fennel Chicken

Prep time: 10 minutes, Cook time: 15 minutes, Serves 4

1 pound (454 g) boneless, skinless chicken thighs, cut crosswise into thirds	1 tsp. ground fennel
	1 tsp. garam masala
	1 tsp. ground turmeric
1 yellow onion, cut into 1½-inch-thick slices	1 tsp. kosher salt
	½ to 1 tsp. cayenne pepper
1 tbsp. coconut oil, melted	olive oil spray
2 tsps. minced fresh ginger	2 tsps. fresh lemon juice
2 tsps. minced garlic	¼ cup chopped fresh cilantro
1 tsp. smoked paprika	or parsley

1. Use a fork to pierce the chicken all over to allow the marinade to penetrate better.
2. In a large bowl, combine the onion, coconut oil, ginger, garlic, paprika, fennel, garam masala, turmeric, salt, and cayenne. Add the chicken, toss to combine, and marinate at room temperature for 30 minutes, or cover and refrigerate for up to 24 hours.
3. Preheat the air fryer to 350°F (177°C).
4. Place the chicken and onion in the air fryer basket. (Discard remaining marinade.) Spray with some olive oil spray. Air fry for 15 minutes. Halfway through the cooking time, remove the basket, spray the chicken and onion with more vegetable oil spray, and toss gently to coat. At the end of the cooking time, use a meat thermometer to ensure the chicken has reached an internal temperature of 165°F (74°C).
5. Transfer the chicken and onion to a serving platter. Sprinkle with the lemon juice and cilantro and serve.

Nutrition Info per Serving:

Calories: 255, Protein: 23g, Fat: 14g, Carbohydrates: 10g, Fiber: 2g, Sugar: 4g, Sodium: 673mg

Glazed Chicken Wings

Prep time: 10 minutes, Cook time: 19 minutes, Serves 4

8 chicken wings
2 tbsps. whole wheat flour
1 tsp. garlic, chopped finely
1 tbsp. fresh lemon juice
1 tbsp. soy sauce
½ tsp. dried oregano, crushed
Salt and freshly ground black pepper, to taste

1. Preheat the Air fryer to 355°F (179°C) and grease an Air fryer basket.
2. Mix all the ingredients except wings in a large bowl.
3. Coat wings generously with the marinade and refrigerate for about 2 hours.
4. Remove the chicken wings from marinade and sprinkle with flour evenly.
5. Transfer the wings in the Air fryer basket and air fry for about 6 minutes, flipping once in between.
6. Dish out the chicken wings in a platter and serve hot.

Nutrition Info per Serving:

Calories: 350, Fat: 12.7g, Carbohydrates: 5.5g, Sugar: 1.8g, Protein: 50.1g, Sodium: 510mg

Sweet Chicken Kabobs

Prep time: 20 minutes, Cook time: 14 minutes, Serves 3

4 scallions, chopped
2 tsps. sesame seeds, toasted
1 pound chicken tenders
Wooden skewers, pres oaked
1 tbsp. fresh ginger, finely grated
4 garlic cloves, minced
½ cup pineapple juice
½ cup soy sauce
¼ cup sesame oil
A pinch of black pepper

1. Preheat the Air fryer to 390°F (199°C) and grease an Air fryer basket.
2. Mix scallion, ginger, garlic, pineapple juice, soy sauce, oil, sesame seeds, and black pepper in a large baking dish.
3. Thread chicken tenders onto pre-soaked wooden skewers.
4. Coat the skewers generously with marinade and refrigerate for about 2 hours.
5. Transfer half of the skewers in the Air fryer basket and roast for about 7 minutes.
6. Repeat with the remaining mixture and dish out to serve warm.

Nutrition Info per Serving:

Calories: 392, Fat: 23g, Carbohydrates: 9.9g, Sugar: 4.1g, Protein: 35.8g, Sodium: 1800mg

Lemon Garlic Chicken

Prep time: 10 minutes, Cook time: 16 to 19 minutes, Serves 4

4 (5-ounce / 142-g) low-sodium boneless, skinless chicken breasts, cut into 4-by-½-inch strips
2 tsps. olive oil
2 tbsps. cornstarch
3 garlic cloves, minced
½ cup low-sodium chicken broth
¼ cup freshly squeezed lemon juice
1 tbsp. honey
½ tsp. dried thyme
Brown rice, cooked (optional)

1. Preheat the air fryer to 400°F (204°C).
2. In a large bowl, mix the chicken and olive oil. Sprinkle with the cornstarch. Toss to coat.
3. Add the garlic and transfer to a metal pan. Bake in the air fryer for 10 minutes, stirring once during cooking.
4. Add the chicken broth, lemon juice, honey, and thyme to the chicken mixture. Bake for 6 to 9 minutes more, or until the sauce is slightly thickened and the chicken reaches an internal temperature of 165°F (74°C) on a meat thermometer. Serve over hot cooked brown rice, if desired.

Nutrition Info per Serving:

Calories: 247, Protein: 27g, Fat: 7g, Carbohydrates: 18g, Fiber: 0.4g, Sugar: 6g, Sodium: 145mg

Chicken Breasts with Chimichurri

Prep time: 15 minutes, Cook time: 35 minutes, Serves 1

1 chicken breast, bone-in, skin-on
½ tbsp. paprika ground
½ tbsp. chili powder
½ tbsp. fennel ground
½ tsp. black pepper, ground
½ tsp. onion powder
1 tsp. salt
½ tsp. garlic powder
½ tsp. cumin ground
½ tbsp. canola oil
For the Chimichurri Sauce:
½ bunch fresh cilantro
¼ bunch fresh parsley
½ shallot, peeled, cut in quarters
2 tbsps. olive oil
4 garlic cloves, peeled
Zest and juice of 1 lemon
1 tsp. kosher salt

1. Preheat the Air fryer to 300°F (149°C) and grease an Air fryer basket.
2. Combine all the spices in a suitable bowl and season the chicken with it.
3. Sprinkle with canola oil and arrange the chicken in the Air fryer basket.
4. Roast for about 35 minutes and dish out in a platter.
5. Put all the ingredients for Chimichurri sauce in the blender and blend until smooth.
6. Serve the chicken with chimichurri sauce.

Nutrition Info per Serving:

Calories: 140, Fats: 7.9g, Carbohydrates: 1.8g, Sugar: 7.1g, Proteins: 7.2g, Sodium: 581mg

Crisp Chicken Wings

Prep time: 15 minutes, Cook time: 20 minutes, Serves 4

1 pound (454 g) chicken wings
3 tbsps. vegetable oil
½ cup whole wheat flour
½ tsp. smoked paprika
½ tsp. garlic powder
½ tsp. kosher salt
1½ tsps. freshly cracked black pepper

1. Preheat the air fryer to 400°F (204°C).
2. Place the chicken wings in a large bowl. Drizzle the vegetable oil over wings and toss to coat.
3. In a separate bowl, whisk together the flour, paprika, garlic powder, salt, and pepper until combined.
4. Dredge the wings in the flour mixture one at a time, coating them well, and place in the air fryer basket. Air fry for 20 minutes, turning the wings halfway through the cooking time, until the breading is browned and crunchy.
5. Serve hot.

Nutrition Info per Serving:

Calories: 380, Protein: 18g, Fat: 27g, Carbohydrates: 18g, Fiber: 3g, Sugar: 0g, Sodium: 398mg

Celery Chicken

Prep time: 10 minutes, Cook time: 15 minutes, Serves 4

½ cup soy sauce
2 tbsps. hoisin sauce
4 tsps. minced garlic
1 tsp. freshly ground black pepper
8 boneless, skinless chicken tenderloins
1 cup chopped celery
1 medium red bell pepper, diced
Olive oil spray

1. Preheat the air fryer to 375°F (191°C). Spray the air fryer basket lightly with olive oil spray.
2. In a large bowl, mix together the soy sauce, hoisin sauce, garlic, and black pepper to make a marinade. Add the chicken, celery, and bell pepper and toss to coat.
3. Shake the excess marinade off the chicken, place it and the vegetables in the air fryer basket, and lightly spray with olive oil spray. You may need to cook them in batches. Reserve the remaining marinade.
4. Air fry for 8 minutes. Turn the chicken over and brush with some of the remaining marinade. Air fry for an additional 5 to 7 minutes, or until the chicken reaches an internal temperature of at least 165°F (74°C). Serve.

Nutrition Info per Serving:

Calories: 673, Protein: 32g, Fat: 3g, Carbohydrates: 8g, Fiber: 1g, Sugar: 5g, Sodium: 832mg

Cranberry Curry Chicken

Prep time: 12 minutes, Cook time: 18 minutes, Serves 4

3 (5-ounce / 142-g) low-sodium boneless, skinless chicken breasts, cut into 1½-inch cubes
2 tsps. olive oil
2 tbsps. cornstarch
1 tbsp. curry powder
1 tart apple, chopped
½ cup low-sodium chicken broth
⅓ cup dried cranberries
2 tbsps. freshly squeezed orange juice
Brown rice, cooked (optional)

1. Preheat the air fryer to 380°F (193°C).
2. In a medium bowl, mix the chicken and olive oil. Sprinkle with the cornstarch and curry powder. Toss to coat. Stir in the apple and transfer to a metal pan. Bake in the air fryer for 8 minutes, stirring once during cooking.
3. Add the chicken broth, cranberries, and orange juice. Bake for about 10 minutes more, or until the sauce is slightly thickened and the chicken reaches an internal temperature of 165°F (74°C) on a meat thermometer. Serve over hot cooked brown rice, if desired.

Nutrition Info per Serving:

Calories: 300, Protein: 29g, Fat: 6g, Carbohydrates: 34g, Fiber: 3g, Sugar: 14g, Sodium: 119mg

Chicken with Apple

Prep time: 10 minutes, Cook time: 20 minutes, Serves 8

1 shallot, thinly sliced
1 tsp. fresh thyme, minced
2 (4-ounces) boneless, skinless chicken thighs, sliced into chunks
1 large apple, cored and cubed
1 tbsp. fresh ginger, finely grated
½ cup apple cider
2 tbsps. maple syrup
Salt and black pepper, as required

1. Preheat the Air fryer to 390°F (199°C) and grease an Air fryer basket.
2. Mix the shallot, ginger, thyme, apple cider, maple syrup, salt, and black pepper in a bowl.
3. Coat the chicken generously with the marinade and refrigerate to marinate for about 8 hours.
4. Arrange the chicken pieces and cubed apples into the Air Fryer basket and air fry for about 20 minutes, flipping once halfway.
5. Dish out the chicken mixture into a serving bowl to serve.

Nutrition Info per Serving:

Calories: 299, Fat: 26.2g, Carbohydrates: 39.9g, Sugar: 30.4g, Protein: 26.2g, Sodium: 125mg

Barbecue Chicken

Prep time: 10 minutes, Cook time: 18 to 20 minutes, Serves 4

⅓ cup no-salt-added tomato sauce
2 tbsps. low-sodium grainy mustard
2 tbsps. apple cider vinegar
1 tbsp. honey
2 garlic cloves, minced
1 jalapeño pepper, minced
3 tbsps. minced onion
4 (5-ounce / 142-g) low-sodium boneless, skinless chicken breasts

1. Preheat the air fryer to 370°F (188°C).
2. In a small bowl, stir together the tomato sauce, mustard, cider vinegar, honey, garlic, jalapeño, and onion.
3. Brush the chicken breasts with some sauce and air fry for 10 minutes.
4. Remove the air fryer basket and turn the chicken; brush with more sauce. Air fry for 5 minutes more.
5. Remove the air fryer basket and turn the chicken again; brush with more sauce. Air fry for 3 to 5 minutes more, or until the chicken reaches an internal temperature of 165°F (74°C) on a meat thermometer. Discard any remaining sauce. Serve immediately.

Nutrition Info per Serving:

Calories: 205, Protein: 26g, Fat: 4g, Carbohydrates: 14g, Fiber: 1g, Sugar: 1g, Sodium: 234mg

Parmesan Chicken Cutlets

Prep time: 15 minutes, Cook time: 30 minutes, Serves 4

¾ cup whole wheat flour
2 large eggs
1½ cups panko breadcrumbs
¼ cup low-fat Parmesan cheese, grated
4 (6-ounces) (¼-inch thick) skinless, boneless chicken cutlets
1 tbsp. mustard powder
Salt and black pepper, to taste

1. Preheat the Air fryer to 355ºF (179ºC) and grease an Air fryer basket.
2. Place the flour in a shallow bowl and whisk the eggs in a second bowl.
3. Mix the breadcrumbs, cheese, mustard powder, salt, and black pepper in a third bowl.
4. Season the chicken with salt and black pepper and coat the chicken with flour.
5. Dip the chicken into whisked eggs and finally dredge into the breadcrumb mixture.
6. Arrange the chicken cutlets into the Air fryer basket and air fry for about 30 minutes.
7. Dish out in a platter and immediately serve.

Nutrition Info per Serving:

Calories: 503, Fat: 42.3g, Carbohydrates: 42g, Sugar: 1.3g, Protein: 49.3g, Sodium: 226mg

Garlic Soy Chicken Thighs

Prep time: 10 minutes, Cook time: 30 minutes, Serves 1 to 2

2 tbsps. chicken stock
2 tbsps. reduced-sodium soy sauce
1½ tbsps. coconut sugar
4 garlic cloves, smashed and peeled
2 large scallions, cut into 2- to 3-inch batons, plus more, thinly sliced, for garnish
2 bone-in, skin-on chicken thighs (7 to 8 ounces / 198 to 227 g each)

1. Preheat the air fryer to 375ºF (191ºC).
2. In a metal cake pan, combine the chicken stock, soy sauce, and sugar and stir until the sugar dissolves. Add the garlic cloves, scallions, and chicken thighs, turning the thighs to coat them in the marinade, then resting them skin-side up. Place the pan in the air fryer and bake, flipping the thighs every 5 minutes after the first 10 minutes, until the chicken is cooked through and the marinade is reduced to a sticky glaze over the chicken, about 30 minutes.
3. Remove the pan from the air fryer and serve the chicken thighs warm, with any remaining glaze spooned over top and sprinkled with more sliced scallions.

Nutrition Info per Serving:

Calories: 507, Protein: 32g, Fat: 33g, Carbohydrates: 19g, Fiber: 1g, Sugar: 12g, Sodium: 815mg

Mayonnaise-Mustard Chicken

Prep time: 10 minutes, Cook time: 15 minutes, Serves 4

6 tbsps. mayonnaise
2 tbsps. coarse-ground mustard
2 tsps. curry powder
1 tsp. kosher salt
1 tsp. cayenne pepper
1 pound (454 g) chicken tenders

1. Preheat the air fryer to 350ºF (177ºC).
2. In a large bowl, whisk together the mayonnaise, mustard, curry powder, salt, and cayenne. Transfer half of the mixture to a serving bowl to serve as a dipping sauce. Add the chicken tenders to the large bowl and toss until well coated.
3. Place the tenders in the air fryer basket and bake for 15 minutes. Use a meat thermometer to ensure the chicken has reached an internal temperature of 165ºF (74ºC).
4. Serve the chicken with the dipping sauce.

Nutrition Info per Serving:

Calories: 315, Protein: 25g, Fat: 22g, Carbohydrates: 3g, Fiber: 0g, Sugar: 2g, Sodium: 744mg

Tandoori Chicken Legs

Prep time: 15 minutes, Cook time: 20 minutes, Serves 4

4 chicken legs
4 tbsps. hung curd
3 tbsps. fresh lemon juice
3 tsps. ginger paste
3 tsps. garlic paste
Salt, as required
2 tbsps. tandoori masala powder
2 tsps. red chili powder
1 tsp. garam masala powder
1 tsp. ground cumin
1 tsp. ground coriander
1 tsp. ground turmeric
Ground black pepper, as required
Pinch of orange food color

1. Preheat the Air fryer to 445ºF (229ºC) and grease an Air fryer basket.
2. Mix chicken legs, lemon juice, ginger paste, garlic paste, and salt in a bowl.
3. Combine the curd, spices, and food color in another bowl.
4. Add the chicken legs into bowl and coat generously with the spice mixture.
5. Cover the bowl of chicken and refrigerate for at least 12 hours.
6. Arrange the chicken legs into the Air fryer basket and roast for about 20 minutes.
7. Dish out the chicken legs onto serving plates and serve hot.

Nutrition Info per Serving:

Calories: 356, Fat: 13.9g, Carbohydrates: 3.7g, Sugar: 0.5g, Protein: 51.5g, Sodium: 259mg

(Note: Hung curd - Hung curd is nothing but yogurt drained of all its water. It can be made very easily at home.)

Hawaiian Tropical Chicken

Prep time: 10 minutes, Cook time: 15 minutes, Serves 4

4 boneless, skinless chicken thighs (about 1½ pounds / 680 g)
1 (8-ounce / 227-g) can pineapple chunks in juice, drained,
¼ cup juice reserved
¼ cup soy sauce
¼ cup coconut sugar
2 tbsps. ketchup
1 tbsp. minced fresh ginger
1 tbsp. minced garlic
¼ cup chopped scallions

1. Use a fork to pierce the chicken all over to allow the marinade to penetrate better. Place the chicken in a large bowl or large resealable plastic bag.
2. Set the drained pineapple chunks aside. In a small microwave-safe bowl, combine the pineapple juice, soy sauce, sugar, ketchup, ginger, and garlic. Pour half the sauce over the chicken; toss to coat. Reserve the remaining sauce. Marinate the chicken at room temperature for 30 minutes, or cover and refrigerate for up to 24 hours.
3. Preheat the air fryer to 350°F (177°C).
4. Place the chicken in the air fryer basket, discarding marinade. Bake for 15 minutes, turning halfway through the cooking time.
5. Meanwhile, microwave the reserved sauce on high for 45 to 60 seconds, stirring every 15 seconds, until the sauce has the consistency of a thick glaze.
6. At the end of the cooking time, use a meat thermometer to ensure the chicken has reached an internal temperature of 165°F (74°C).
7. Transfer the chicken to a serving platter. Pour the sauce over the chicken. Garnish with the pineapple chunks and scallions before serving.

Nutrition Info per Serving:

Calories: 363, Protein: 25g, Fat: 16g, Carbohydrates: 32g, Fiber: 1g, Sugar: 26g, Sodium: 796mg

Air-Fried Chicken Wings

Prep time: 5 minutes, Cook time: 19 minutes, Serves 6

2 pounds (907 g) chicken wings, tips removed
⅛ tsp. salt

1. Preheat the air fryer to 400°F (204°C). Season the wings with salt.
2. Working in 2 batches, place half the chicken wings in the basket and air fry for 15 minutes, or until the skin is browned and cooked through, turning the wings with tongs halfway through cooking.
3. Combine both batches in the air fryer and air fry for 4 minutes more. Transfer to a large bowl and serve immediately.

Nutrition Info per Serving:

Calories: 283, Protein: 21g, Fat: 21g, Carbohydrates: 0g, Fiber: 0g, Sugar: 0g, Sodium: 112mg

Curried Orange Honey Chicken

Prep time: 10 minutes, Cook time: 16 to 19 minutes, Serves 4

¾ pound (340 g) boneless, skinless chicken thighs, cut into 1-inch pieces
1 yellow bell pepper, cut into 1½-inch pieces
1 small red onion, sliced
Olive oil for misting
¼ cup chicken stock
2 tbsps. honey
¼ cup orange juice
1 tbsp. cornstarch
2 to 3 tsps. curry powder

1. Preheat the air fryer to 370°F (188°C).
2. Put the chicken thighs, pepper, and red onion in the air fryer basket and mist with olive oil.
3. Roast for 12 to 14 minutes or until the chicken is cooked to 165°F (74°C), shaking the basket halfway through cooking time.
4. Remove the chicken and vegetables from the air fryer basket and set aside.
5. In a metal bowl, combine the stock, honey, orange juice, cornstarch, and curry powder, and mix well. Add the chicken and vegetables, stir, and put the bowl in the basket.
6. Return the basket to the air fryer and roast for 2 minutes. Remove and stir, then roast for 2 to 3 minutes or until the sauce is thickened and bubbly.
7. Serve warm.

Nutrition Info per Serving:

Calories: 236, Protein: 20g, Fat: 7g, Carbohydrates: 26g, Fiber: 2g, Sugar: 17g, Sodium: 207mg

Buffalo Chicken Wings

Prep time: 20 minutes, Cook time: 22 minutes, Serves 6

2 pounds chicken wings, cut into drumettes and flats
1 tsp. chicken seasoning
1 tsp. garlic powder
Ground black pepper, to taste
1 tbsp. olive oil
¼ cup red hot sauce
2 tbsps. low-sodium soy sauce

1. Preheat the Air fryer to 400°F (204°C) and grease an Air fryer basket.
2. Season each chicken wing evenly with chicken seasoning, garlic powder, and black pepper.
3. Arrange the chicken wings into the Air Fryer basket and drizzle with olive oil.
4. Roast for about 10 minutes and dish out the chicken wings onto a serving platter.
5. Pour the red hot sauce and soy sauce on the chicken wings and toss to coat well.
6. Roast for about 12 minutes and dish out to serve hot.

Nutrition Info per Serving:

Calories: 311, Fat: 13.6g, Carbohydrates: 0.6g, Sugar: 0.3g, Protein: 44g, Sodium: 491mg

Spiced Roasted Chicken

Prep time: 15 minutes, Cook time: 1 hour, Serves 2

1 (5-pounds) whole chicken, necks and giblets removed
2 tsps. dried thyme
2 tsps. paprika
1 tsp. cayenne pepper
1 tsp. ground white pepper
1 tsp. onion powder
1 tsp. garlic powder
Salt and ground black pepper, as required
3 tbsps. olive oil

1. Preheat the Air fryer to 350°F (177°C) and grease an Air fryer basket.
2. Mix the thyme, spices and other seasoning in a bowl.
3. Coat the chicken generously with olive oil and rub with spice mixture.
4. Arrange the chicken into the Air Fryer basket, breast side down and roast for about 30 minutes.
5. Flip the chicken and roast for 30 more minutes.
6. Dish out the chicken in a platter and cut into desired size pieces to serve.

Nutrition Info per Serving:

Calories: 871, Fat: 60g, Carbohydrates: 1.7g, Sugar: 0.4g, Protein: 70.6g, Sodium: 296mg

Fajita Chicken Strips

Prep time: 10 minutes, Cook time: 15 minutes, Serves 4

1 pound (454 g) boneless, skinless chicken tenderloins, cut into strips
3 bell peppers, any color, cut into chunks
1 onion, cut into chunks
1 tbsp. olive oil
1 tbsp. fajita seasoning mix
Cooking spray

1. Preheat the air fryer to 370°F (188°C).
2. In a large bowl, mix together the chicken, bell peppers, onion, olive oil, and fajita seasoning mix until completely coated.
3. Spray the air fryer basket lightly with cooking spray.
4. Place the chicken and vegetables in the air fryer basket and lightly spray with cooking spray.
5. Air fry for 7 minutes. Shake the basket and air fry for an additional 5 to 8 minutes, until the chicken is cooked through and the veggies are starting to char.
6. Serve warm.

Nutrition Info per Serving:

Calories: 186, Protein: 26g, Fat: 6g, Carbohydrates: 9g, Fiber: 3g, Sugar: 5g, Sodium: 285mg

Chicken and Mushroom Casserole

Prep time: 15 minutes, Cook time: 20 minutes, Serves 4

4 chicken breasts
1 tbsp. curry powder
1 cup nonfat coconut milk
Salt, to taste
1 broccoli, cut into florets
1 cup mushrooms
½ cup shredded low-fat Parmesan cheese
Cooking spray

1. Preheat the air fryer to 350°F (177°C). Spritz a casserole dish with cooking spray.
2. Cube the chicken breasts and combine with curry powder and coconut milk in a bowl. Season with salt.
3. Add the broccoli and mushroom and mix well.
4. Pour the mixture into the casserole dish. Top with the cheese.
5. Transfer to the air fryer and bake for about 20 minutes.
6. Serve warm.

Nutrition Info per Serving:

Calories: 304, Protein: 38g, Fat: 10g, Carbohydrates: 15g, Fiber: 4g, Sugar: 3g, Sodium: 431mg

Chicken and Veggie Kabobs

Prep time: 20 minutes, Cook time: 30 minutes, Serves 3

1 lb. skinless, boneless chicken thighs, cut into cubes
½ cup low-fat plain Greek yogurt
2 small tomatoes, seeded and cut into large chunks
1 large red onion, cut into large chunks
Wooden skewers, presoaked
1 tbsp. olive oil
2 tsps. curry powder
½ tsp. smoked paprika
¼ tsp. cayenne pepper
Salt, to taste

1. Preheat the Air fryer to 360°F (182°C) and grease an Air fryer basket.
2. Mix the chicken, oil, yogurt, and spices in a large baking dish.
3. Thread chicken cubes, tomatoes and onion onto presoaked wooden skewers.
4. Coat the skewers generously with marinade and refrigerate for about 3 hours.
5. Transfer half of the skewers in the Air fryer basket and roast for about 15 minutes.
6. Repeat with the remaining mixture and dish out to serve warm.

Nutrition Info per Serving:

Calories: 222, Fat: 8.2g, Carbohydrates: 8.7g, Sugar: 5.3g, Protein: 27.9g, Sodium: 104mg

Thai Cornish Game Hens

Prep time: 15 minutes, Cook time: 20 minutes, Serves 4

1 cup chopped fresh cilantro leaves and stems
¼ cup fish sauce
1 tbsp. soy sauce
1 serrano chile, seeded and chopped
8 garlic cloves, smashed
2 tbsps. coconut sugar
2 tbsps. lemongrass paste
2 tsps. black pepper
2 tsps. ground coriander
1 tsp. kosher salt
1 tsp. ground turmeric
2 Cornish game hens, giblets removed, split in half lengthwise

1. In a blender, combine the cilantro, fish sauce, soy sauce, serrano, garlic, sugar, lemongrass, black pepper, coriander, salt, and turmeric. Blend until smooth.
2. Place the game hen halves in a large bowl. Pour the cilantro mixture over the hen halves and toss to coat. Marinate at room temperature for 30 minutes, or cover and refrigerate for up to 24 hours.
3. Preheat the air fryer to 400°F (204°C).
4. Arrange the hen halves in a single layer in the air fryer basket. Roast for 20 minutes. Use a meat thermometer to ensure the game hens have reached an internal temperature of 165°F (74°C). Serve warm.

Nutrition Info per Serving:

Calories: 380, Protein: 40g, Fat: 17g, Carbohydrates: 18g, Fiber: 1g, Sugar: 11g, Sodium: 892mg

Spiced Turkey Tenderloin

Prep time: 20 minutes, Cook time: 30 minutes, Serves 4

½ tsp. paprika
½ tsp. garlic powder
½ tsp. salt
½ tsp. freshly ground black pepper
Pinch cayenne pepper
1½ pounds (680 g) turkey breast tenderloin
Olive oil spray

1. Preheat the air fryer to 370ºF (188ºC). Spray the air fryer basket lightly with olive oil spray.
2. In a small bowl, combine the paprika, garlic powder, salt, black pepper, and cayenne pepper. Rub the mixture all over the turkey.
3. Place the turkey in the air fryer basket and lightly spray with olive oil spray.
4. Air fry for 15 minutes. Flip the turkey over and lightly spray with olive oil spray. Air fry until the internal temperature reaches at least 170ºF (77ºC) for an additional 10 to 15 minutes.
5. Let the turkey rest for 10 minutes before slicing and serving.

Nutrition Info per Serving:

Calories: 180, Protein: 39g, Fat: 2g, Carbohydrates: 1g, Fiber: 0g, Sugar: 0g, Sodium: 316mg

Chicken with Pineapple and Peach

Prep time: 10 minutes, Cook time: 14 to 15 minutes, Serves 4

1 pound (454 g) low-sodium boneless, skinless chicken breasts, cut into 1-inch pieces
1 medium red onion, chopped
1 (8-ounce / 227-g) can pineapple chunks, drained, ¼ cup juice reserved
1 tbsp. peanut oil or safflower oil
1 peach, peeled, pitted, and cubed
1 tbsp. cornstarch
½ tsp. ground ginger
¼ tsp. ground allspice
Brown rice, cooked (optional)

1. Preheat the air fryer to 380ºF (193ºC).
2. In a medium metal bowl, mix the chicken, red onion, pineapple, and peanut oil. Bake in the air fryer for 9 minutes. Remove and stir.
3. Add the peach and return the bowl to the air fryer. Bake for 3 minutes more. Remove and stir again.
4. In a small bowl, whisk the reserved pineapple juice, the cornstarch, ginger, and allspice well. Add to the chicken mixture and stir to combine.
5. Bake for 2 to 3 minutes more, or until the chicken reaches an internal temperature of 165ºF (74ºC) on a meat thermometer and the sauce is slightly thickened.
6. Serve immediately over hot cooked brown rice, if desired.

Nutrition Info per Serving:

Calories: 234, Protein: 24g, Fat: 6g, Carbohydrates: 21g, Fiber: 2g, Sugar: 14g, Sodium: 58mg

Blackened Chicken Breasts

Prep time: 10 minutes, Cook time: 20 minutes, Serves 4

1 large egg, beaten
¾ cup Blackened seasoning
2 whole boneless, skinless chicken breasts (about 1 pound / 454 g each), halved
Cooking spray

1. Preheat the air fryer to 360ºF (182ºC). Line the air fryer basket with parchment paper.
2. Place the beaten egg in one shallow bowl and the Blackened seasoning in another shallow bowl.
3. One at a time, dip the chicken pieces in the beaten egg and the Blackened seasoning, coating thoroughly.
4. Place the chicken pieces on the parchment and spritz with cooking spray.
5. Air fry for 10 minutes. Flip the chicken, spritz it with cooking spray, and air fry for 10 minutes more until the internal temperature reaches 165ºF (74ºC) and the chicken is no longer pink inside. Let sit for 5 minutes before serving.

Nutrition Info per Serving:

Calories: 257, Protein: 36g, Fat: 8g, Carbohydrates: 7g, Fiber: 3g, Sugar: 1g, Sodium: 815mg

Crispy Chicken Strips

Prep time: 15 minutes, Cook time: 20 minutes, Serves 4

1 tbsp. olive oil
1 pound (454 g) boneless, skinless chicken tenderloins
1 tsp. salt
½ tsp. freshly ground black pepper
½ tsp. paprika
½ tsp. garlic powder
½ cup whole-wheat seasoned bread crumbs
1 tsp. dried parsley
Cooking spray

1. Preheat the air fryer to 370ºF (188ºC). Spray the air fryer basket lightly with cooking spray.
2. In a medium bowl, toss the chicken with the salt, pepper, paprika, and garlic powder until evenly coated.
3. Add the olive oil and toss to coat the chicken evenly.
4. In a separate, shallow bowl, mix together the bread crumbs and parsley.
5. Coat each piece of chicken evenly in the bread crumb mixture.
6. Place the chicken in the air fryer basket in a single layer and spray it lightly with cooking spray. You may need to cook them in batches.
7. Air fry for 10 minutes. Flip the chicken over, lightly spray it with cooking spray, and air fry for an additional 8 to 10 minutes, until golden brown. Serve.

Nutrition Info per Serving:

Calories: 201, Protein: 24g, Fat: 7g, Carbohydrates: 9g, Fiber: 1g, Sugar: 1g, Sodium: 665mg

CHAPTER 9
LAMB

Spicy Lamb Kebabs

Prep time: 20 minutes, Cook time: 8 minutes, Serves 6

4 eggs, beaten
1 cup pistachios, chopped
1 pound ground lamb
4 tbsps. plain flour
4 tbsps. flat-leaf parsley, chopped
2 tsps. chili flakes
4 garlic cloves, minced
2 tbsps. fresh lemon juice
2 tsps. cumin seeds
1 tsp. fennel seeds
2 tsps. dried mint
2 tsps. salt
Olive oil
1 tsp. coriander seeds
1 tsp. freshly ground black pepper

1. Preheat the Air fryer to 355ºF (179ºC) and grease an Air fryer basket.
2. Mix lamb, pistachios, eggs, lemon juice, chili flakes, flour, cumin seeds, fennel seeds, coriander seeds, mint, parsley, salt and black pepper in a large bowl.
3. Thread the lamb mixture onto metal skewers to form sausages and coat with olive oil.
4. Place the skewers in the Air fryer basket and grill for about 8 minutes.
5. Dish out in a platter and serve hot.

Nutrition Info per Serving:
Calories: 284, Fat: 15.8g, Carbohydrates: 8.4g, Sugar: 1.1g, Protein: 27.9g, Sodium: 932mg

Garlicky Lamb Chops

Prep time: 20 minutes, Cook time: 22 minutes, Serves 4

1 tbsp. fresh oregano, chopped
1 tbsp. fresh thyme, chopped
8 (4-ounce) lamb chops
¼ cup olive oil, divided
1 bulb garlic
Salt and black pepper, to taste

1. Preheat the Air fryer to 390ºF (199ºC) and grease an Air fryer basket.
2. Rub the garlic bulb with about 2 tbsps. of the olive oil.
3. Arrange the garlic bulb in the Air fryer basket and air fry for about 12 minutes.
4. Mix remaining oil, herbs, salt and black pepper in a large bowl.
5. Coat the lamb chops with about 1 tbsp. of the herb mixture.
6. Place half of the chops in the Air fryer basket with garlic bulb and roast for about 5 minutes.
7. Repeat with the remaining lamb chops and serve with herb mixture.

Nutrition Info per Serving:
Calories: 551, Fat: 29.4g, Carbohydrates: 4.7g, Sugar: 0.9g, Protein: 64.5g, Sodium: 175mg

Air Fried Lamb Ribs

Prep time: 5 minutes, Cook time: 18 minutes, Serves 4

2 tbsps. mustard
1 pound (454 g) lamb ribs
1 tsp. rosemary, chopped
Salt and ground black pepper, to taste
¼ cup mint leaves, chopped
1 cup nonfat Greek yogurt

1. Preheat the air fryer to 350ºF (177ºC).
2. Use a brush to apply the mustard to the lamb ribs, and season with rosemary, salt, and pepper.
3. Air fry the ribs in the air fryer for 18 minutes.
4. Meanwhile, combine the mint leaves and yogurt in a bowl.
5. Remove the lamb ribs from the air fryer when cooked and serve with the mint yogurt.

Nutrition Info per Serving:
Calories: 318, Protein: 31g, Fat: 18g, Carbohydrates: 4g, Fiber: 0g, Sugar: 3g, Sodium: 215mg

Pesto Coated Rack of Lamb

Prep time: 15 minutes, Cook time: 15 minutes, Serves 4

½ bunch fresh mint   ¼ cup extra-virgin olive oil
1 (1½-pounds) rack of lamb ½ tbsp. honey
1 garlic clove   Salt and black pepper, to taste

1. Preheat the Air fryer to 200ºF (93ºC) and grease an Air fryer basket.
2. Put the mint, garlic, oil, honey, salt, and black pepper in a blender and pulse until smooth to make pesto.
3. Coat the rack of lamb with this pesto on both sides and arrange in the Air fryer basket.
4. Roast for about 15 minutes and cut the rack into individual chops to serve.

Nutrition Info per Serving:
Calories: 406, Fat: 27.7g, Carbohydrates: 2.9g, Sugar: 2.2g, Protein: 34.9g, Sodium: 161mg

Simple Lamb Chops

Prep time: 10 minutes, Cook time: 15 minutes, Serves 2

4 (4-ounces) lamb chops
Salt and black pepper, to taste
1 tbsp. olive oil

1. Preheat the Air fryer to 390ºF (199ºC) and grease an Air fryer basket.
2. Mix the olive oil, salt, and black pepper in a large bowl and add chops.
3. Arrange the chops in the Air fryer basket and roast for about 15 minutes.
4. Dish out the lamb chops and serve hot.

Nutrition Info per Serving:
Calories: 486, Fat: 31.7g, Carbohydrates: 0.8g, Sugar: 0g, Protein: 63.8g, Sodium: 250mg

Nut Crusted Rack of Lamb

Prep time: 15 minutes, Cook time: 35 minutes, Serves 6

1¾ pounds rack of lamb
1 egg
1 tbsp. breadcrumbs
3-ounce almonds, chopped finely
1 tbsp. fresh rosemary, chopped
1 tbsp. olive oil
1 garlic clove, minced
Salt and black pepper, to taste

1. Preheat the Air fryer to 220°F (104°C) and grease an Air fryer basket.
2. Mix garlic, olive oil, salt and black pepper in a bowl.
3. Whisk the egg in a shallow dish and mix breadcrumbs, almonds and rosemary in another shallow dish.
4. Coat the rack of lamb with garlic mixture evenly, dip into the egg and dredge into the breadcrumb mixture.
5. Arrange the rack of lamb in the Air fryer basket and air fry for about 30 minutes.
6. Set the Air fryer to 390°F (199°C) and roast for about 5 more minutes.
7. Dish out and serve warm.

Nutrition Info per Serving:

Calories: 366, Fat: 20g, Carbohydrates: 4.4g, Sugar: 0.7g, Protein: 41.3g, Sodium: 120mg

Scrumptious Lamb Chops

Prep time: 20 minutes, Cook time: 8 minutes, Serves 4

2 tbsps. fresh mint leaves, minced
4 (6-ounce) lamb chops
2 carrots, peeled and cubed
1 parsnip, peeled and cubed
1 fennel bulb, cubed
1 garlic clove, minced
2 tbsps. dried rosemary
3 tbsps. olive oil
Salt and black pepper, to taste

1. Preheat the Air fryer to 390°F (199°C) and grease an Air fryer basket.
2. Mix herbs, garlic and oil in a large bowl and coat lamp chops generously with this mixture.
3. Marinate in the refrigerator for about 3 hours.
4. Soak the vegetables in a large pan of water for about 15 minutes.
5. Arrange the chops in the Air fryer basket and roast for about 2 minutes.
6. Remove the chops and place the vegetables in the Air fryer basket.
7. Top with the chops and air fry for about 6 minutes.
8. Dish out and serve warm.

Nutrition Info per Serving:

Calories: 470, Fat: 23.5g, Carbohydrates: 14.8g, Sugar: 3.1g, Protein: 49.4g, Sodium: 186mg

Za'atar Lamb Loin Chops

Prep time: 10 minutes, Cook time: 15 minutes, Serves 4

8 (3½-ounces) bone-in lamb loin chops, trimmed
3 garlic cloves, crushed
1 tbsp. fresh lemon juice
1 tsp. olive oil
1 tbsp. Za'atar
Salt and black pepper, to taste

1. Preheat the Air fryer to 400°F (204°C) and grease an Air fryer basket.
2. Mix the garlic, lemon juice, oil, Za'atar, salt, and black pepper in a large bowl.
3. Coat the chops generously with the herb mixture and arrange the chops in the Air fryer basket.
4. Roast for about 15 minutes, flipping twice in between and dish out the lamb chops to serve hot.

Nutrition Info per Serving:

Calories: 433, Fat: 17.6g, Carbohydrates: 0.6g, Sugar: 0.2g, Protein: 64.1g, Sodium: 201mg

(Note: Za'atar - Za'atar is generally made with ground dried thyme, oregano, marjoram, or some combination thereof, mixed with toasted sesame seeds, and salt, though other spices such as sumac might also be added. Some commercial varieties also include roasted flour.)

Leg of Lamb with Brussels Sprouts

Prep time: 20 minutes, Cook time: 1 hour 30 minutes, Serves 6

2¼ pounds leg of lamb
1 tbsp. fresh rosemary, minced
1 tbsp. fresh lemon thyme
1½ pounds Brussels sprouts, trimmed
3 tbsps. olive oil, divided
1 garlic clove, minced
Salt and ground black pepper, as required
2 tbsps. honey

1. Preheat the Air fryer to 300°F (149°C) and grease an Air fryer basket.
2. Make slits in the leg of lamb with a sharp knife.
3. Mix 2 tbsps. of oil, herbs, garlic, salt, and black pepper in a bowl.
4. Coat the leg of lamb with oil mixture generously and arrange in the Air fryer basket.
5. Roast for about 75 minutes and set the Air fryer to 390°F (199°C).
6. Coat the Brussels sprouts evenly with the remaining oil and honey and arrange them in the Air fryer basket with leg of lamb.
7. Roast for about 15 minutes and dish out to serve warm.

Nutrition Info per Serving:

Calories: 449, Fats: 19.9g, Carbohydrates: 16.6g, Sugar: 8.2g, Proteins: 51.7g, Sodium: 185mg

Herbed Lamb Chops

Prep time: 10 minutes, Cook time: 15 minutes, Serves 2

4 (4-ounces) lamb chops
1 tbsp. fresh lemon juice
1 tbsp. olive oil
1 tsp. dried rosemary
1 tsp. dried thyme
1 tsp. dried oregano
½ tsp. ground cumin
½ tsp. ground coriander
Salt and black pepper, to taste

1. Preheat the Air fryer to 390ºF (199ºC) and grease an Air fryer basket.
2. Mix the lemon juice, oil, herbs, and spices in a large bowl.
3. Coat the chops generously with the herb mixture and refrigerate to marinate for about 1 hour.
4. Arrange the chops in the Air fryer basket and roast for about 15 minutes, flipping once in between.
5. Dish out the lamb chops in a platter and serve hot.

Nutrition Info per Serving:

Calories: 491, Fat: 24g, Carbohydrates: 1.6g, Sugar: 0.2g, Protein: 64g, Sodium: 253mg

Spiced Lamb Steaks

Prep time: 15 minutes, Cook time: 15 minutes, Serves 3

½ onion, roughly chopped
1½ pounds boneless lamb sirloin steaks
5 garlic cloves, peeled
1 tbsp. fresh ginger, peeled
1 tsp. garam masala
1 tsp. ground fennel
½ tsp. ground cumin
½ tsp. ground cinnamon
½ tsp. cayenne pepper
Salt and black pepper, to taste

1. Preheat the Air fryer to 330ºF (166ºC) and grease an Air fryer basket.
2. Put the onion, garlic, ginger, and spices in a blender and pulse until smooth.
3. Coat the lamb steaks with this mixture on both sides and refrigerate to marinate for about 24 hours.
4. Arrange the lamb steaks in the Air fryer basket and roast for about 15 minutes, flipping once in between.
5. Dish out the steaks in a platter and serve warm.

Nutrition Info per Serving:

Calories: 252, Fat: 16.7g, Carbohydrates: 4.2g, Sugar: 0.7g, Protein: 21.7g, Sodium: 42mg

Lollipop Lamb Chops

Prep time: 15 minutes, Cook time: 7 minutes, Serves 4

½ small clove garlic
¼ cup packed fresh parsley
¾ cup packed fresh mint
½ tsp. lemon juice
¼ cup grated low-fat Parmesan cheese
⅓ cup shelled pistachios
¼ tsp. salt
½ cup olive oil
8 lamb chops (1 rack)
2 tbsps. vegetable oil
Salt and freshly ground black pepper, to taste
1 tbsp. dried rosemary, chopped
1 tbsp. dried thyme

1. Make the pesto by combining the garlic, parsley and mint in a food processor and process until finely chopped. Add the lemon juice, Parmesan cheese, pistachios and salt. Process until all the ingredients have turned into a paste. With the processor running, slowly pour the olive oil in. Scrape the sides of the processor with a spatula and process for another 30 seconds.
2. Preheat the air fryer to 400ºF (204ºC).
3. Rub both sides of the lamb chops with vegetable oil and season with salt, pepper, rosemary and thyme, pressing the herbs into the meat gently with the fingers. Transfer the lamb chops to the air fryer basket.
4. Air fry the lamb chops for 5 minutes. Flip the chops over and air fry for an additional 2 minutes.
5. Serve the lamb chops with mint pesto drizzled on top.

Nutrition Info per Serving:

Calories: 505, Protein: 25g, Fat: 40g, Carbohydrates: 5g, Fiber: 2g, Sugar: 1g, Sodium: 419mg

Mustard Lamb Loin Chops

Prep time: 15 minutes, Cook time: 30 minutes, Serves 4

8 (4-ounces) lamb loin chops
2 tbsps. Dijon mustard
1 tbsp. fresh lemon juice
½ tsp. olive oil
1 tsp. dried tarragon
Salt and black pepper, to taste

1. Preheat the Air fryer to 390ºF (199ºC) and grease an Air fryer basket.
2. Mix the mustard, lemon juice, oil, tarragon, salt, and black pepper in a large bowl.
3. Coat the chops generously with the mustard mixture and arrange in the Air fryer basket.
4. Roast for about 15 minutes, flipping once in between and dish out to serve hot.

Nutrition Info per Serving:

Calories: 433, Fat: 17.6g, Carbohydrates: 0.6g, Sugar: 0.2g, Protein: 64.1g, Sodium: 201mg

Fast Lamb Satay

Prep time: 5 minutes, Cook time: 8 minutes, Serves 2

¼ tsp. cumin
1 tsp. ginger
½ tsp. nutmeg
Salt and ground black pepper, to taste
2 boneless lamb steaks
Cooking spray

1. Combine the cumin, ginger, nutmeg, salt and pepper in a bowl.
2. Cube the lamb steaks and massage the spice mixture into each one.
3. Leave to marinate for 10 minutes, then transfer onto metal skewers.
4. Preheat the air fryer to 400°F (204°C).
5. Spritz the skewers with the cooking spray, then air fry them in the air fryer for 8 minutes.
6. Take care when removing them from the air fryer and serve.

Nutrition Info per Serving:

Calories: 274, Protein: 28g, Fat: 16g, Carbohydrates: 2g, Fiber: 1g, Sugar: 0g, Sodium: 120mg

Fantastic Leg of Lamb

Prep time: 10 minutes, Cook time: 1 hour 15 minutes, Serves 4

2 pounds leg of lamb
2 fresh rosemary sprigs
2 fresh thyme sprigs
2 tbsps. olive oil
Salt and black pepper, to taste

1. Preheat the Air fryer to 300°F (149°C) and grease an Air fryer basket.
2. Sprinkle the leg of lamb with oil, salt and black pepper and wrap with herb sprigs.
3. Arrange the leg of lamb in the Air fryer basket and air fry for about 75 minutes.
4. Dish out and serve warm.

Nutrition Info per Serving:

Calories: 534, Fat: 25.8g, Carbohydrates: 2.4g, Sugar: 0g, Protein: 69.8g, Sodium: 190mg

Roasted Lamb

Prep time: 15 minutes, Cook time: 1 hour 30 minutes, Serves 4

2½ pounds half lamb leg roast, slits carved
2 garlic cloves, sliced into smaller slithers
1 tbsp. dried rosemary
1 tbsp. olive oil
Cracked Himalayan rock salt and cracked peppercorns, to taste

1. Preheat the Air fryer to 400°F (204°C) and grease an Air fryer basket.
2. Insert the garlic slithers in the slits and brush with rosemary, oil, salt, and black pepper.
3. Arrange the lamb in the Air fryer basket and air fry for about 15 minutes.
4. Set the Air fryer to 350°F (177°C) and roast for 1 hour and 15 minutes.
5. Dish out the lamb and serve hot.

Nutrition Info per Serving:

Calories: 246, Fat: 7.4g, Carbohydrates: 9.4g, Sugar: 6.5g, Protein: 37.2g, Sodium: 353mg

Italian Lamb Chops with Avocado Mayo

Prep time: 5 minutes, Cook time: 12 minutes, Serves 2

2 lamb chops
2 tsps. Italian herbs
2 avocados
½ cup mayonnaise
1 tbsp. lemon juice

1. Season the lamb chops with the Italian herbs, then set aside for 5 minutes.
2. Preheat the air fryer to 400°F (204°C) and place the rack inside.
3. Put the chops on the rack and air fry for 12 minutes.
4. In the meantime, halve the avocados and open to remove the pits. Spoon the flesh into a blender.
5. Add the mayonnaise and lemon juice and pulse until a smooth consistency is achieved.
6. Take care when removing the chops from the air fryer, then plate up and serve with the avocado mayo.

Nutrition Info per Serving:

Calories: 566, Protein: 29g, Fat: 42g, Carbohydrates: 11g, Fiber: 7g, Sugar: 1g, Sodium: 340mg

CHAPTER 10
PORK

Flavorsome Pork Chops with Peanut Sauce

Prep time: 30 minutes, Cook time: 21 minutes, Serves 4

For the Pork:
1 pound pork chops, cubed into 1-inch size
1 tsp. fresh ginger, minced
1 garlic clove, minced
2 tbsps. soy sauce
1 tbsp. olive oil
1 tsp. hot pepper sauce
For the Peanut Sauce:
2 tbsps. olive oil, divided
1 shallot, chopped finely
1 garlic clove, minced
1 tsp. ground coriander
1 tsp. hot pepper sauce
¾ cup ground peanuts
¾ cup nonfat coconut milk

1. Preheat the Air fryer to 390ºF (199ºC) and grease an Air fryer basket.
2. For the Pork: Mix all the ingredients in a bowl and keep aside for about 30 minutes.
3. Arrange the chops in the Air fryer basket and roast for about 12 minutes, flipping once in between.
4. For the Peanut Sauce: Heat 1 tbsp. olive oil in a pan on medium heat and add shallot and garlic. Sauté for about 3 minutes and stir in coriander. Sauté for about 1 minute and add rest of the ingredients. Cook for about 5 minutes and pour over the pork chops to serve.

Nutrition Info per Serving:

Calories: 725, Fat: 62.9g, Carbohydrates: 9.5g, Sugar: 2.8g, Protein: 34.4g, Sodium: 543mg

Pork Chops with Rinds

Prep time: 5 minutes, Cook time: 15 minutes, Serves 4

1 tsp. chili powder
½ tsp. garlic powder
1½ ounces (43 g) pork rinds, finely ground
4 (4-ounce / 113-g) pork chops
1 tbsp. coconut oil, melted

1. Preheat the air fryer to 400ºF (204ºC).
2. Combine the chili powder, garlic powder, and ground pork rinds.
3. Coat the pork chops with the coconut oil, followed by the pork rind mixture, taking care to cover them completely. Then place the chops in the air fryer basket.
4. Air fry the chops for 15 minutes or until the internal temperature of the chops reaches at least 145ºF (63ºC), turning halfway through.
5. Serve immediately.

Nutrition Info per Serving:

Calories: 231, Protein: 26g, Fat: 13g, Carbohydrates: 1g, Fiber: 0g, Sugar: 0g, Sodium: 290mg

Sun-dried Tomato Crusted Chops

Prep time: 15 minutes, Cook time: 10 minutes, Serves 4

½ cup oil-packed sun-dried tomatoes
½ cup toasted almonds
¼ cup grated low-fat Parmesan cheese
½ cup olive oil, plus more for brushing the air fryer basket
2 tbsps. water
½ tsp. salt
Freshly ground black pepper, to taste
4 center-cut boneless pork chops (about 1¼ pounds / 567 g)

1. Put the sun-dried tomatoes into a food processor and pulse them until they are coarsely chopped. Add the almonds, Parmesan cheese, olive oil, water, salt and pepper. Process into a smooth paste. Spread most of the paste (leave a little in reserve) onto both sides of the pork chops and then pierce the meat several times with a needle-style meat tenderizer or a fork. Let the pork chops sit and marinate for at least 1 hour (refrigerate if marinating for longer than 1 hour).
2. Preheat the air fryer to 370ºF (188ºC).
3. Brush more olive oil on the bottom of the air fryer basket. Transfer the pork chops into the air fryer basket, spooning a little more of the sun-dried tomato paste onto the pork chops if there are any gaps where the paste may have been rubbed off. Air fry the pork chops for 10 minutes, turning the chops over halfway through.
4. When the pork chops have finished cooking, transfer them to a serving plate and serve.

Nutrition Info per Serving:

Calories: 511, Protein: 31g, Fat: 38g, Carbohydrates: 8g, Fiber: 3g, Sugar: 3g, Sodium: 620mg

Garlic Butter Pork Chops

Prep time: 10 minutes, Cook time: 8 minutes, Serves 4

4 pork chops
1 tbsp. coconut butter
2 tsps. parsley
1 tbsp. coconut oil
2 tsps. garlic, grated
Salt and black pepper, to taste

1. Preheat the Air fryer to 350ºF (177ºC) and grease an Air fryer basket.
2. Mix all the seasonings, coconut oil, garlic, butter, and parsley in a bowl and coat the pork chops with it.
3. Cover the chops with foil and refrigerate to marinate for about 1 hour.
4. Remove the foil and arrange the chops in the Air fryer basket.
5. Roast for about 8 minutes and dish out in a bowl to serve warm.

Nutrition Info per Serving:

Calories: 311, Fat: 25.5g, Carbohydrates: 1.4g, Sugar: 0.3g, Protein: 18.4g, Sodium: 58mg

Citrus Pork Loin Roast

Prep time: 10 minutes, Cook time: 45 minutes, Serves 8

1 tbsp. lime juice
1 tbsp. orange marmalade
1 tsp. coarse brown mustard
1 tsp. curry powder
1 tsp. dried lemongrass
2 pounds (907 g) boneless pork loin roast
Salt and ground black pepper, to taste
Cooking spray

1. Preheat the air fryer to 360ºF (182ºC).
2. Mix the lime juice, marmalade, mustard, curry powder, and lemongrass.
3. Rub mixture all over the surface of the pork loin. Season with salt and pepper.
4. Spray air fryer basket with cooking spray and place pork roast diagonally in the basket.
5. Air fry for approximately 45 minutes, until the internal temperature reaches at least 145ºF (63ºC).
6. Wrap roast in foil and let rest for 10 minutes before slicing.
7. Serve immediately.

Nutrition Info per Serving:
Calories: 209, Protein: 29g, Fat: 8g, Carbohydrates: 4g, Fiber: 0g, Sugar: 3g, Sodium: 88mg

Filling Pork Chops

Prep time: 20 minutes, Cook time: 12 minutes, Serves 2

2 (1-inch thick) pork chops
½ tbsp. fresh cilantro, chopped
½ tbsp. fresh rosemary, chopped
½ tbsp. fresh parsley, chopped
2 garlic cloves, minced
2 tbsps. olive oil
¾ tbsp. Dijon mustard
1 tbsp. ground coriander
1 tsp. coconut sugar
Salt, to taste

1. Preheat the Air fryer to 390ºF (199ºC) and grease an Air fryer basket.
2. Mix all the ingredients in a large bowl except the chops.
3. Coat the pork chops with marinade generously and cover to refrigerate for about 3 hours.
4. Keep the pork chops at room temperature for about 30 minutes and transfer into the Air fryer basket.
5. Air fry for about 12 minutes, flipping once in between and dish out to serve hot.

Nutrition Info per Serving:
Calories: 276, Fat: 19.1g, Carbohydrates: 3.9g, Sugar: 2.1g, Protein: 22.6g, Sodium: 185mg

Barbecue Pork Ribs

Prep time: 5 minutes, Cook time: 30 minutes, Serves 4

1 tbsp. barbecue dry rub   1 tsp. sesame oil
1 tsp. mustard   1 pound (454 g) pork
1 tbsp. apple cider vinegar   ribs, chopped

1. Combine the dry rub, mustard, apple cider vinegar, and sesame oil, then coat the ribs with this mixture. Refrigerate the ribs for 20 minutes.
2. Preheat the air fryer to 360ºF (182ºC).
3. When the ribs are ready, place them in the air fryer and air fry for 15 minutes. Flip them and air fry on the other side for a further 15 minutes.
4. Serve immediately.

Nutrition Info per Serving:
Calories: 210, Protein: 14g, Fat: 15g, Carbohydrates: 2g, Fiber: 0g, Sugar: 1g, Sodium: 220mg

Chinese Style Pork Meatballs

Prep time: 15 minutes, Cook time: 10 minutes, Serves 3

1 egg, beaten   ½ tsp. sesame oil
6-ounce ground pork   ¼ tsp. five spice powder
¼ cup cornstarch   ½ tbsp. olive oil
1 tsp. oyster sauce   ¼ tsp. honey
½ tbsp. light soy sauce

1. Preheat the Air fryer to 390ºF (199ºC) and grease an Air fryer basket.
2. Mix all the ingredients in a bowl except cornstarch until well combined.
3. Shape the mixture into equal-sized balls and place the cornstarch in a shallow dish.
4. Roll the meatballs evenly into cornstarch mixture and arrange in the Air fryer basket.
5. Roast for about 10 minutes and dish out to serve warm.

Nutrition Info per Serving:
Calories: 171, Fat: 6.6g, Carbohydrates: 10.8g, Sugar: 0.7g, Protein: 16.9g, Sodium: 254mg

Air Fried Baby Back Ribs

Prep time: 5 minutes, Cook time: 30 minutes, Serves 2

2 tsps. red pepper flakes
¾ ground ginger
3 cloves minced garlic
Salt and ground black pepper, to taste
2 baby back ribs

1. Preheat the air fryer to 350ºF (177ºC).
2. Combine the red pepper flakes, ginger, garlic, salt and pepper in a bowl, making sure to mix well. Massage the mixture into the baby back ribs.
3. Air fry the ribs in the air fryer for 30 minutes.
4. Take care when taking the rubs out of the air fryer. Put them on a serving dish and serve.

Nutrition Info per Serving:
Calories: 548, Protein: 28g, Fat: 43g, Carbohydrates: 6g, Fiber: 1g, Sugar: 1g, Sodium: 156mg

Five Spice Pork

Prep time: 15 minutes, Cook time: 20 minutes, Serves 4

1-pound pork belly	2 tsps. garlic, minced
1 tsp. stevia	2 tsps. ginger, minced
2 tbsps. dark soy sauce	1 tbsp. hoisin sauce
1 tbsp. Shaoxing (cooking wine)	1 tsp. Chinese Five Spice

1. Preheat the Air fryer to 390°F (199°C) and grease an Air fryer basket.
2. Mix all the ingredients in a bowl and place in the Ziplock bag.
3. Seal the bag, shake it well and refrigerate to marinate for about 1 hour.
4. Remove the pork from the bag and arrange it in the Air fryer basket.
5. Air fry for about 15 minutes and dish out in a bowl to serve warm.

Nutrition Info per Serving:

Calories: 604, Fat: 30.6g, Carbohydrates: 1.4g, Sugar: 20.3g, Protein: 19.8g, Sodium: 834mg

Orange Pork Tenderloin

Prep time: 15 minutes, Cook time: 23 minutes, Serves 3 to 4

2 tbsps. coconut sugar
2 tsps. cornstarch
2 tsps. Dijon mustard
½ cup orange juice
½ tsp. soy sauce
2 tsps. grated fresh ginger
¼ cup white wine
Zest of 1 orange
1 pound (454 g) pork tenderloin
Salt and freshly ground black pepper, to taste
Oranges, halved, for garnish
Fresh parsley, for garnish

1. Combine the coconut sugar, cornstarch, Dijon mustard, orange juice, soy sauce, ginger, white wine and orange zest in a small saucepan and bring the mixture to a boil on the stovetop. Lower the heat and simmer while you air fry the pork tenderloin or until the sauce has thickened.
2. Preheat the air fryer to 370°F (188°C).
3. Season all sides of the pork tenderloin with salt and freshly ground black pepper. Transfer the tenderloin to the air fryer basket.
4. Air fry for 20 to 23 minutes, or until the internal temperature reaches 145°F (63°C). Flip the tenderloin over halfway through the cooking process and baste with the sauce.
5. Transfer the tenderloin to a cutting board and let it rest for 5 minutes. Slice the pork at a slight angle and serve garnished with orange halves and fresh parsley.

Nutrition Info per Serving:

Calories: 199, Protein: 25g, Fat: 6g, Carbohydrates: 10g, Fiber: 0g, Sugar: 7g, Sodium: 168mg

Pork Spare Ribs

Prep time: 15 minutes, Cook time: 20 minutes, Serves 6

12 (1-inch) pork spare ribs
½ cup cornstarch
5-6 garlic cloves, minced
½ cup rice vinegar
2 tbsps. soy sauce
2 tbsps. olive oil
Salt and black pepper, to taste

1. Preheat the Air fryer to 390°F (199°C) and grease an Air fryer basket.
2. Mix the garlic, vinegar, soy sauce, salt, and black pepper in a large bowl.
3. Coat the ribs generously with this mixture and refrigerate to marinate overnight.
4. Place the cornstarch in a shallow bowl and dredge the ribs in it.
5. Drizzle with olive oil and arrange the ribs in the Air fryer basket.
6. Air fry for about 20 minutes, flipping once in between.
7. Dish out and serve hot.

Nutrition Info per Serving:

Calories: 557, Fat: 51.3g, Carbohydrates: 11g, Sugar: 0.1g, Protein: 35g, Sodium: 997mg

Cheese Crusted Chops

Prep time: 10 minutes, Cook time: 12 minutes, Serves 4 to 6

¼ tsp. pepper
½ tsp. salt
4 to 6 thick boneless pork chops
1 cup pork rind crumbs
¼ tsp. chili powder
½ tsp. onion powder
1 tsp. smoked paprika
2 beaten eggs
3 tbsps. grated low-fat Parmesan cheese
Cooking spray

1. Preheat the air fryer to 400°F (205°C).
2. Rub the pepper and salt on both sides of pork chops.
3. In a food processor, pulse pork rinds into crumbs. Mix crumbs with chili powder, onion powder, and paprika in a bowl.
4. Beat eggs in another bowl.
5. Dip pork chops into eggs then into pork rind crumb mixture.
6. Spritz the air fryer with cooking spray and add pork chops to the basket.
7. Air fry for 12 minutes.
8. Serve garnished with the Parmesan cheese.

Nutrition Info per Serving:

Calories: 286, Protein: 41g, Fat: 12g, Carbohydrates: 2g, Fiber: 0g, Sugar: 0g, Sodium: 564mg

Breaded Pork Chops

Prep time: 15 minutes, Cook time: 15 minutes, Serves 2

2 (6-ounces) pork chops
¼ cup plain flour
1 egg
4 ounces breadcrumbs
Salt and black pepper, to taste
1 tbsp. vegetable oil

1. Preheat the Air fryer to 400ºF (204ºC) and grease an Air fryer basket.
2. Season the chops with salt and black pepper.
3. Place the flour in a shallow bowl and whisk an egg in a second bowl.
4. Mix the breadcrumbs and vegetable oil in a third bowl.
5. Coat the pork chops with flour, dip into egg and dredge into the breadcrumb mixture.
6. Arrange the chops in the Air fryer basket and roast for about 15 minutes, flipping once in between.
7. Dish out and serve hot.

Nutrition Info per Serving:

Calories: 621, Fat: 26.1g, Carbohydrates: 53.3g, Sugar: 3.7g, Protein: 43.9g, Sodium: 963mg

Pork Chop Stir Fry

Prep time: 10 minutes, Cook time: 30 minutes, Serves 4 to 6

¼ cup olive oil
¼ cup soy sauce
¼ cup freshly squeezed lemon juice
1 garlic clove, minced
1 tbsp. Dijon mustard
1 tsp. salt
½ tsp. freshly ground black pepper
2 pounds (907 g) pork tenderloin

1. In a large mixing bowl, make the marinade: Mix the olive oil, soy sauce, lemon juice, minced garlic, Dijon mustard, salt, and pepper. Reserve ¼ cup of the marinade.
2. Put the tenderloin in a large bowl and pour the remaining marinade over the meat. Cover and marinate in the refrigerator for about 1 hour.
3. Preheat the air fryer to 400ºF (204ºC).
4. Put the marinated pork tenderloin into the air fryer basket. Roast for 10 minutes. Flip the pork and baste it with half of the reserved marinade. Roast for 10 minutes more.
5. Flip the pork, then baste with the remaining marinade. Roast for another 10 minutes, for a total cooking time of 30 minutes.
6. Serve immediately.

Nutrition Info per Serving:

Calories: 306, Protein: 36g, Fat: 15g, Carbohydrates: 4g, Fiber: 0g, Sugar: 1g, Sodium: 773mg

Marinated Pork Tenderloin

Prep time: 10 minutes, Cook time: 30 minutes, Serves 4 to 6

¼ cup olive oil
¼ cup soy sauce
¼ cup freshly squeezed lemon juice
1 garlic clove, minced
1 tbsp. Dijon mustard
1 tsp. salt
½ tsp. freshly ground black pepper
2 pounds (907 g) pork tenderloin

1. In a large mixing bowl, make the marinade: Mix the olive oil, soy sauce, lemon juice, minced garlic, Dijon mustard, salt, and pepper. Reserve ¼ cup of the marinade.
2. Put the tenderloin in a large bowl and pour the remaining marinade over the meat. Cover and marinate in the refrigerator for about 1 hour.
3. Preheat the air fryer to 400ºF (204ºC).
4. Put the marinated pork tenderloin into the air fryer basket. Roast for 10 minutes. Flip the pork and baste it with half of the reserved marinade. Roast for 10 minutes more.
5. Flip the pork, then baste with the remaining marinade. Roast for another 10 minutes, for a total cooking time of 30 minutes.
6. Serve immediately.

Nutrition Info per Serving:

Calories: 306, Protein: 36g, Fat: 15g, Carbohydrates: 4g, Fiber: 0g, Sugar: 1g, Sodium: 773mg

Sweet and Sour Pork Chops

Prep time: 10 minutes, Cook time: 16 minutes, Serves 4

6 pork loin chops
Salt and black pepper, to taste
2 garlic cloves, minced
2 tbsps. honey
2 tbsps. soy sauce
1 tbsp. balsamic vinegar
¼ tsp. ground ginger

1. Preheat the Air fryer to 355ºF (179ºC) and grease a baking tray.
2. Season the chops with a little salt and black pepper.
3. Mix rest of the ingredients in a large bowl and add chops.
4. Coat with marinade generously and cover to refrigerate for about 8 hours.
5. Arrange the chops in the baking tray and transfer into the Air fryer basket.
6. Roast for about 16 minutes, flipping once in between and dish out to serve hot.

Nutrition Info per Serving:

Calories: 282, Fats: 19.9g, Carbohydrates: 6.6g, Sugar: 5.9g, Proteins: 18.4g, Sodium: 357mg

Moist Stuffed Pork Roll

Prep time: 20 minutes, Cook time: 15 minutes, Serves 4

1 scallion, chopped
¼ cup sun-dried tomatoes, chopped finely
2 tbsps. fresh parsley, chopped
4 (6-ounce) pork cutlets, pounded slightly
Salt and black pepper, to taste
2 tsps. paprika
½ tbsp. olive oil

1. Preheat the Air fryer to 390ºF (199ºC) and grease an Air fryer basket.
2. Mix scallion, tomatoes, parsley, salt and black pepper in a large bowl.
3. Coat the cutlets with tomato mixture and roll each cutlet.
4. Secure the cutlets with cocktail sticks and rub with paprika, salt and black pepper.
5. Coat evenly with oil and transfer into the Air fryer basket.
6. Roast for about 15 minutes, flipping once in between and dish out to serve hot.

Nutrition Info per Serving:

Calories: 265, Fats: 7.9g, Carbohydrates: 1.4g, Sugar: 0.5g, Proteins: 44.9g, Sodium: 100mg

Char Siew

Prep time: 10 minutes, Cook time: 20 minutes, Serves 4 to 6

1 strip of pork shoulder butt with a good amount of fat marbling
Olive oil, for brushing the pan
For the Marinade:
1 tsp. sesame oil
2 tbsps. raw honey
1 tsp. low-sodium dark soy sauce
1 tsp. light soy sauce
1 tbsp. rose wine
2 tbsps. Hoisin sauce

1. Combine all the marinade ingredients together in a Ziploc bag. Put pork in bag, making sure all sections of pork strip are engulfed in the marinade. Chill for 3 to 24 hours.
2. Take out the strip 30 minutes before planning to roast and preheat the air fryer to 350ºF (177ºC).
3. Put foil on small pan and brush with olive oil. Put marinated pork strip onto prepared pan.
4. Roast in the preheated air fryer for 20 minutes.
5. Glaze with marinade every 5 to 10 minutes.
6. Remove strip and leave to cool a few minutes before slicing.
7. Serve immediately.

Nutrition Info per Serving:

Calories: 253, Protein: 13g, Fat: 13g, Carbohydrates: 22g, Fiber: 0g, Sugar: 10g, Sodium: 300mg

Pepper Pork Chops

Prep time: 15 minutes, Cook time: 6 minutes, Serves 2

2 pork chops
1 egg white
¾ cup xanthum gum
½ tsp. sea salt
¼ tsp. freshly ground black pepper
1 oil mister

1. Preheat the Air fryer to 400ºF (204ºC) and grease an Air fryer basket.
2. Whisk egg white with salt and black pepper in a bowl and dip the pork chops in it.
3. Cover the bowl and marinate for about 20 minutes.
4. Pour the xanthum gum over both sides of the chops and spray with oil mister.
5. Arrange the chops in the Air fryer basket and roast for about 6 minutes.
6. Dish out in a bowl and serve warm.

Nutrition Info per Serving:

Calories: 541, Fat: 34g, Carbohydrates: 3.4g, Sugar: 1g, Protein: 20.3g, Sodium: 547mg

Pork Chop Stir Fry

Prep time: 10 minutes, Cook time: 20 minutes, Serves 4

3 tbsps. olive oil, divided
¼ tsp. ground black pepper
½ tsp. salt
1 egg white
4 (4-ounce / 113-g) pork chops
¾ cup almond flour
2 sliced jalapeño peppers
2 sliced scallions
¼ tsp. ground white pepper
1 tsp. sea salt

1. Coat the air fryer basket with 1 tbsp. olive oil.
2. Whisk black pepper, salt, and egg white together until foamy.
3. Cut pork chops into pieces, leaving just a bit on bones. Pat dry.
4. Add pieces of pork to egg white mixture, coating well. Let sit for marinade 20 minutes.
5. Preheat the air fryer to 360ºF (182ºC).
6. Put marinated chops into a large bowl and add almond flour. Dredge and shake off excess and place into air fryer.
7. Air fry the chops in the preheated air fryer for 12 minutes.
8. Turn up the heat to 400ºF (205ºC) and air fry for another 6 minutes until pork chops are nice and crisp.
9. Meanwhile, remove jalapeño seeds and chop up. Chop scallions and mix with jalapeño pieces.
10. Heat a skillet with the remaining olive oil. Stir-fry the white pepper, salt, scallions, and jalapeños for 60 seconds. Then add fried pork pieces to skills and toss with scallion mixture. Stir-fry for 1 to 2 minutes until well coated and hot.
11. Serve immediately.

Nutrition Info per Serving:

Calories: 441, Protein: 29g, Fat: 30g, Carbohydrates: 13g, Fiber: 6g, Sugar: 2g, Sodium: 605mg

CHAPTER 11
BEEF

Beef and Veggie Kebabs

Prep time: 20 minutes, Cook time: 12 minutes, Serves 4

1 pound sirloin steak, cut into 1-inch chunks
8 ounces baby Bella mushrooms, stems removed
1 large bell pepper, seeded and cut into 1-inch pieces
1 red onion, cut into 1-inch pieces
¼ cup soy sauce
¼ cup olive oil
1 tbsp. garlic, minced
1 tsp. coconut sugar
½ tsp. ground cumin
Salt and black pepper, to taste

1. Preheat the Air fryer to 390°F (199°C) and grease an Air fryer basket.
2. Mix soy sauce, oil, garlic, coconut sugar, cumin, salt, and black pepper in a large bowl.
3. Coat the steak cubes generously with marinade and refrigerate to marinate for about 30 minutes.
4. Thread the steak cubes, mushrooms, bell pepper, and onion onto metal skewers.
5. Place the skewers in the Air fryer basket and grill for about 12 minutes, flipping once in between.
6. Dish out in a platter and serve hot.

Nutrition Info per Serving:

Calories: 369, Fat: 20g, Carbohydrates: 10.5g, Sugar: 4.7g, Protein: 37.6g, Sodium: 1018mg

Perfect Skirt Steak

Prep time: 15 minutes, Cook time: 10 minutes, Serves 4

1 cup fresh parsley leaves, chopped finely
3 tbsps. fresh oregano, chopped finely
3 tbsps. fresh mint leaves, chopped finely
2 (8-ounce) grass-fed skirt steaks
3 garlic cloves, minced
1 tbsp. ground cumin
2 tsps. smoked paprika
1 tsp. cayenne pepper
1 tsp. red pepper flakes, crushed
Salt and freshly ground black pepper, to taste
¾ cup olive oil
3 tbsps. red wine vinegar

1. Preheat the Air fryer to 390°F (199°C) and grease an Air fryer basket.
2. Season the steaks with a little salt and black pepper.
3. Mix all the ingredients in a large bowl except the steaks.
4. Put ¼ cup of the herb mixture and steaks in a resealable bag and shake well.
5. Refrigerate for about 24 hours and reserve the remaining herb mixture.
6. Keep the steaks at room temperature for about 30 minutes and transfer into the Air fryer basket.
7. Roast for about 10 minutes and sprinkle with remaining herb mixture to serve.

Nutrition Info per Serving:

Calories: 561, Fat: 50.3g, Carbohydrates: 6.1g, Sugar: 0.6g, Protein: 31.9g, Sodium: 297mg

Air Fried Ribeye Steak

Prep time: 5 minutes, Cook time: 15 minutes, Serves 1

1 (1-pound / 454-g) grass-fed ribeye steak
Salt and ground black pepper, to taste
1 tbsp. peanut oil
½ tbsp. peanut butter
½ tsp. thyme, chopped

1. Preheat a skillet in the air fryer at 400°F (204°C).
2. Season the steaks with salt and pepper. Remove the skillet from the air fryer once preheated.
3. Put the skillet on the stovetop burner on a medium heat and drizzle with the peanut oil.
4. Sear the steak for 2 minutes.
5. Turn over the steak and place in the air fryer for 6 minutes.
6. Take out the steak from the air fryer and place it back on the stove top on low heat to keep warm.
7. Toss in the butter and thyme and air fry for 3 minutes.
8. Rest for 5 minutes and serve.

Nutrition Info per Serving:

Calories: 715, Protein: 59g, Fat: 48g, Carbohydrates: 1g, Fiber: 0g, Sugar: 0g, Sodium: 116mg

Beef Egg Rolls

Prep time: 15 minutes, Cook time: 12 minutes, Makes 8 egg rolls

½ chopped onion
2 garlic cloves, chopped
½ packet taco seasoning
Salt and ground black pepper, to taste
1 pound (454 g) grass-fed lean ground beef
½ can cilantro lime rotel
16 egg roll wrappers
1 cup shredded low-fat Mexican cheese
1 tbsp. olive oil
1 tsp. cilantro

1. Preheat the air fryer to 400°F (205°C).
2. Add onions and garlic to a skillet, cooking until fragrant. Then add taco seasoning, pepper, salt, and beef, cooking until beef is broke up into tiny pieces and cooked thoroughly.
3. Add rotel and stir well.
4. Lay out egg wrappers and brush with a touch of water to soften a bit.
5. Load wrappers with beef filling and add cheese to each.
6. Fold diagonally to close and use water to secure edges.
7. Brush filled egg wrappers with olive oil and add to the air fryer.
8. Air fry 8 minutes, flip, and air fry for another 4 minutes.
9. Serve sprinkled with cilantro.

Nutrition Info per Serving:

Calories: 208, Protein: 10g, Fat: 10g, Carbohydrates: 20g, Fiber: 2g, Sugar: 1g, Sodium: 319mg

Veggie Stuffed Beef Rolls

Prep time: 20 minutes, Cook time: 14 minutes, Serves 6

2 pounds grass-fed beef flank steak, pounded to ⅛-inch thickness
6 low-fat Provolone cheese slices
3-ounce roasted red bell peppers
¾ cup fresh baby spinach
3 tbsps. prepared pesto
Salt and black pepper, to taste

1. Preheat the Air fryer to 400ºF (204ºC) and grease an Air fryer basket.
2. Place the steak onto a smooth surface and spread evenly with pesto.
3. Top with the cheese slices, red peppers and spinach.
4. Roll up the steak tightly around the filling and secure with the toothpicks.
5. Arrange the roll in the Air fryer basket and roast for about 14 minutes, flipping once in between.
6. Dish out in a platter and serve warm.

Nutrition Info per Serving:

Calories: 447, Fats: 23.4g, Carbohydrates: 1.8g, Sugar: 0.6g, Proteins: 53.2g, Sodium: 472mg

Beef and Vegetable Cubes

Prep time: 15 minutes, Cook time: 17 minutes, Serves 4

2 tbsps. olive oil
1 tbsp. apple cider vinegar
1 tsp. fine sea salt
½ tsp. ground black pepper
1 tsp. shallot powder
¾ tsp. smoked cayenne pepper
½ tsp. garlic powder
¼ tsp. ground cumin
1 pound (454 g) grass-fed top round steak, cut into cubes
4 ounces (113 g) broccoli, cut into florets
4 ounces (113 g) mushrooms, sliced
1 tsp. dried basil
1 tsp. celery seeds

1. Massage the olive oil, vinegar, salt, black pepper, shallot powder, cayenne pepper, garlic powder, and cumin into the cubed steak, ensuring to coat each piece evenly.
2. Allow to marinate for a minimum of 3 hours.
3. Preheat the air fryer to 365ºF (185ºC).
4. Put the beef cubes in the air fryer basket and air fry for 12 minutes.
5. When the steak is cooked through, place it in a bowl.
6. Wipe the grease from the basket and pour in the vegetables. Season them with basil and celery seeds.
7. Increase the temperature of the air fryer to 400ºF (204ºC) and air fry for 5 to 6 minutes. When the vegetables are hot, serve them with the steak.

Nutrition Info per Serving:

Calories: 252, Protein: 20g, Fat: 16g, Carbohydrates: 6g, Fiber: 2g, Sugar: 2g, Sodium: 654mg

Holiday Spicy Beef Roast

Prep time: 10 minutes, Cook time: 45 minutes, Serves 8

2 pounds (907 g) roast beef, at room temperature
2 tbsps. extra-virgin olive oil
1 tsp. sea salt flakes
1 tsp. black pepper, preferably freshly ground
1 tsp. smoked paprika
A few dashes of liquid smoke
2 jalapeño peppers, thinly sliced

1. Preheat the air fryer to 330ºF (166ºC).
2. Pat the roast dry using kitchen towels. Rub with extra-virgin olive oil and all seasonings along with liquid smoke.
3. Roast for 30 minutes in the preheated air fryer. Turn the roast over and roast for additional 15 minutes.
4. Check for doneness using a meat thermometer and serve sprinkled with sliced jalapeños. Bon appétit!

Nutrition Info per Serving:

Calories: 272, Protein: 24g, Fat: 18g, Carbohydrates: 1g, Fiber: 0g, Sugar: 0g, Sodium: 390mg

Tasty Beef Stuffed Bell Peppers

Prep time: 20 minutes, Cook time: 26 minutes, Serves 4

½ medium onion, chopped
1 pound grass-fed lean ground beef
½ cup jasmine rice, cooked
⅔ cup light Mexican cheese, shredded and divided
4 bell peppers, tops and seeds removed
1 tsp. olive oil
2 garlic cloves, minced
1 tsp. dried basil, crushed
1 tsp. garlic salt
½ tsp. red chili powder
Ground black pepper, as required
8 ounces tomato sauce, divided
2 tsps. Worcestershire sauce

1. Preheat the Air fryer to 400ºF (204ºC) and grease an Air fryer basket.
2. Heat olive oil in a medium skillet over medium heat and add onion and garlic.
3. Sauté for about 5 minutes and add the ground beef, basil, and spices.
4. Cook for about 10 minutes and drain off the excess grease from skillet.
5. Stir in the rice, half of the cheese, ⅔ of the tomato sauce and Worcestershire sauce and mix well.
6. Stuff the beef mixture in each bell pepper and arrange the bell peppers in the Air fryer basket.
7. Air fry for about 7 minutes and top with the remaining tomato sauce and cheese.
8. Air fry for 4 more minutes and dish out in a bowl to serve warm.

Nutrition Info per Serving:

Calories: 439, Fat: 3.1g, Carbohydrates: 34.4g, Sugar: 1.6g, Protein: 11.3g, Sodium: 160mg

Swedish Beef Meatballs

Prep time: 10 minutes, Cook time: 12 minutes, Serves 8

1 pound (454 g) grass-fed ground beef
1 egg, beaten
2 carrots, shredded
2 whole wheat bread slices, crumbled
1 small onion, minced
½ tsp. garlic salt
Pepper and salt, to taste
1 cup tomato sauce
2 cups pasta sauce

1. Preheat the air fryer to 400°F (204°C).
2. In a bowl, combine the ground beef, egg, carrots, crumbled bread, onion, garlic salt, pepper and salt.
3. Divide the mixture into equal amounts and shape each one into a small meatball.
4. Put them in the air fryer basket and air fry for 7 minutes.
5. Transfer the meatballs to an oven-safe dish and top with the tomato sauce and pasta sauce.
6. Set the dish into the air fryer basket and allow to air fry at 320°F (160°C) for 5 more minutes. Serve hot.

Nutrition Info per Serving:

Calories: 182, Protein: 12g, Fat: 10g, Carbohydrates: 12g, Fiber: 2g, Sugar: 4g, Sodium: 559mg

Steak with Bell Peppers

Prep time: 20 minutes, Cook time: 22 minutes, Serves 4

1¼ pounds grass-fed beef steak, cut into thin strips
2 green bell peppers, seeded and cubed
1 red bell pepper, seeded and cubed
1 red onion, sliced
1 tsp. dried oregano, crushed
1 tsp. onion powder
1 tsp. garlic powder
1 tsp. red chili powder
1 tsp. paprika
Salt, to taste
2 tbsps. olive oil

1. Preheat the Air fryer to 390°F (199°C) and grease an Air fryer basket.
2. Mix the oregano and spices in a bowl.
3. Add bell peppers, onion, oil, and beef strips and mix until well combined.
4. Transfer half of the steak strips in the Air fryer basket and air fry for about 11 minutes, flipping once in between.
5. Repeat with the remaining mixture and dish out to serve hot.

Nutrition Info per Serving:

Calories: 372, Fats: 16.3g, Carbohydrates: 11.2g, Sugar: 6.2g, Proteins: 44.6g, Sodium: 143mg

Spinach and Beef Braciole

Prep time: 25 minutes, Cook time: 1 hour 32 minutes, Serves 4

½ onion, finely chopped
1 tsp. olive oil
⅓ cup red wine
2 cups crushed tomatoes
1 tsp. Italian seasoning
½ tsp. garlic powder
¼ tsp. crushed red pepper flakes
2 tbsps. chopped fresh parsley
2 grass-fed top round steaks (about 1½ pounds / 680 g)
salt and freshly ground black pepper
2 cups fresh spinach, chopped
1 clove minced garlic
½ cup roasted red peppers, julienned
½ cup grated low-fat pecorino cheese
¼ cup pine nuts, toasted and roughly chopped
2 tbsps. olive oil

1. Preheat the air fryer to 400°F (204°C).
2. Toss the onions and olive oil together in a baking pan or casserole dish. Air fry at 400°F (204°C) for 5 minutes, stirring a couple times during the cooking process. Add the red wine, crushed tomatoes, Italian seasoning, garlic powder, red pepper flakes and parsley and stir. Cover the pan tightly with aluminum foil, lower the air fryer temperature to 350°F (177°C) and continue to air fry for 15 minutes.
3. While the sauce is simmering, prepare the beef. Using a meat mallet, pound the beef until it is ¼-inch thick. Season both sides of the beef with salt and pepper. Combine the spinach, garlic, red peppers, pecorino cheese, pine nuts and olive oil in a medium bowl. Season with salt and freshly ground black pepper. Disperse the mixture over the steaks. Starting at one of the short ends, roll the beef around the filling, tucking in the sides as you roll to ensure the filling is completely enclosed. Secure the beef rolls with toothpicks.
4. Remove the baking pan with the sauce from the air fryer and set it aside. Preheat the air fryer to 400°F (204°C).
5. Brush or spray the beef rolls with a little olive oil and air fry at 400°F (204°C) for 12 minutes, rotating the beef during the cooking process for even browning. When the beef is browned, submerge the rolls into the sauce in the baking pan, cover the pan with foil and return it to the air fryer. Reduce the temperature of the air fryer to 250°F (121°C) and air fry for 60 minutes.
6. Remove the beef rolls from the sauce. Cut each roll into slices and serve, ladling some sauce overtop.

Nutrition Info per Serving:

Calories: 517, Protein: 43g, Fat: 29g, Carbohydrates: 18g, Fiber: 4g, Sugar: 8g, Sodium: 784mg

Honey Mustard Cheesy Meatballs

Prep time: 15 minutes, Cook time: 15 minutes, Serves 8

2 onions, chopped
1 pound grass-fed ground beef
4 tbsps. fresh basil, chopped
2 tbsps. low-fat cheddar cheese, grated
2 tsps. garlic paste
2 tsps. honey
Salt and black pepper, to taste
2 tsps. mustard

1. Preheat the Air fryer to 385°F (196°C) and grease an Air fryer basket.
2. Mix all the ingredients in a bowl until well combined.
3. Shape the mixture into equal-sized balls gently and arrange the meatballs in the Air fryer basket.
4. Air fry for about 15 minutes and dish out to serve warm.

Nutrition Info per Serving:

Calories: 134, Fat: 4.4g, Carbohydrates: 4.6g, Sugar: 2.7g, Protein: 18.2g, Sodium: 50mg

Super Simple Steaks

Prep time: 5 minutes, Cook time: 14 minutes, Serves 2

½ pound grass-fed quality cuts steak
Salt and black pepper, to taste

1. Preheat the Air fryer to 390°F (199°C) and grease an Air fryer basket.
2. Season the steaks evenly with salt and black pepper and transfer into the Air fryer basket.
3. Roast for about 14 minutes and dish out to serve.

Nutrition Info per Serving:

Calories: 211, Fat: 7.1g, Carbohydrates: 0g, Sugar: 0g, Protein: 34.4g, Sodium: 75mg

Herbed Beef Roast

Prep time: 10 minutes, Cook time: 45 minutes, Serves 5

2 pounds beef roast
1 tbsp. olive oil
1 tsp. dried rosemary, crushed
1 tsp. dried thyme, crushed
Salt, to taste

1. Preheat the Air fryer to 360°F (182°C) and grease an Air fryer basket.
2. Rub the roast generously with herb mixture and coat with olive oil.
3. Arrange the roast in the Air fryer basket and air fry for about 45 minutes.
4. Dish out the roast and cover with foil for about 10 minutes.
5. Cut into desired size slices and serve.

Nutrition Info per Serving:

Calories: 362, Fat: 14.2g, Carbohydrates: 0.3g, Sugar: 0g, Protein: 55.1g, Sodium: 151mg

Provolone Stuffed Beef and Pork Meatballs

Prep time: 15 minutes, Cook time: 12 minutes, Serves 4 to 6

1 tbsp. olive oil
1 small onion, finely chopped
1 to 2 cloves garlic, minced
¾ pound (340 g) grass-fed ground beef
¾ pound (340 g) ground pork
¾ cup bread crumbs
¼ cup grated low-fat Parmesan cheese
¼ cup finely chopped fresh parsley
½ tsp. dried oregano
1½ tsps. salt
Freshly ground black pepper, to taste
2 eggs, lightly beaten
5 ounces (142 g) sharp or aged provolone cheese, cut into 1-inch cubes

1. Preheat a skillet over medium-high heat. Add the oil and cook the onion and garlic until tender, but not browned.
2. Transfer the onion and garlic to a large bowl and add the beef, pork, bread crumbs, Parmesan cheese, parsley, oregano, salt, pepper and eggs. Mix well until all the ingredients are combined. Divide the mixture into 12 evenly sized balls. Make one meatball at a time, by pressing a hole in the meatball mixture with the finger and pushing a piece of provolone cheese into the hole. Mold the meat back into a ball, enclosing the cheese.
3. Preheat the air fryer to 380°F (193°C).
4. Working in two batches, transfer six of the meatballs to the air fryer basket and air fry for 12 minutes, shaking the basket and turning the meatballs twice during the cooking process. Repeat with the remaining 6 meatballs. Serve warm.

Nutrition Info per Serving:

Calories: 344, Protein: 29g, Fat: 21g, Carbohydrates: 11g, Fiber: 1g, Sugar: 1g, Sodium: 798mg

Easy Beef Schnitzel

Prep time: 5 minutes, Cook time: 12 minutes, Serves 1

½ cup friendly bread crumbs
2 tbsps. olive oil
Pepper and salt, to taste
1 egg, beaten
1 thin beef schnitzel

1. Preheat the air fryer to 350°F (177°C).
2. In a shallow dish, combine the bread crumbs, oil, pepper, and salt.
3. In a second shallow dish, place the beaten egg.
4. Dredge the schnitzel in the egg before rolling it in the bread crumbs.
5. Put the coated schnitzel in the air fryer basket and air fry for 12 minutes. Flip the schnitzel halfway through.
6. Serve immediately.

Nutrition Info per Serving:

Calories: 479, Protein: 28g, Fat: 33g, Carbohydrates: 22g, Fiber: 1g, Sugar: 2g, Sodium: 706mg

Crumbed Golden Filet Mignon

Prep time: 15 minutes, Cook time: 12 minutes, Serves 2

½ pound (227 g) grass-fed filet mignon
Sea salt and ground black pepper, to taste
½ tsp. cayenne pepper
1 tsp. dried basil
1 tsp. dried rosemary
1 tsp. dried thyme
1 tbsp. sesame oil
1 small egg, whisked
½ cup bread crumbs

1. Preheat the air fryer to 360ºF (182ºC).
2. Cover the filet mignon with the salt, black pepper, cayenne pepper, basil, rosemary, and thyme. Coat with sesame oil.
3. Put the egg in a shallow plate.
4. Pour the bread crumbs in another plate.
5. Dip the filet mignon into the egg. Roll it into the crumbs.
6. Transfer the steak to the air fryer and air fry for 12 minutes or until it turns golden.
7. Serve immediately.

Nutrition Info per Serving:

Calories: 380, Protein: 30g, Fat: 23g, Carbohydrates: 11g, Fiber: 1g, Sugar: 1g, Sodium: 480mg

Beef Steak Fingers

Prep time: 5 minutes, Cook time: 8 minutes, Serves 4

4 small grass-fed beef cube steaks
Salt and ground black pepper, to taste
½ cup whole wheat flour
Cooking spra

1. Preheat the air fryer to 390ºF (199ºC).
2. Cut cube steaks into 1-inch-wide strips.
3. Sprinkle lightly with salt and pepper to taste.
4. Roll in flour to coat all sides.
5. Spritz air fryer basket with cooking spray. Put steak strips in air fryer basket in a single layer. Spritz top of steak strips with cooking spray.
6. Air fry for 4 minutes, turn strips over, and spritz with cooking spray.
7. Air fry 4 more minutes and test with fork for doneness. Steak fingers should be crispy outside with no red juices inside.
8. Repeat steps 5 through 7 to air fry remaining strips.
9. Serve immediately.

Nutrition Info per Serving:

Calories: 200, Protein: 25g, Fat: 8g, Carbohydrates: 9g, Fiber: 1.5g, Sugar: 0.2g, Sodium: 350mg

Beef Meatballs

Prep time: 5 minutes, Cook time: 18 minutes, Serves

1 pound (454 g) grass-fed ground beef
½ cup grated low-fat Parmesan cheese
1 tbsp. minced garlic
½ cup low-fat Mozzarella cheese
1 tsp. freshly ground pepper

1. Preheat the air fryer to 400ºF (204ºC).
2. In a bowl, mix all the ingredients together.
3. Roll the meat mixture into 5 generous meatballs.
4. Air fry inside the air fryer at 165ºF (74ºC) for about 18 minutes.
5. Serve immediately.

Nutrition Info per Serving:

Calories: 220, Protein: 18g, Fat: 13g, Carbohydrates: 4g, Fiber: 1g, Sugar: 1g, Sodium: 374mg

Miso Marinated Steak

Prep time: 5 minutes, Cook time: 12 minutes, Serves 4

¾ pound (340 g) grass-fed flank steak
1½ tbsps. sake
1 tbsp. brown miso paste
1 tsp. honey
2 cloves garlic, pressed
1 tbsp. olive oil

1. Put all the ingredients in a Ziploc bag. Shake to cover the steak well with the seasonings and refrigerate for at least 1 hour.
2. Preheat the air fryer to 400ºF (204ºC). Coat all sides of the steak with cooking spray. Put the steak in the baking pan.
3. Air fry for 12 minutes, turning the steak twice during the cooking time, then serve immediately.

Nutrition Info per Serving:

Calories: 190, Protein: 17g, Fat: 11g, Carbohydrates: 5g, Fiber: 0g, Sugar: 3g, Sodium: 467mg

Simple New York Strip Steak

Prep time: 10 minutes, Cook time: 10 minutes, Serves 2

1 (9½-ounces) grass-fed New York strip steak
1 tsp. olive oil
Crushed red pepper flakes, to taste
Salt and black pepper, to taste

1. Preheat the Air fryer to 400ºF (204ºC) and grease an Air fryer basket.
2. Rub the steak generously with red pepper flakes, salt and black pepper and coat with olive oil.
3. Transfer the steak in the Air fryer basket and roast for about 10 minutes, flipping once in between.
4. Dish out the steak and cut into desired size slices to serve.

Nutrition Info per Serving:

Calories: 186, Fat: 7g, Carbohydrates: 0g, Sugar: 0g, Protein: 30.2g, Sodium: 177mg

Classic Skirt Steak Strips with Veggies

Prep time: 10 minutes, Cook time: 17 minutes, Serves 4

1 (12-ounce) grass-fed skirt steak, cut into thin strips
½ pound fresh mushrooms, quartered
6-ounce snow peas
1 onion, cut into half rings
¼ cup olive oil, divided
2 tbsps. soy sauce
2 tbsps. honey
Salt and black pepper, to taste

1. Preheat the Air fryer to 390ºF (199ºC) and grease an Air fryer basket.
2. Mix 2 tbsps. of oil, soy sauce and honey in a bowl and coat steak strips with this marinade.
3. Put vegetables, remaining oil, salt and black pepper in another bowl and toss well.
4. Transfer the steak strips and vegetables in the Air fryer basket and roast for about 17 minutes.
5. Dish out and serve warm.

Nutrition Info per Serving:
Calories: 360, Fat: 21.5g, Carbohydrates: 16.7g, Sugar: 12.6g, Protein: 26.7g, Sodium: 522mg

Italian Beef Meatballs

Prep time: 10 minutes, Cook time: 15 minutes, Serves 6

2 large eggs
2 pounds ground beef
¼ cup fresh parsley, chopped
1¼ cups panko breadcrumbs
¼ cup Parmigiano Reggiano, grated
1 tsp. dried oregano
1 small garlic clove, chopped
Salt and black pepper, to taste
1 tsp. vegetable oil

1. Preheat the Air fryer to 350ºF (177ºC) and grease an Air fryer basket.
2. Mix beef with all other ingredients in a bowl until well combined.
3. Make equal-sized balls from the mixture and arrange the balls in the Air fryer basket.
4. Air fry for about 13 minutes and dish out to serve warm.

Nutrition Info per Serving:
Calories: 398, Fat: 13.8g, Carbohydrates: 3.6g, Sugar: 1.3g, Protein: 51.8g, Sodium: 272mg

Easy Rib Steak

Prep time: 10 minutes, Cook time: 14 minutes, Serves 4

2 lbs. rib steak
2 cups steak rub
1 tbsp. olive oil

1. Preheat the Air fryer to 400ºF (204ºC) and grease an Air fryer basket.
2. Rub the steak generously with steak rub, salt and black pepper, and coat with olive oil.
3. Transfer the steak in the Air fryer basket and roast for about 14 minutes, flipping once in between.
4. Dish out the steak and cut into desired size slices to serve.

Nutrition Info per Serving:
Calories: 438, Fat: 35.8g, Carbohydrates: 0g, Sugar: 0g, Protein: 26.8g, Sodium: 157mg

(Note: To prepare the Steak Rub - 2 tbsps. fresh cracked black pepper, 2 tbsps. kosher salt, 2 tbsps. paprika, 1 tbsp. crushed red pepper flakes, 1 tbsp. crushed coriander seeds (not ground), 1 tbsp. garlic powder, 1 tbsp. onion powder, 2 tsps. cayenne pepper. Mix all ingredients in a medium bowl and stir well to combine.)

Air Fried Beef Ribs

Prep time: 20 minutes, Cook time: 8 minutes, Serves 4

1 pound (454 g) grass-fed meaty beef ribs, rinsed and drained
3 tbsps. apple cider vinegar
1 cup coriander, finely chopped
1 tbsp. fresh basil leaves, chopped
2 garlic cloves, finely chopped
1 chipotle powder
1 tsp. fennel seeds
1 tsp. hot paprika
Kosher salt and black pepper, to taste
½ cup olive oil

1. Coat the ribs with the remaining ingredients and re-frigerate for at least 3 hours.
2. Preheat the air fryer to 360ºF (182ºC).
3. Separate the ribs from the marinade and put them on a grill pan. Air fry for 8 minutes.
4. Pour the remaining marinade over the ribs before serving.

Nutrition Info per Serving:
Calories: 380, Protein: 18g, Fat: 32g, Carbohydrates: 6g, Fiber: 2g, Sugar: 0.5g, Sodium: 453mg

Air Fried London Broil

Prep time: 15 minutes, Cook time: 25 minutes, Serves 8

2 pounds (907 g) grass-fed London broil
3 large garlic cloves, minced
3 tbsps. balsamic vinegar
3 tbsps. Dijon mustard
2 tbsps. olive oil
Sea salt and ground black pepper, to taste
½ tsp. dried hot red pepper flakes

1. Wash and dry the London broil. Score its sides with a knife.
2. Mix the remaining ingredients. Rub this mixture into the broil, coating it well. Allow to marinate for a minimum of 3 hours.
3. Preheat the air fryer to 400ºF (204ºC).
4. Air fry the meat for 15 minutes. Turn it over and air fry for an additional 10 minutes before serving.

Nutrition Info per Serving:

Calories: 230, Protein: 24g, Fat: 12g, Carbohydrates: 3g, Fiber: 0g, Sugar: 1g, Sodium: 309mg

Beef Chuck with Brussels Sprouts

Prep time: 20 minutes, Cook time: 25 minutes, Serves 4

1 pound (454 g) grass-fed beef chuck shoulder steak
2 tbsps. olive oil
1 tbsp. red wine vinegar
1 tsp. fine sea salt
½ tsp. ground black pepper
1 tsp. smoked paprika
1 tsp. onion powder
½ tsp. garlic powder
½ pound (227 g) Brussels sprouts, cleaned and halved
½ tsp. fennel seeds
1 tsp. dried basil
1 tsp. dried sage

1. Massage the beef with the olive oil, wine vinegar, salt, black pepper, paprika, onion powder, and garlic powder, coating it well.
2. Allow to marinate for a minimum of 3 hours.
3. Preheat the air fryer to 390ºF (199ºC).
4. Remove the beef from the marinade and put in the preheated air fryer. Air fry for 10 minutes. Flip the beef halfway through.
5. Put the prepared Brussels sprouts in the air fryer along with the fennel seeds, basil, and sage.
6. Lower the heat to 380ºF (193ºC) and air fry everything for another 5 minutes.
7. Give them a good stir. Air fry for an additional 10 minutes.
8. Serve immediately.

Nutrition Info per Serving:

Calories: 318, Protein: 22g, Fat: 20g, Carbohydrates: 12g, Fiber: 4g, Sugar: 2g, Sodium: 629mg

Beef Pot Pie

Prep time: 10 minutes, Cook time: 1 hour 27 minutes, Serves 3

1 pound grass-fed beef stewing steak, cubed
1 can ale mixed into 1 cup water
2 beef bouillon cubes
1 tbsp. plain flour
1 prepared short crust pastry
1 tbsp. olive oil
1 tbsp. tomato puree
2 tbsps. onion paste
Salt and black pepper, to taste

1. Preheat the Air fryer to 390ºF (199ºC) and grease 2 ramekins lightly.
2. Heat olive oil in a pan and add steak cubes.
3. Cook for about 5 minutes and stir in the onion paste and tomato puree.
4. Cook for about 6 minutes and add the ale mixture, bouillon cubes, salt and black pepper.
5. Bring to a boil and reduce the heat to simmer for about 1 hour.
6. Mix flour and 3 tbsps. of warm water in a bowl and slowly add this mixture into the beef mixture.
7. Roll out the short crust pastry and line 2 ramekins with pastry.
8. Divide the beef mixture evenly in the ramekins and top with extra pastry.
9. Transfer into the Air fryer basket and bake for about 10 minutes.
10. Set the Air fryer to 335ºF (168ºC) and bake for about 6 more minutes.
11. Dish out and serve warm.

Nutrition Info per Serving:

Calories: 442, Fat: 14.2g, Carbohydrates: 19g, Sugar: 1.2g, Protein: 50.6g, Sodium: 583mg

Beef and Mushroom Meatloaf

Prep time: 15 minutes, Cook time: 25 minutes, Serves 4

1 pound grass-fed lean ground beef
1 small onion, finely chopped
3 tbsps. dry breadcrumbs
1 egg, lightly beaten
2 mushrooms, thickly sliced
Salt and ground black pepper, as required
1 tbsp. olive oil

1. Preheat the Air fryer to 390ºF (199ºC) and grease an Air fryer basket.
2. Mix the beef, onion, olive oil, breadcrumbs, egg, salt, and black pepper in a bowl until well combined.
3. Shape the mixture into loaves and top with mushroom slices.
4. Arrange the loaves in the Air fryer basket and bake for about 25 minutes.
5. Cut into desired size wedges and serve warm.

Nutrition Info per Serving:

Calories: 267, Fat: 12g, Carbohydrates: 6.1g, Sugar: 1.3g, Protein: 37g, Sodium: 167mg

Smoked Beef

Prep time: 10 minutes, Cook time: 45 minutes, Serves 8

2 pounds (907 g) roast beef, at room temperature
2 tbsps. extra-virgin olive oil
1 tsp. sea salt flakes
1 tsp. ground black pepper
1 tsp. smoked paprika
Few dashes of liquid smoke
2 jalapeño peppers, thinly sliced

1. Preheat the air fryer to 330°F (166°C).
2. With kitchen towels, pat the beef dry.
3. Massage the extra-virgin olive oil, salt, black pepper, and paprika into the meat. Cover with liquid smoke.
4. Put the beef in the air fryer and roast for 30 minutes. Flip the roast over and allow to roast for another 15 minutes.
5. When cooked through, serve topped with sliced jalapeños.

Nutrition Info per Serving:

Calories: 193, Protein: 27g, Fat: 9g, Carbohydrates: 1g, Fiber: 0g, Sugar: 0g, Sodium: 251mg

Carne Asada Tacos

Prep time: 5 minutes, Cook time: 14 minutes, Serves 4

⅓ cup olive oil
1½ pounds (680 g) grass-fed flank steak
Salt and freshly ground black pepper, to taste
⅓ cup freshly squeezed lime juice
½ cup chopped fresh cilantro
4 tsps. minced garlic
1 tsp. ground cumin
1 tsp. chili powder

1. Brush the air fryer basket with olive oil.
2. Put the flank steak in a large mixing bowl. Season with salt and pepper.
3. Add the lime juice, cilantro, garlic, cumin, and chili powder and toss to coat the steak.
4. For the best flavor, let the steak marinate in the refrigerator for about 1 hour.
5. Preheat the air fryer to 400°F (204°C)
6. Put the steak in the air fryer basket. Air fry for 7 minutes. Flip the steak. Air fry for 7 minutes more or until an internal temperature reaches at least 145°F (63°C).
7. Let the steak rest for about 5 minutes, then cut into strips to serve.

Nutrition Info per Serving:

Calories: 407, Protein: 33g, Fat: 28g, Carbohydrates: 4g, Fiber: 1g, Sugar: 0g, Sodium: 282mg

Beef Tips with Onion

Prep time: 15 minutes, Cook time: 10 minutes, Serves 2

1 pound grass-fed top round beef, cut into 1½-inch cubes
½ yellow onion, chopped
2 tbsps. Worcestershire sauce
1 tbsp. avocado oil
1 tsp. onion powder
1 tsp. garlic powder
Salt and black pepper, to taste

1. Preheat the Air fryer to 360°F (182°C) and grease an Air fryer basket.
2. Mix the beef tips, onion, Worcestershire sauce, avocado oil, and spices in a bowl.
3. Arrange the beef mixture in the Air fryer basket and roast for about 10 minutes.
4. Dish out the steak mixture onto serving plates and cut into desired size slices to serve.

Nutrition Info per Serving:

Calories: 266, Fat: 10.5g, Carbohydrates: 4g, Sugar: 2.5g, Protein: 36.3g, Sodium: 192mg

Beef Roast

Prep time: 10 minutes, Cook time: 50 minutes, Serves 6

2½ pounds grass-fed beef eye of round roast, trimmed
2 tbsps. olive oil
½ tsp. onion powder
½ tsp. garlic powder
½ tsp. cayenne pepper
½ tsp. ground black pepper
Salt, to taste

1. Preheat the Air fryer to 360°F (182°C) and grease an Air fryer basket.
2. Rub the roast generously with all the spices and coat with olive oil.
3. Arrange the roast in the Air fryer basket and air fry for about 50 minutes.
4. Dish out the roast and cover with foil.
5. Cut into desired size slices and serve.

Nutrition Info per Serving:

Calories: 397, Fat: 12.4g, Carbohydrates: 0.5g, Sugar: 0.2g, Protein: 55.5g, Sodium: 99mg

CHAPTER 12
SNACK

Spicy Kale Chips

Prep time: 5 minutes, Cook time: 8 to 12 minutes, Serves 4

5 cups kale, large stems removed and chopped
2 tsps. canola oil
¼ tsp. smoked paprika
¼ tsp. kosher salt
Cooking spray

1. Preheat the air fryer to 390°F (199°C).
2. In a large bowl, toss the kale, canola oil, smoked paprika, and kosher salt.
3. Spray the air fryer basket with cooking spray, then place half the kale in the basket and air fry for 2 to 3 minutes.
4. Shake the basket and air fry for 2 to 3 more minutes, or until crispy. Repeat this process with the remaining kale.
5. Remove the kale and allow to cool on a wire rack for 3 to 5 minutes before serving.

Nutrition Info per Serving:

Calories: 35, Protein: 1g, Fat: 2g, Carbohydrates: 4g, Fiber: 1g, Sugar: 0g, Sodium: 168mg

Coconut-Crusted Shrimp

Prep time: 10 minutes, Cook time: 4 minutes, Serves 2 to 4

½ pound (227 g) medium shrimp, peeled and deveined (tails intact)
1 cup canned nonfat coconut milk
Finely grated zest of 1 lime
Kosher salt, to taste
½ cup panko bread crumbs
½ cup unsweetened shredded coconut
Freshly ground black pepper, to taste
Cooking spray
1 small or ½ medium cucumber, halved and deseeded
1 cup nonfat coconut yogurt
1 serrano chile, deseeded and minced

1. Preheat the air fryer to 400°F (204°C).
2. In a bowl, combine the shrimp, coconut milk, lime zest, and ½ tsp. kosher salt. Let the shrimp stand for 10 minutes.
3. Meanwhile, in a separate bowl, stir together the bread crumbs and shredded coconut and season with salt and pepper.
4. A few at a time, add the shrimp to the bread crumb mixture and toss to coat completely. Transfer the shrimp to a wire rack set over a baking sheet. Spray the shrimp all over with cooking spray.
5. Transfer the shrimp to the air fryer and air fry for 4 minutes, or until golden brown and cooked through. Transfer the shrimp to a serving platter and season with more salt.
6. Grate the cucumber into a small bowl. Stir in the coconut yogurt and chile and season with salt and pepper. Serve alongside the shrimp while they're warm.

Nutrition Info per Serving:

Calories: 240, Protein: 16g, Fat: 10g, Carbohydrates: 21g, Fiber: 2g, Sugar: 6g, Sodium: 400mg

Chicken Nuggets

Prep time: 15 minutes, Cook time: 10 minutes, Serves 4

20-ounce chicken breast, cut into chunks
1 cup whole wheat flour
2 tbsps. low-fat milk
1 egg
1 cup panko breadcrumbs
½ tbsp. mustard powder
1 tbsp. garlic powder
1 tbsp. onion powder
Salt and black pepper, to taste

1. Preheat the Air fryer to 390°F (199°C) and grease an Air fryer basket.
2. Put chicken along with mustard powder, garlic powder, onion powder, salt and black pepper in a food processor and pulse until combined.
3. Place flour in a shallow dish and whisk the eggs with milk in a second dish.
4. Place breadcrumbs in a third shallow dish.
5. Coat the nuggets evenly in flour and dip in the egg mixture.
6. Roll into the breadcrumbs evenly and arrange the nuggets in the Air fryer basket.
7. Bake for about 10 minutes and dish out to serve warm.

Nutrition Info per Serving:

Calories: 220, Fat: 17.1g, Carbohydrates: 6g, Sugar: 3.5g, Protein: 12.8g, Sodium: 332mg

Nutty Cauliflower Poppers

Prep time: 10 minutes, Cook time: 15 minutes, Serves 4

¼ cup golden raisins
1 cup boiling water
¼ cup toasted pine nuts
1 head of cauliflower, cut into small florets
½ cup olive oil, divided
1 tbsp. curry powder
¼ tsp. salt

1. Preheat the Air fryer to 390°F (199°C) and grease an Air fryer basket.
2. Put raisins in boiling water in a bowl and keep aside.
3. Drizzle 1 tsp. olive oil on the pine nuts in another bowl.
4. Place the pine nuts in the Air fryer basket and air fry for about 2 minutes.
5. Remove the pine nuts from the Air fryer and keep aside.
6. Mix together cauliflower, salt, curry powder and remaining olive oil in a large bowl.
7. Transfer this mixture into the Air fryer basket and air fry for about 12 minutes
8. Dish out the cauliflower in a serving bowl and stir in the pine nuts.
9. Drain raisins and add to the serving bowl.

Nutrition Info per Serving:

Calories: 322, Fat: 31.3g, Carbohydrates: 12.7g, Sugar: 7.3g, Protein: 3g, Sodium: 171mg

Old-Fashioned Eggplant Slices

Prep time: 10 minutes, Cook time: 8 minutes, Serves 2

1 medium eggplant, peeled and cut into ½-inch round slices
½ cup whole wheat flour
1 cup Italian-style whole wheat breadcrumbs
2 eggs, beaten
2 tbsps. low-fat milk
Salt, to taste
¼ cup olive oil

1. Preheat the Air fryer to 390°F (199°C) and grease in an Air fryer basket.
2. Season the eggplant slices with salt and keep aside for 1 hour.
3. Place flour in a shallow dish.
4. Whisk the eggs with milk in a second dish.
5. Mix together oil and breadcrumbs in a third shallow dish.
6. Coat the eggplant slices evenly with flour, then dip in the egg mixture and finally coat with breadcrumb mixture.
7. Transfer the eggplant slices in the Air fryer basket and air fry for about 8 minutes.
8. Dish out and serve warm.

Nutrition Info per Serving:

Calories: 685, Fat: 36.9g, Carbohydrates: 49.1g, Sugar: 5.3g, Protein: 42.1g, Sodium: 2391mg

Cajun Zucchini Chips

Prep time: 5 minutes, Cook time: 15 to 16 minutes, Serves 4

2 large zucchinis, cut into ⅛-inch-thick slices
2 tsps. Cajun seasoning
Cooking spray

1. Preheat the air fryer to 370°F (188°C).
2. Spray the air fryer basket lightly with cooking spray.
3. Put the zucchini slices in a medium bowl and spray them generously with cooking spray.
4. Sprinkle the Cajun seasoning over the zucchini and stir to make sure they are evenly coated with oil and seasoning.
5. Place the slices in a single layer in the air fryer basket, making sure not to overcrowd. You will need to cook these in several batches.
6. Air fry for 8 minutes. Flip the slices over and air fry for an additional 7 to 8 minutes, or until they are as crisp and brown as you prefer.
7. Serve immediately.

Nutrition Info per Serving:

Calories: 31, Protein: 1g, Fat: 0.6g, Carbohydrates: 7g, Fiber: 2g, Sugar: 3g, Sodium: 226mg

Crispy Kale Chips

Prep time: 10 minutes, Cook time: 3 minutes, Serves 4

1 head fresh kale, stems and ribs removed and cut into 1½ inch pieces
1 tbsp. olive oil
1 tsp. soy sauce

1. Preheat the Air fryer to 380°F (193°C) and grease an Air fryer basket.
2. Mix together all the ingredients in a bowl until well combined.
3. Arrange the kale in the Air fryer basket and air fry for about 3 minutes, flipping in between.
4. Dish out and serve warm.

Nutrition Info per Serving:

Calories: 143, Fats: 3.5g, Carbohydrates: 23.8g, Sugar: 0g, Proteins: 6.9g, Sodium: 173mg

Crunchy Spicy Chickpeas

Prep time: 5 minutes, Cook time: 20 minutes, Serves 4

1 (15-ounce) can chickpeas, rinsed and drained
1 tbsp. olive oil
½ tsp. ground cumin
½ tsp. cayenne pepper
½ tsp. smoked paprika
Salt, taste

1. Preheat the Air fryer to 390°F (199°C) and grease an Air fryer basket.
2. Mix together all the ingredients in a bowl and toss to coat well.
3. Place half of the chickpeas in the Air fryer basket and air fry for about 10 minutes.
4. Repeat with the remaining chickpeas and dish out to serve warm.

Nutrition Info per Serving:

Calories: 419, Fat: 10g, Carbohydrates: 64.9g, Sugar: 11.4g, Protein: 20.6g, Sodium: 65mg

Tortilla Chips

Prep time: 10 minutes, Cook time: 6 minutes, Serves 6

8 whole-grain corn tortillas, cut into triangles
1 tbsp. olive oil
Salt, to taste

1. Preheat the Air fryer to 390°F (199°C) and grease an Air fryer basket.
2. Drizzle the tortilla chips with olive oil and season with salt.
3. Arrange half of the tortilla chips in the Air fryer basket and air fry for about 3 minutes, flipping in between.
4. Repeat with the remaining tortilla chips and dish out to serve warm.

Nutrition Info per Serving:

Calories: 90, Fat: 3.2g, Carbohydrates: 14.3g, Sugar: 0.3g, Protein: 1.8g, Sodium: 42mg

Pineapple Bites with Yogurt Dip

Prep time: 15 minutes, Cook time: 10 minutes, Serves 4

½ of pineapple, cut into long 1-2 inch thick sticks
¼ cup desiccated coconut
1 tbsp. fresh mint leaves, minced
1 green chili, chopped
1 cup nonfat vanilla yogurt
1 tbsp. honey

1. Preheat the Air fryer to 390°F (199°C) and grease an Air fryer basket.
2. Place the coconut in a shallow dish.
3. Dip pineapple sticks in the honey and then dredge in the coconut.
4. Transfer the pineapple sticks in the Air fryer basket and air fry for about 10 minutes.
5. For yogurt dip: Mix together mint, chili and vanilla yogurt in a bowl.
6. Serve these pineapple sticks with yogurt dip.

Nutrition Info per Serving:

Calories: 518, Fat: 34.9g, Carbohydrates: 20g, Sugar: 0.6g, Protein: 29.9g, Sodium: 1475mg

Croissant Rolls

Prep time: 10 minutes, Cook time: 6 minutes, Serves 8

1 (8-ounces) can croissant rolls
4 tbsps. almond butter, melted
1 tbsp. olive oil

1. Preheat the Air fryer to 320°F (160°C) and grease an Air fryer basket with olive oil.
2. Coat the croissant rolls with almond butter and arrange into the Air fryer basket.
3. Bake for about 6 minutes, flipping once in between.
4. Dish out in a platter and serve hot.

Nutrition Info per Serving:

Calories: 167, Fat: 12.6g, Carbohydrates: 11.1g, Sugar: 3g, Protein: 2.1g, Sodium: 223mg

Warm Spiced Apple Chips

Prep time: 10 minutes, Cook time: 16 minutes, Serves 2

1 apple, peeled, cored and thinly sliced
1 tbsp. coconut sugar
½ tsp. ground cinnamon
Pinch of ground cardamom
Pinch of ground ginger
Pinch of salt

1. Preheat the Air fryer to 390°F (199°C) and grease an Air fryer basket.
2. Mix together all the ingredients in a bowl until well combined.
3. Arrange the apple slices in the Air fryer basket.
4. Air fry for about 8 minutes, flipping in between.
5. Dish out and serve warm.

Nutrition Info per Serving:

Calories: 72, Fat: 0.2g, Carbohydrates: 19.2g, Sugar: 15.5g, Protein: 0.3g, Sodium: 78mg

Lemony Chicken Drumsticks

Prep time: 5 minutes, Cook time: 30 minutes, Serves 2

2 tsps. freshly ground coarse black pepper
1 tsp. baking powder
½ tsp. garlic powder
4 chicken drumsticks (4 ounces / 113 g each)
Kosher salt, to taste
1 lemon

1. In a small bowl, stir together the pepper, baking powder, and garlic powder. Place the drumsticks on a plate and sprinkle evenly with the baking powder mixture, turning the drumsticks so they're well coated. Let the drumsticks stand in the refrigerator for at least 1 hour or up to overnight.
2. Preheat the air fryer to 375°F (191°C).
3. Sprinkle the drumsticks with salt, then transfer them to the air fryer, standing them bone-end up and leaning against the wall of the air fryer basket. Air fry for 30 minutes, or until cooked through and crisp on the outside.
4. Transfer the drumsticks to a serving platter and finely grate the zest of the lemon over them while they're hot. Cut the lemon into wedges and serve with the warm drumsticks.

Nutrition Info per Serving:

Calories: 220, Protein: 21g, Fat: 14g, Carbohydrates: 3g, Fiber: 1g, Sugar: 0g, Sodium: 340mg

Peppery Chicken Meatballs

Prep time: 5 minutes, Cook time: 13 to 20 minutes, Makes 16 meatballs

2 tsps. olive oil
¼ cup minced onion
¼ cup minced red bell pepper
2 vanilla wafers, crushed
1 egg white
½ tsp. dried thyme
½ pound (227 g) ground chicken breast

1. Preheat the air fryer to 370°F (188°C).
2. In a baking pan, mix the olive oil, onion, and red bell pepper. Put the pan in the air fryer. Air fry for 3 to 5 minutes, or until the vegetables are tender.
3. In a medium bowl, mix the cooked vegetables, crushed wafers, egg white, and thyme until well combined
4. Mix in the chicken, gently but thoroughly, until everything is combined.
5. Form the mixture into 16 meatballs and place them in the air fryer basket. Air fry for 10 to 15 minutes, or until the meatballs reach an internal temperature of 165°F (74°C) on a meat thermometer.
6. Serve immediately.

Nutrition Info per Serving:

Calories: 90, Protein: 8g, Fat: 5g, Carbohydrates: 4g, Fiber: 0.5g, Sugar: 1g, Sodium: 65mg

Crispy Breaded Beef Cubes

Prep time: 10 minutes, Cook time: 12 to 16 minutes, Serves 4

1 pound (454 g) sirloin tip, cut into 1-inch cubes
1 cup cheese pasta sauce
1½ cups soft bread crumbs
2 tbsps. olive oil
½ tsp. dried marjoram

1. Preheat the air fryer to 360°F (182°C).
2. In a medium bowl, toss the beef with the pasta sauce to coat.
3. In a shallow bowl, combine the bread crumbs, oil, and marjoram, and mix well. Drop the beef cubes, one at a time, into the bread crumb mixture to coat thoroughly.
4. Air fry the beef in two batches for 6 to 8 minutes, shaking the basket once during cooking time, until the beef is at least 145°F (63°C) and the outside is crisp and brown.
5. Serve hot.

Nutrition Info per Serving:

Calories: 387, Protein: 29g, Fat: 18g, Carbohydrates: 26g, Fiber: 1g, Sugar: 3g, Sodium: 635mg

Vegetable Nuggets

Prep time: 15 minutes, Cook time: 10 minutes, Serves 4

1 zucchini, chopped roughly
½ of carrot, chopped roughly
1 cup whole wheat flour
1 egg
1 tbsp. nonfat milk
1 cup panko breadcrumbs
1 tbsp. garlic powder
½ tbsp. mustard powder
1 tbsp. onion powder
Salt and black pepper, to taste

1. Preheat the Air fryer to 380°F (193°C) and grease an Air fryer basket.
2. Put zucchini, carrot, mustard powder, garlic powder, onion powder, salt and black pepper in a food processor and pulse until combined.
3. Place flour in a shallow dish and whisk the eggs with milk in a second dish.
4. Place breadcrumbs in a third shallow dish.
5. Coat the vegetable nuggets evenly in flour and dip in the egg mixture.
6. Roll into the breadcrumbs evenly and arrange the nuggets in the Air fryer basket.
7. Bake for about 10 minutes and dish out to serve warm.

Nutrition Info per Serving:

Calories: 281, Fat: 13g, Carbohydrates: 15.4g, Sugar: 1.8g, Protein: 26.2g, Sodium: 249mg

Spinach and Crab Meat Cups

Prep time: 10 minutes, Cook time: 10 minutes, Makes 30 cups

1 (6-ounce / 170-g) can crab meat, drained to yield ⅓ cup meat
¼ cup frozen spinach, thawed, drained, and chopped
1 clove garlic, minced
½ cup grated low-fat Parmesan cheese
3 tbsps. low-fat plain yogurt
¼ tsp. lemon juice
½ tsp. Worcestershire sauce
30 mini frozen phyllo shells, thawed
Cooking spray

1. Preheat the air fryer to 390°F (199°C).
2. Remove any bits of shell that might remain in the crab meat.
3. Mix the crab meat, spinach, garlic, and cheese together.
4. Stir in the yogurt, lemon juice, and Worcestershire sauce and mix well.
5. Spoon a tsp. of filling into each phyllo shell.
6. Spray the air fryer basket with cooking spray and arrange half the shells in the basket. Air fry for 5 minutes. Repeat with the remaining shells.
7. Serve immediately.

Nutrition Info per Serving:

Calories: 47, Protein: 3g, Fat: 2g, Carbohydrates: 5g, Fiber: 0.3g, Sugar: 0.3g, Sodium: 82mg

Veggie Shrimp Toast

Prep time: 15 minutes, Cook time: 3 to 6 minutes, Serves 4

8 large raw shrimp, peeled and finely chopped
1 egg white
2 garlic cloves, minced
3 tbsps. minced red bell pepper
1 medium celery stalk, minced
2 tbsps. cornstarch
¼ tsp. Chinese five-spice powder
3 slices firm thin-sliced no-sodium whole-wheat bread

1. Preheat the air fryer to 350°F (177°C).
2. In a small bowl, stir together the shrimp, egg white, garlic, red bell pepper, celery, cornstarch, and five-spice powder. Top each slice of bread with one-third of the shrimp mixture, spreading it evenly to the edges. With a sharp knife, cut each slice of bread into 4 strips.
3. Place the shrimp toasts in the air fryer basket in a single layer. You may need to cook them in batches. Air fry for 3 to 6 minutes, until crisp and golden brown.
4. Serve hot.

Nutrition Info per Serving:

Calories: 125, Protein: 11g, Fat: 1g, Carbohydrates: 18g, Fiber: 2g, Sugar: 2g, Sodium: 259mg

Air Fried Chicken Tenders

Prep time: 15 minutes, Cook time: 10 minutes, Serves 4

12 oz. chicken breasts, cut into tenders
1 egg white
⅛ cup whole wheat flour
½ cup panko bread crumbs
Salt and black pepper, to taste

1. Preheat the Air fryer to 350ºF (177ºC) and grease an Air fryer basket.
2. Season the chicken tenders with salt and black pepper.
3. Coat the chicken tenders with flour, then dip in egg whites and then dredge in the panko bread crumbs.
4. Arrange in the Air fryer basket and roast for about 10 minutes.
5. Dish out in a platter and serve warm.

Nutrition Info per Serving:
Calories: 220, Fat: 17.1g, Carbohydrates: 6g, Sugar: 3.5g, Protein: 12.8g, Sodium: 332mg

Seasoned Crab Sticks

Prep time: 10 minutes, Cook time: 12 minutes, Serves 4

1 packet crab sticks, shred into small pieces
2 tsps. sesame oil
Cajun seasoning, to taste

1. Preheat the Air fryer to 320ºF (160ºC) and grease an Air fryer basket.
2. Drizzle crab stick pieces with sesame oil and arrange in the Air fryer basket.
3. Air fry for about 12 minutes and serve, sprinkled with Cajun seasoning.

Nutrition Info per Serving:
Calories: 91.9, Fat: 2.41g, Carbohydrates: 8.8g, Sugar: 2.4g, Protein: 5.6g, Sodium: 2mg

Crispy Zucchini Fries

Prep time: 10 minutes, Cook time: 10 minutes, Serves 4

1 pound zucchini, sliced into 2½-inch sticks
¾ cup panko breadcrumbs
Salt, to taste
2 tbsps. olive oil

1. Preheat the Air fryer to 425ºF (218ºC) and grease an Air fryer basket
2. Season zucchini with salt and keep aside for about 10 minutes.
3. Place breadcrumbs in a shallow dish and coat zucchini fries in it.
4. Arrange the zucchini fries in the Air fryer basket and air fry for about 10 minutes.
5. Dish out and serve warm.

Nutrition Info per Serving:
Calories: 158, Fat: 8.3g, Carbohydrates: 18.4g, Sugar: 3.2g, Protein: 4.1g, Sodium: 198mg

Butternut Squash Fries

Prep time: 15 minutes, Cook time: 40 minutes, Serves 2

2 pounds butternut squash, peeled and cut into ½ inch strips
1 tsp. chili powder
½ tsp. ground cinnamon
¼ tsp. garlic salt

1. Preheat the Air fryer to 390ºF (199ºC) and grease an Air fryer basket
2. Season butternut squash with all other ingredients in a bowl until well combined.
3. Arrange half of the squash fries in the Air fryer basket and air fry for about 20 minutes.
4. Repeat with the remaining fries and dish out to serve warm.

Nutrition Info per Serving:
Calories: 110, Fat: 7.1g, Carbohydrates: 5g, Sugar: 0g, Protein: 3.8g, Sodium: 69mg

Simple and Easy Croutons

Prep time: 5 minutes, Cook time: 8 minutes, Serves 4

2 slices whole wheat friendly bread
1 tbsp. olive oil
Hot soup, for serving

1. Preheat the air fryer to 390ºF (199ºC).
2. Cut the slices of bread into medium-size chunks.
3. Brush the air fryer basket with the oil.
4. Place the chunks inside and air fry for at least 8 minutes.
5. Serve with hot soup.

Nutrition Info per Serving:
Calories: 45, Protein: 1g, Fat: 2g, Carbohydrates: 6g, Fiber: 1g, Sugar: 1g, Sodium: 60mg

Easy Crispy Prawns

Prep time: 15 minutes, Cook time: 10 minutes, Serves 4

1 egg
½ pound nacho chips, crushed
18 prawns, peeled and deveined
Salt and black pepper, to taste

1. Preheat the Air fryer to 355ºF (179ºC) and grease an Air fryer basket.
2. Crack egg in a shallow dish and beat well.
3. Place the crushed nacho chips in another shallow dish.
4. Coat prawns with egg, salt and black pepper, then roll into nacho chips.
5. Place the coated prawns into the Air fryer basket and air fry for about 10 minutes.
6. Dish out and serve warm.

Nutrition Info per Serving:
Calories: 425, Fat: 17.6g, Carbohydrates: 36.6g, Sugar: 2.2g, Protein: 28.6g, Sodium: 606mg

Spicy Broccoli Poppers

Prep time: 35 minutes, Cook time: 10 minutes, Serves 4

2 tbsps. nonfat plain yogurt	½ tsp. red chili powder
1 pound broccoli, cut into small florets	¼ tsp. ground cumin
	¼ tsp. ground turmeric
2 tbsps. chickpea flour	Salt, to taste

1. Preheat the Air fryer to 400°F (204°C) and grease an Air fryer basket.
2. Mix together the yogurt, red chili powder, cumin, turmeric and salt in a bowl until well combined.
3. Stir in the broccoli and generously coat with marinade.
4. Refrigerate for about 30 minutes and sprinkle the broccoli florets with chickpea flour.
5. Arrange the broccoli florets in the Air fryer basket and air fry for about 10 minutes, flipping once in between.
6. Dish out and serve warm.

Nutrition Info per Serving:

Calories: 69, Fat: 0.9g, Carbohydrates: 12.2g, Sugar: 3.2g, Protein: 4.9g, Sodium: 87mg

Honey Sriracha Chicken Wings

Prep time: 5 minutes, Cook time: 30 minutes, Serves 4

1 tbsp. Sriracha hot sauce	½ tsp. kosher salt
1 tbsp. honey	16 chicken wings and drumettes
1 garlic clove, minced	Cooking spray

1. Preheat the air fryer to 360°F (182°C).
2. In a large bowl, whisk together the Sriracha hot sauce, honey, minced garlic, and kosher salt, then add the chicken and toss to coat.
3. Spray the air fryer basket with cooking spray, then place 8 wings in the basket and air fry for 15 minutes, turning halfway through. Repeat this process with the remaining wings.
4. Remove the wings and allow to cool on a wire rack for 10 minutes before serving.

Nutrition Info per Serving:

Calories: 247, Protein: 17g, Fat: 18g, Carbohydrates: 5g, Fiber: 0g, Sugar: 4g, Sodium: 343mg

Ranch Dipped Fillets

Prep time: 5 minutes, Cook time: 13 minutes, Serves 2

¼ cup panko breadcrumbs	1¼ tbsps. olive oil
1 egg beaten	For Garnish:
2 tilapia fillets	Herbs and chilies
½ packet ranch dressing mix powder	

1. Preheat the Air fryer to 350°F (177°C) and grease an Air fryer basket.
2. Mix ranch dressing with panko breadcrumbs in a bowl.
3. Whisk eggs in a shallow bowl and dip the fish fillet in the eggs.
4. Dredge in the breadcrumbs and transfer into the Air fryer basket.
5. Air fry for about 13 minutes and garnish with chilies and herbs to serve.

Nutrition Info per Serving:

Calories: 301, Fat: 12.2g, Carbohydrates: 1.5g, Sugar: 1.4g, Protein: 28.8g, Sodium: 276mg

Crispy Shrimps

Prep time: 15 minutes, Cook time: 8 minutes, Serves 2

1 egg
¼ pound nacho chips, crushed
10 shrimps, peeled and deveined
1 tbsp. olive oil
Salt and black pepper, to taste

1. Preheat the Air fryer to 365°F (185°C) and grease an Air fryer basket.
2. Crack egg in a shallow dish and beat well.
3. Place the nacho chips in another shallow dish.
4. Season the shrimps with salt and black pepper, coat into egg and then roll into nacho chips.
5. Place the coated shrimps into the Air fryer basket and air fry for about 8 minutes.
6. Dish out and serve warm.

Nutrition Info per Serving:

Calories: 514, Fat: 25.8g, Carbohydrates: 36.9g, Sugar: 2.3g, Protein: 32.5g, Sodium: 648mg

Avocado Fries

Prep time: 20 minutes, Cook time: 7 minutes, Serves 2

¼ cup whole wheat flour	1 avocado, peeled, pitted and sliced into 8 pieces
1 egg	
1 tsp. water	Salt and black pepper, to taste
½ cup panko breadcrumbs	

1. Preheat the Air fryer to 400°F (204°C) and grease an Air fryer basket.
2. Place flour, salt and black pepper in a shallow dish and whisk the egg with water in a second dish.
3. Place the breadcrumbs in a third shallow dish.
4. Coat the avocado slices evenly in flour and dip in the egg mixture.
5. Roll into the breadcrumbs evenly and arrange the avocado slices in the Air fryer basket.
6. Air fry for about 7 minutes, flipping once in between and dish out to serve warm.

Nutrition Info per Serving:

Calories: 363, Fat: 22.4g, Carbohydrates: 35.7g, Sugar: 1.2g, Protein: 8.3g, Sodium: 225mg

Crispy Apple Chips

Prep time: 5 minutes, Cook time: 25 to 35 minutes, Serves 1

1 Honeycrisp or Pink Lady apple

1. Preheat the air fryer to 300°F (149°C).
2. Core the apple with an apple corer, leaving apple whole. Cut the apple into ⅛-inch-thick slices.
3. Arrange the apple slices in the basket, staggering slices as much as possible. Air fry for 25 to 35 minutes, or until the chips are dry and some are lightly browned, turning 4 times with tongs to separate and rotate them from top to bottom.
4. Place the chips in a single layer on a wire rack to cool. Apples will become crisper as they cool. Serve immediately.

Nutrition Info per Serving:

Calories: 95, Protein: 0g, Fat: 0g, Carbohydrates: 25g, Fiber: 4g, Sugar: 19g, Sodium: 1mg

Cheesy Mushroom Pizza

Prep time: 15 minutes, Cook time: 6 minutes, Serves 2

2 Portobello mushroom caps, stemmed
2 tbsps. canned tomatoes, chopped
2 tbsps. Monterey Jack cheese, shredded
2 jalapeno peppers, pitted and sliced
2 tbsps. onions, chopped
2 tbsps. olive oil
1 tsp. dried oregano
Salt and white pepper, to taste

1. Preheat the Air fryer to 320ºF (160ºC) and grease an Air fryer basket.
2. Coat both sides of all Portobello mushroom cap with olive oil.
3. Season the inside of each mushroom cap with salt and white pepper.
4. Divide pasta sauce and garlic inside each mushroom.
5. Arrange mushroom caps into the Air fryer basket and top with canned tomatoes, jalapeno peppers, onions and cheese.
6. Sprinkle with dried oregano and bake for about 6 minutes.
7. Remove from the Air fryer and serve warm.

Nutrition Info per Serving:
Calories: 251, Fat: 21g, Carbohydrates: 5.7g, Sugar: 0.7g, Protein: 13.4g, Sodium: 330mg

Rosemary Baked Cashews

Prep time: 5 minutes, Cook time: 3 minutes, Makes 2 cups

2 sprigs of fresh rosemary (1 chopped and 1 whole)
1 tsp. olive oil
1 tsp. kosher salt
½ tsp. honey
2 cups roasted and unsalted whole cashews
Cooking spray

1. Preheat the air fryer to 300ºF (149ºC).
2. In a medium bowl, whisk together the chopped rosemary, olive oil, kosher salt, and honey. Set aside.
3. Spray the air fryer basket with cooking spray, then place the cashews and the whole rosemary sprig in the basket and bake for 3 minutes.
4. Remove the cashews and rosemary from the air fryer, then discard the rosemary and add the cashews to the olive oil mixture, tossing to coat.
5. Allow to cool for 15 minutes before serving.

Nutrition Info per Serving:
Calories: 182, Protein: 5g, Fat: 15g, Carbohydrates: 9g, Fiber: 1g, Sugar: 2g, Sodium: 293mg

Crispy Cauliflower Poppers

Prep time: 10 minutes, Cook time: 20 minutes, Serves 4

1 large egg white
¾ cup panko breadcrumbs
4 cups cauliflower florets
3 tbsps. ketchup
2 tbsps. hot sauce

1. Preheat the Air fryer to 320ºF (160ºC) and grease an Air fryer basket.
2. Mix together the egg white, ketchup, and hot sauce in a bowl until well combined.
3. Stir in the cauliflower florets and generously coat with marinade.
4. Place breadcrumbs in a shallow dish and dredge the cauliflower florets in it.
5. Arrange the cauliflower florets in the Air fryer basket and air fry for about 20 minutes, flipping once in between.
6. Dish out and serve warm.

Nutrition Info per Serving:
Calories: 94, Fat: 0.5g, Carbohydrates: 19.6g, Sugar: 5.5g, Protein: 4.6g, Sodium: 457mg

Delightful Fish Nuggets

Prep time: 15 minutes, Cook time: 10 minutes, Serves 4

1 cup whole wheat flour
2 eggs
¾ cup whole wheat breadcrumbs
1 pound cod, cut into 1x2½-inch strips
Pinch of salt
2 tbsps. olive oil

1. Preheat the Air fryer to 380ºF (193ºC) and grease an Air fryer basket.
2. Place flour in a shallow dish and whisk the eggs in a second dish.
3. Mix breadcrumbs, salt and oil in a third shallow dish.
4. Coat the fish strips evenly in flour and dip in the egg.
5. Roll into the breadcrumbs evenly and arrange the nuggets in the Air fryer basket.
6. Air fry for about 10 minutes and dish out to serve warm.

Nutrition Info per Serving:
Calories: 404, Fat: 11.6g, Carbohydrates: 36.8g, Sugar: 1.5g, Protein: 34.6g, Sodium: 307mg

Air Fried Spicy Olives

Prep time: 10 minutes, Cook time: 5 minutes, Serves 4

12 ounces (340 g) pitted black extra-large olives
¼ cup whole wheat flour
1 cup panko bread crumbs
2 tsps. dried thyme
1 tsp. red pepper flakes
1 tsp. smoked paprika
1 egg beaten with 1 tbsp. water
Vegetable oil for spraying

1. Preheat the air fryer to 400°F (204°C).
2. Drain the olives and place them on a paper towel–lined plate to dry.
3. Put the flour on a plate. Combine the panko, thyme, red pepper flakes, and paprika on a separate plate. Dip an olive in the flour, shaking off any excess, then coat with egg mixture. Dredge the olive in the panko mixture, pressing to make the crumbs adhere, and place the breaded olive on a platter. Repeat with the remaining olives.
4. Spray the olives with oil and place them in a single layer in the air fryer basket. Work in batches if necessary so as not to overcrowd the basket. Air fry for 5 minutes until the breading is browned and crispy. Serve warm

Nutrition Info per Serving:

Calories: 165, Protein: 3g, Fat: 10g, Carbohydrates: 15g, Fiber: 2g, Sugar: 1g, Sodium: 384mg

Spiced Soy Curls

Prep time: 15 minutes, Cook time: 10 minutes, Serves 2

4 ounces soy curls, soaked in boiling water for about 10 minutes and drained
¼ cup fine ground cornmeal
¼ cup nutritional yeast
2 tsps. Cajun seasoning
1 tsp. poultry seasoning
Salt and ground white pepper, to taste

1. Preheat the Air fryer to 385°F (196°C) and grease an Air fryer basket.
2. Mix together cornmeal, nutritional yeast, Cajun seasoning, poultry seasoning, salt and white pepper in a bowl.
3. Coat the soy curls generously with this mixture and arrange in the Air fryer basket.
4. Air fry for about 10 minutes, flipping in between and dis out in a serving platter.

Nutrition Info per Serving:

Calories: 317, Fat: 10.2g, Carbohydrates: 30.8g, Sugar: 2g, Protein: 29.4g, Sodium: 145mg

Crispy Cajun Dill Pickle Chips

Prep time: 5 minutes, Cook time: 10 minutes, Makes 16 slices

¼ cup whole wheat flour
½ cup panko bread crumbs
1 large egg, beaten
2 tsps. Cajun seasoning
2 large dill pickles, sliced into 8 rounds each
Cooking spray

1. Preheat the air fryer to 390°F (199°C).
2. Place the whole wheat flour, panko bread crumbs, and egg into 3 separate shallow bowls, then stir the Cajun seasoning into the flour.
3. Dredge each pickle chip in the flour mixture, then the egg, and finally the bread crumbs. Shake off any excess, then place each coated pickle chip on a plate.
4. Spritz the air fryer basket with cooking spray, then place 8 pickle chips in the basket and air fry for 5 minutes, or until crispy and golden brown. Repeat this process with the remaining pickle chips.
5. Remove the chips and allow to slightly cool on a wire rack before serving.

Nutrition Info per Serving:

Calories: 40, Protein: 1g, Fat: 1g, Carbohydrates: 7g, Fiber: 1g, Sugar: 0g, Sodium: 296mg

Lemony Pear Chips

Prep time: 15 minutes, Cook time: 9 to 13 minutes, Serves 4

2 firm Bosc pears, cut crosswise into ⅛-inch-thick slices
1 tbsp. freshly squeezed lemon juice
½ tsp. ground cinnamon
⅛ tsp. ground cardamom

1. Preheat the air fryer to 380°F (193°C).
2. Separate the smaller stem-end pear rounds from the larger rounds with seeds. Remove the core and seeds from the larger slices. Sprinkle all slices with lemon juice, cinnamon, and cardamom.
3. Put the smaller chips into the air fryer basket. Air fry for 3 to 5 minutes, or until light golden brown, shaking the basket once during cooking. Remove from the air fryer.
4. Repeat with the larger slices, air frying for 6 to 8 minutes, or until light golden brown, shaking the basket once during cooking.
5. Remove the chips from the air fryer. Cool and serve or store in an airtight container at room temperature up for to 2 days.

Nutrition Info per Serving:

Calories: 49, Protein: 0.3g, Fat: 0.2g, Carbohydrates: 13g, Fiber: 2.4g, Sugar: 7.5g, Sodium: 1mg

Cheese Stuffed Tomatoes

Prep time: 15 minutes, Cook time: 15 minutes, Serves 2

2 large tomatoes, sliced in half and pulp scooped out
½ cup broccoli, finely chopped
½ cup low-fat cheddar cheese, shredded
1 tbsp. almond butter, melted
½ tsp. dried thyme, crushed

1. Preheat the Air fryer to 355ºF (179ºC) and grease an Air fryer basket.
2. Mix together broccoli and cheese in a bowl.
3. Stuff the broccoli mixture in each tomato.
4. Arrange the stuffed tomatoes into the Air fryer basket and drizzle evenly with almond butter.
5. Air fry for about 15 minutes and dish out in a serving platter.
6. Garnish with thyme and serve warm.

Nutrition Info per Serving:
Calories: 206, Fat: 15.6g, Carbohydrates: 9.1g, Sugar: 5.3g, Protein: 9.4g, Sodium: 233mg

Tofu in Sweet and Spicy Sauce

Prep time: 15 minutes, Cook time: 6 minutes, Serves 2

1 (14-ounces) block firm tofu, pressed and cubed
½ cup arrowroot flour
2 scallions (green part), chopped
½ tsp. sesame oil
4 tbsps. low-sodium soy sauce
1½ tbsps. rice vinegar
1½ tbsps. chili sauce
1 tbsp. agave nectar
2 large garlic cloves, minced
1 tsp. fresh ginger, peeled and grated

1. Preheat the Air fryer to 360ºF (182ºC) and grease an Air fryer basket.
2. Mix together tofu, arrowroot flour, and sesame oil in a bowl.
3. Arrange the tofu into the Air fryer basket and air fry for about 20 minutes.
4. Meanwhile, mix together remaining ingredients except scallions in a bowl to make a sauce.
5. Place the tofu and sauce in a skillet and cook for about 3 minutes, stirring occasionally.
6. Garnish with green parts of scallions and serve hot.

Nutrition Info per Serving:
Calories: 153, Fat: 6.4g, Carbohydrates: 13.5g, Sugar: 13.4g, Protein: 13.4g, Sodium: 1300mg

Crispy Spiced Chickpeas

Prep time: 5 minutes, Cook time: 6 to 12 minutes, Makes 1½ cups

1 can (15-ounce / 425-g) chickpeas, rinsed and dried with paper towels
1 tbsp. olive oil
½ tsp. dried rosemary
½ tsp. dried parsley
½ tsp. dried chives
¼ tsp. mustard powder
¼ tsp. sweet paprika
¼ tsp. cayenne pepper
Kosher salt and freshly ground black pepper, to taste

1. Preheat the air fryer to 350ºF (177ºC).
2. In a large bowl, combine all the ingredients, except for the kosher salt and black pepper, and toss until the chickpeas are evenly coated in the herbs and spices.
3. Scrape the chickpeas and seasonings into the air fryer and air fry for 6 to 12 minutes, or until browned and crisp, shaking the basket halfway through.
4. Transfer the crispy chickpeas to a bowl, sprinkle with kosher salt and black pepper, and serve warm.

Nutrition Info per Serving:
Calories: 129, Protein: 4g, Fat: 4.5g, Carbohydrates: 17.6g, Fiber: 4g, Sugar: 2.6g, Sodium: 11mg

Party Time Mixed Nuts

Prep time: 15 minutes, Cook time: 14 minutes, Serves 3

½ cup raw peanuts
½ cup raw almonds
½ cup raw cashew nuts
½ cup raisins
½ cup pecans
1 tbsp. olive oil
Salt, to taste

1. Preheat the Air fryer to 320ºF (160ºC) and grease an Air fryer basket.
2. Place the nuts in the Air fryer basket and roast for about 9 minutes, tossing twice in between.
3. Remove the nuts from the Air fryer basket and transfer into a bowl.
4. Drizzle with olive oil and salt and toss to coat well.
5. Return the nuts mixture into the Air fryer basket and roast for about 5 minutes.
6. Dish out and serve warm.

Nutrition Info per Serving:
Calories: 489, Fat: 36.9g, Carbohydrates: 34.2g, Sugar: 17.2g, Protein: 14.1g, Sodium: 11mg

Ricotta and Parsley Filo Triangles

Prep time: 15 minutes, Cook time: 5 minutes, Serves 6

1 egg yolk
4-ounce low-fat Ricotta cheese, crumbled
1 scallion, chopped finely
2 tbsps. fresh parsley, chopped finely
2 frozen filo pastry sheets, thawed and cut into three strips
2 tbsps. olive oil
Salt and black pepper, to taste

1. Preheat the Air fryer to 390°F (199°C) and grease an Air fryer basket.
2. Whisk egg yolk in a large bowl and beat well.
3. Stir in Ricotta cheese, scallion, parsley, salt and black pepper.
4. Brush pastry with olive oil and put a tbsp. of feta mixture over one corner of filo strip.
5. Fold diagonally to create a triangle and keep folding until filling is completely wrapped.
6. Repeat with the remaining strips and filling and coat the triangles with olive oil.
7. Place the triangles in the Air fryer basket and bake for about 3 minutes.
8. Now, set the Air fryer to 360°F (182°C) and bake for another 2 minutes.
9. Dish out and serve warm.

Nutrition Info per Serving:

Calories: 141, Fat: 9.8g, Carbohydrates: 9.2g, Sugar: 1g, Protein: 4.3g, Sodium: 213mg

Herbed Pita Chips

Prep time: 5 minutes, Cook time: 5 to 6 minutes, Serves 4

¼ tsp. dried basil
¼ tsp. marjoram
¼ tsp. ground oregano
¼ tsp. garlic powder
¼ tsp. ground thyme
¼ tsp. salt
2 whole wheat 6-inch pitas
Cooking spray

1. Preheat the air fryer to 330°F (166°C).
2. Mix all the seasonings together.
3. Cut each pita half into 4 wedges. Break apart wedges at the fold.
4. Mist one side of pita wedges with oil. Sprinkle with half of seasoning mix.
5. Turn pita wedges over, mist the other side with oil, and sprinkle with remaining seasonings.
6. Place pita wedges in air fryer basket and bake for 2 minutes.
7. Shake the basket and bake for 2 minutes longer. Shake again, and if needed, bake for 1 or 2 more minutes, or until crisp. Watch carefully because at this point they will cook very quickly.
8. Serve hot.

Nutrition Info per Serving:

Calories: 80, Protein: 3g, Fat: 1g, Carbohydrates: 16g, Fiber: 2g, Sugar: 0g, Sodium: 200mg

Breaded Artichoke Hearts

Prep time: 5 minutes, Cook time: 8 minutes, Serves 14

14 whole artichoke hearts, packed in water
1 egg
½ cup whole wheat flour
⅓ cup panko bread crumbs
1 tsp. Italian seasoning
Cooking spray

1. Preheat the air fryer to 380°F (193°C)
2. Squeeze excess water from the artichoke hearts and place them on paper towels to dry.
3. In a small bowl, beat the egg. In another small bowl, place the flour. In a third small bowl, combine the bread crumbs and Italian seasoning, and stir.
4. Spritz the air fryer basket with cooking spray.
5. Dip the artichoke hearts in the flour, then the egg, and then the bread crumb mixture.
6. Place the breaded artichoke hearts in the air fryer. Spray them with cooking spray. Air fry for 8 minutes, or until the artichoke hearts have browned and are crisp, flipping once halfway through.
7. Let cool for 5 minutes before serving.

Nutrition Info per Serving:

Calories: 35, Protein: 1g, Fat: 1g, Carbohydrates: 5g, Fiber: 1g, Sugar: 0g, Sodium: 70mg

Basic Salmon Croquettes

Prep time: 15 minutes, Cook time: 14 minutes, Serves 16

1 large can red salmon, drained
2 eggs, lightly beaten
2 tbsps. fresh parsley, chopped
1 cup breadcrumbs
2 tbsps. low-fat milk
Salt and black pepper, to taste
⅓ cup vegetable oil

1. Preheat the Air fryer to 390°F (199°C) and grease an Air fryer basket.
2. Mash the salmon completely in a bowl and stir in eggs, parsley, breadcrumbs, milk, salt and black pepper.
3. Mix until well combined and make 16 equal-sized croquettes from the mixture.
4. Mix together oil and breadcrumbs in a shallow dish and coat the croquettes in this mixture.
5. Place half of the croquettes in the Air fryer basket and bake for about 7 minutes.
6. Repeat with the remaining croquettes and serve warm.

Nutrition Info per Serving:

Calories: 110, Fat: 7.1g, Carbohydrates: 5g, Sugar: 0g, Protein: 3.8g, Sodium: 69mg

CHAPTER 13
DESSERT

Zucchini Brownies

Prep time: 5 minutes, Cook time: 35 minutes, Serves 2

1 cup peanut butter
1 cup dark sugar free chocolate chips
1½ cups zucchini, shredded
¼ tsp. baking soda
1 egg
1 tsp. vanilla extract
⅓ cup applesauce, unsweetened
1 tsp. ground cinnamon
½ tsp. ground nutmeg

1. Preheat the Air fryer to 345°F (174°C) and grease 3 large ramekins.
2. Mix all the ingredients in a large bowl until well combined.
3. Pour evenly into the prepared ramekins and smooth the top surface with the back of spatula.
4. Transfer the ramekin in the Air fryer basket and bake for about 35 minutes.
5. Dish out and cut into slices to serve.

Nutrition Info per Serving:

Calories: 195, Fat: 18.4g, Carbohydrates: 8.2g, Sugar: 6.4g, Protein: 1.5g, Sodium: 143mg

Chickpea Brownies

Prep time: 10 minutes, Cook time: 20 minutes, Serves 6

Vegetable oil
1 (15-ounce / 425-g) can chickpeas, drained and rinsed
4 large eggs
⅓ cup coconut oil, melted
1 tsp. stevia
3 tbsps. unsweetened cocoa powder
1 tbsp. espresso powder (optional)
1 tsp. baking powder
1 tsp. baking soda
½ cup sugar free chocolate chips

1. Preheat the air fryer to 325°F (163°C).
2. Generously grease a baking pan with vegetable oil.
3. In a blender or food processor, combine the chickpeas, eggs, coconut oil, stevia, cocoa powder, espresso powder (if using), baking powder, and baking soda. Blend or process until smooth. Transfer to the prepared pan and stir in the chocolate chips by hand.
4. Set the pan in the air fryer basket and bake for 20 minutes, or until a toothpick inserted into the center comes out clean.
5. Let cool in the pan on a wire rack for 30 minutes before cutting into squares.
6. Serve immediately.

Nutrition Info per Serving:

Calories: 220, Protein: 6g, Fat: 14g, Carbohydrates: 18g, Fiber: 4g, Sugar: 2g, Sodium: 345mg

Chocolate Croissants

Prep time: 5 minutes, Cook time: 24 minutes, Serves 8

1 sheet frozen puff pastry, thawed
⅓ cup chocolate-hazelnut spread
1 large egg, beaten

1. On a lightly floured surface, roll puff pastry into a 14-inch square. Cut pastry into quarters to form 4 squares. Cut each square diagonally to form 8 triangles.
2. Spread 2 tsps. chocolate-hazelnut spread on each triangle; from wider end, roll up pastry. Brush egg on top of each roll.
3. Preheat the air fryer to 375°F (191°C). Air fry rolls in batches, 3 or 4 at a time, 8 minutes per batch, or until pastry is golden brown.
4. Cool on a wire rack; serve while warm or at room temperature.

Nutrition Info per Serving:

Calories: 218, Protein: 3g, Fat: 15g, Carbohydrates: 18g, Fiber: 1g, Sugar: 6g, Sodium: 125mg

Pumpkin Bars

Prep time: 10 minutes, Cook time: 25 minutes, Serves 6

¼ cup almond butter
1 tbsp. unsweetened almond milk
½ cup coconut flour
¾ tsp. baking soda
½ cup dark sugar free chocolate chips, divided
1 cup canned sugar free pumpkin puree
1 tbsp. stevia
1 tsp. cinnamon
1 tsp. vanilla extract
¼ tsp. nutmeg
½ tsp. ginger
⅛ tsp. salt
⅛ tsp. ground cloves

1. Preheat the Air fryer to 360°F (182°C) and layer a baking pan with wax paper.
2. Mix pumpkin puree, stevia, vanilla extract, milk, and butter in a bowl.
3. Combine coconut flour, spices, salt, and baking soda in another bowl.
4. Combine the two mixtures and mix well until smooth.
5. Add about ⅓ cup of the sugar free chocolate chips and transfer this mixture into the baking pan.
6. Transfer into the Air fryer basket and bake for about 25 minutes.
7. Microwave sugar free chocolate bits on low heat and dish out the baked cake from the pan.
8. Top with melted chocolate and slice to serve.

Nutrition Info per Serving:

Calories: 249, Fat: 11.9g, Carbohydrates: 1.8g, Sugar: 0.3g, Protein: 5g, Sodium: 79mg

Sunflower Seeds Bread

Prep time: 15 minutes, Cook time: 18 minutes, Serves 4

⅔ cup whole wheat flour
⅔ cup almond flour
⅓ cup sunflower seeds
1 cup lukewarm water
½ sachet instant yeast
1 tsp. salt

1. Preheat the Air fryer to 390°F (199°C) and grease a cake pan.
2. Mix together flours, sunflower seeds, yeast and salt in a bowl.
3. Add water slowly and knead for about 5 minutes until a dough is formed.
4. Cover the dough with a plastic wrap and keep in warm place for about half an hour.
5. Arrange the dough into a cake pan and transfer into an Air fryer basket.
6. Bake for about 18 minutes and dish out to serve warm.

Nutrition Info per Serving:

Calories: 156, Fat: 2.4g, Carbohydrates: 28.5g, Sugar: 0.5g, Protein: 4.6g, Sodium: 582mg

Walnut Banana Cake

Prep time: 5 minutes, Cook time: 40 minutes, Serves 6

1½ cups almond flour
1 tsp. baking soda
2 eggs
3 medium bananas, peeled and mashed
½ cup walnuts, chopped
½ tsp. ground cinnamon
Salt, to taste
½ cup olive oil
½ cup coconut sugar
½ tsp. vanilla extract

1. Preheat the Air fryer to 300°F (149°C) and grease a 6-inch round baking pan lightly.
2. Mix flour, baking soda, cinnamon and salt in a bowl until well combined.
3. Whisk egg with oil, vanilla extract, sugar and bananas in another bowl.
4. Stir in the flour mixture slowly until fully combined.
5. Fold in the chopped walnuts.
6. Pour the mixture into the baking pan and spread evenly.
7. Cover with the foil paper and transfer the baking pan into the Air fryer.
8. Bake for about 30 minutes and remove the foil.
9. Bake for 10 more minutes and cut into slices to serve.

Nutrition Info per Serving:

Calories: 462, Fat: 23.2g, Carbohydrates: 59.6g, Sugar: 27.8g, Protein: 7.2g, Sodium: 260mg

Cinnamon Almonds

Prep time: 5 minutes, Cook time: 8 minutes, Serves 4

1 cup whole almonds
2 tbsps. almond butter, melted
1 tbsp. coconut sugar
½ tsp. ground cinnamon

1. Preheat the air fryer to 300°F (149°C).
2. In a medium bowl, combine the almonds, almond butter, sugar, and cinnamon. Mix well to ensure all the almonds are coated with the spiced butter.
3. Transfer the almonds to the air fryer basket and shake so they are in a single layer. Bake for 8 minutes, stirring the almonds halfway through the cooking time.
4. Let cool completely before serving.

Nutrition Info per Serving:

Calories: 217, Protein: 6g, Fat: 18g, Carbohydrates: 9g, Fiber: 4g, Sugar: 3g, Sodium: 3mg

Simple Pineapple Sticks

Prep time: 5 minutes, Cook time: 10 minutes, Serves 4

½ fresh pineapple, cut into sticks
¼ cup desiccated coconut

1. Preheat the air fryer to 400°F (204°C).
2. Coat the pineapple sticks in the desiccated coconut and put each one in the air fryer basket.
3. Air fry for 10 minutes.
4. Serve immediately

Nutrition Info per Serving:

Calories: 66, Protein: 0.5g, Fat: 2g, Carbohydrates: 13g, Fiber: 1.5g, Sugar: 9g, Sodium: 2mg

Brownies Muffins

Prep time: 10 minutes, Cook time: 10 minutes, Serves 12

1 package Betty Crocker fudge brownie mix
¼ cup walnuts, chopped
1 egg
2 tsps. water
⅓ cup vegetable oil

1. Preheat the Air fryer to 300°F (149°C) and grease 12 muffin molds lightly.
2. Mix all the ingredients in a bowl and divide evenly into the muffin molds.
3. Arrange the molds in the Air Fryer basket and bake for about 10 minutes.
4. Dish out and invert the muffins onto wire rack to completely cool before serving.

Nutrition Info per Serving:

Calories: 241, Fat: 9.6g, Carbohydrates: 36.9g, Sugar: 25g, Protein: 2.8g, Sodium: 155mg

Lemony Blackberry Crisp

Prep time: 5 minutes, Cook time: 20 minutes, Serves 1

2 tbsps. lemon juice
⅓ cup powdered erythritol
¼ tsp. xantham gum
2 cups blackberries
1 cup crunchy granola

1. Preheat the air fryer to 350°F (177°C).
2. In a bowl, combine the lemon juice, erythritol, xantham gum, and blackberries. Transfer to a round baking dish and cover with aluminum foil.
3. Put the dish in the air fryer and bake for 12 minutes.
4. Take care when removing the dish from the air fryer. Give the blackberries a stir and top with the granola.
5. Return the dish to the air fryer and bake for an additional 3 minutes, this time at 320°F (160°C). Serve once the granola has turned brown and enjoy.

Nutrition Info per Serving:

Calories: 256, Protein: 5g, Fat: 7g, Carbohydrates: 48g, Fiber: 8g, Sugar: 15g, Sodium: 21mg

Easy Almond Shortbread

Prep time: 5 minutes, Cook time: 12 minutes, Serves 8

½ cup almond butter
½ cup coconut sugar
1 tsp. pure almond extract
1 cup whole wheat flour

1. Preheat the air fryer to 375°F (191°C).
2. In a bowl of a stand mixer fitted with the paddle attachment, beat the almond butter and sugar on medium speed until fluffy, 3 to 4 minutes. Add the almond extract and beat until combined, about 30 seconds. Turn the mixer to low. Add the flour a little at a time and beat for about 2 minutes more until well incorporated.
3. Pat the dough into an even layer in a round baking pan. Put the pan in the air fryer basket and bake for 12 minutes.
4. Carefully remove the pan from air fryer basket. While the shortbread is still warm and soft, cut it into 8 wedges.
5. Let cool in the pan on a wire rack for 5 minutes. Remove the wedges from the pan and let cool on the rack before serving.

Nutrition Info per Serving:

Calories: 205, Protein: 4g, Fat: 11g, Carbohydrates: 24g, Fiber: 2g, Sugar: 10g, Sodium: 17mg

Fiesta Pastries

Prep time: 15 minutes, Cook time: 20 minutes, Serves 8

½ of apple, peeled, cored and chopped
1 tsp. fresh orange zest, grated finely
7.05-ounce prepared frozen puff pastry, cut into 16 squares
½ tbsp. coconut sugar
½ tsp. ground cinnamon

1. Preheat the Air fryer to 390°F (199°C) and grease an Air fryer basket.
2. Mix all ingredients in a bowl except puff pastry.
3. Arrange about 1 tsp. of this mixture in the center of each square.
4. Fold each square into a triangle and slightly press the edges with a fork.
5. Arrange the pastries in the Air fryer basket and bake for about 10 minutes.
6. Dish out and serve immediately.

Nutrition Info per Serving:

Calories: 147, Fat: 9.5g, Carbohydrates: 13.8g, Sugar: 2.1g, Protein: 1.9g, Sodium: 62mg

Ninja Pop-Tarts

Prep time: 10 minutes, Cook time: 1 hour, Serves 6

For the Pop-tarts:	½ tsp. vanilla extract
1 cup coconut flour	For the Lemon Glaze:
1 cup almond flour	2 tbsps. stevia
½ cup of ice-cold water	2 tbsps. lemon juice
¼ tsp. salt	zest of 1 lemon
1 tsp. stevia	1 tsp. coconut oil, melted
⅔ cup very cold coconut oil	¼ tsp. vanilla extract

1. For the Pop-tarts:
2. Preheat the Air fryer to 375°F (191°C) and grease an Air fryer basket.
3. Mix all the flours, stevia, and salt in a bowl and stir in the coconut oil.
4. Mix well with a fork until an almond meal mixture is formed.
5. Stir in vanilla and 1 tbsp. of cold water and mix until a firm dough is formed.
6. Cut the dough into two equal pieces and spread in a thin sheet.
7. Cut each sheet into 12 equal sized rectangles and transfer 4 rectangles in the Air fryer basket.
8. Bake for about 10 minutes and repeat with the remaining rectangles.
9. For the Lemon Glaze:
10. Meanwhile, mix all the ingredients for the lemon glaze and pour over the cooked tarts.
11. Top with sprinkles and serve.

Nutrition Info per Serving:

Calories: 368, Fat: 6g, Carbohydrates: 2.8g, Sugar: 2.9g, Protein: 7.2g, Sodium: 103mg

Dark Chocolate Cake

Prep time: 10 minutes, Cook time: 10 minutes, Serves 4

1½ tbsps. almond flour
3½ oz. peanut butter
3½ oz. sugar free dark chocolate, chopped
2 eggs
1 tbsp. stevia

1. Preheat the Air fryer to 375ºF (191ºC) and grease 4 regular sized ramekins.
2. Microwave all chocolate bits with peanut butter in a bowl for about 3 minutes.
3. Remove from the microwave and whisk in the eggs and stevia.
4. Stir in the flour and mix well until smooth.
5. Transfer the mixture into the ramekins and arrange in the Air fryer basket.
6. Bake for about 10 minutes and dish out to serve.

Nutrition Info per Serving:

Calories: 379, Fat: 29.7g, Carbohydrates: 3.7g, Sugar: 1.3g, Protein: 5.2g, Sodium: 193mg

Cheesy Dinner Rolls

Prep time: 10 minutes, Cook time: 5 minutes, Serves 2

2 whole wheat dinner rolls
½ cup low-fat Parmesan cheese, grated
2 tbsps. almond butter, melted
½ tsp. garlic bread seasoning mix

1. Preheat the Air fryer to 355ºF (179ºC) and grease an Air fryer basket.
2. Cut the dinner rolls in slits and stuff cheese in the slits.
3. Top with almond butter and garlic bread seasoning mix.
4. Arrange the dinner rolls into the Air fryer basket and bake for about 5 minutes.
5. Dish out in a platter and serve hot.

Nutrition Info per Serving:

Calories: 608, Fat: 33.1g, Carbohydrates: 48.8g, Sugar: 4.8g, Protein: 33.5g, Sodium: 2000mg

Cinnamon Balls

Prep time: 10 minutes, Cook time: 12 minutes, Serves 6

1 cup almond flour
1 tsp. baking powder
2 tbsps. water
¼ cup nonfat almond milk
2 tbsps. stevia, divided
½ tsp. salt
1 tbsp. coconut oil, melted
2 tsps. cinnamon

1. Preheat the Air fryer to 360ºF (182ºC) and grease an Air fryer basket.
2. Mix flour, 1 tbsp. stevia, salt, cinnamon and baking powder in a bowl.
3. Stir in the coconut oil, water, and soy milk until a smooth dough is formed.
4. Cover this dough and refrigerate for about 1 hour.
5. Mix ground cinnamon with 1 tbsp. stevia in another bowl and keep aside.
6. Divide the dough into 12 equal balls and roll each ball in the cinnamon stevia mixture.
7. Transfer 6 balls in the Air fryer basket and bake for about 6 minutes.
8. Repeat with the remaining balls and dish out to serve.

Nutrition Info per Serving:

Calories: 166, Fat: 4.9g, Carbohydrates: 9.3g, Sugar: 2.7g, Protein: 2.4g, Sodium: 3mg

APPENDIX 1: 30-DAY MEAL PLAN

Meal Plan	Breakfast	Lunch	Dinner	Snack/Dessert
Day-1	Spinach Omelet	Lime-Chili Shrimp Bowl	Lemon Chicken and Spinach Salad	Walnut Banana Cake
Day-2	Golden Avocado Tempura	Brussels Sprouts Salad	Spicy Green Crusted Chicken	Crispy Zucchini Fries
Day-3	Cheesy Greens Sandwich	Broccoli with Cauliflower	Leg of Lamb with Brussels Sprouts	Zucchini Brownies
Day-4	Spinach with Scrambled Eggs	Lemony Green Beans	Almond-Crusted Chicken Nuggets	Crispy Kale Chips
Day-5	Delish Mushroom Frittata	Carne Asada Tacos	Herb-Roasted Veggies	Herbed Pita Chips
Day-6	Zucchini Fritters	Roasted Fish with Almond-Lemon Crumbs	Jerk Chicken, Pineapple and Veggie Kabobs	Cinnamon Balls
Day-7	Veggie Pita Sandwich	Orange Pork Tenderloin	Radish and Mozzarella Salad	Basic Salmon Croquettes
Day-8	Tomato and Mozzarella Bruschetta	Spicy Cauliflower Roast	Roasted Salmon Fillets	Cinnamon Almonds
Day-9	Lettuce Fajita Meatball Wraps	Crab Cakes with Sriracha Mayonnaise	Steak with Bell Peppers	Vegetable Nuggets
Day-10	Breakfast Zucchini	Scallops with Capers Sauce	Chicken with Veggies	Crispy Shrimps

Meal Plan	Breakfast	Lunch	Dinner	Snack/Dessert
Day-11	Tofu and Mushroom Omelet	Simple Salmon	Apricot-Glazed Chicken	Chicken Nuggets
Day-12	Tuna and Lettuce Wraps	Mini Turkey Meatloaves with Carrot	Couscous Stuffed Tomatoes	Ninja Pop-Tarts
Day-13	Supreme Breakfast Burrito	Sun-dried Tomato Crusted Chops	Zucchini Salad	Air Fried Spicy Olives
Day-14	Veggie Salsa Wraps	Cod with Asparagus	Beef Tips with Onion	Chocolate Croissants
Day-15	Gold Avocado	Mediterranean Air Fried Veggies	Crispy Coconut Shrimp	Coconut-Crusted Shrimp
Day-16	Fluffy Cheesy Omelet	Scrumptious Lamb Chops	Crab Cakes with Lettuce and Apple Salad	Dark Chocolate Cake
Day-17	Avocado Quesadillas	Veggies Stuffed Eggplants	Swordfish Skewers with Caponata	Butternut Squash Fries
Day-18	Luscious Scrambled Eggs	Barbecue Chicken	Beef and Veggie Kebabs	Chickpea Brownies
Day-19	Tuna and Lettuce Wraps	Beet Salad with Lemon Vinaigrette	Cajun Fish Fillets	Avocado Fries
Day-20	Air Fryer Breakfast Bake	Chicken with Apple	Sesame Seeds Bok Choy	Fiesta Pastries

Meal Plan	Breakfast	Lunch	Dinner	Snack/Dessert
Day-21	Onion Omelet	Fried Shrimp	Chicken and Mushroom Casserole	Crispy Cauliflower Poppers
Day-22	Heirloom Tomato Sandwiches with Pesto	Pork Chop Stir Fry	Fig, Chickpea, and Arugula Salad	Lemony Blackberry Crisp
Day-23	Mustard Meatballs	Tofu with Veggies	Crunchy Air Fried Cod Fillets	Old-Fashioned Eggplant Slices
Day-24	Pumpkin and Yogurt Bread	Beef Pot Pie	Lush Vegetable Salad	Crispy Spiced Chickpeas
Day-25	Pumpkin and Yogurt Bread	Homemade Fish Sticks	Chicken and Veggie Kabobs	Sunflower Seeds Bread
Day-26	Air Fryer Breakfast Bake	Chermoula Beet Roast	Air Fried Lamb Ribs	Delightful Fish Nuggets
Day-27	Indian Masala Omelet	Pecan-Crusted Tilapia	Almond Asparagus	Spinach and Crab Meat Cups
Day-28	Zucchini Fritters	Tasty Beef Stuffed Bell Peppers	Glazed Veggies	Simple Pineapple Sticks
Day-29	Cauliflower Hash Brown	Spinach Stuffed Chicken Breasts	Mixed Veggie Salad	Cheese Stuffed Tomatoes
Day-30	Lettuce Fajita Meatball Wraps	Sesame Seeds Coated Tuna	Chicken with Pineapple and Peach	Pumpkin Bars

APPENDIX 2:
BASIC KITCHEN CONVERSIONS & EQUIVALENTS

DRY MEASUREMENTS CONVERSION CHART

3 teaspoons = 1 tablespoon = 1/16 cup

6 teaspoons = 2 tablespoons = 1/8 cup

12 teaspoons = 4 tablespoons = ¼ cup

24 teaspoons = 8 tablespoons = ½ cup

36 teaspoons = 12 tablespoons = ¾ cup

48 teaspoons = 16 tablespoons = 1 cup

METRIC TO US COOKING CONVERSIONS

OVEN TEMPERATURES

120 ºC = 250 ºF

160 ºC = 320 ºF

180 ºC = 350 ºF

205 ºC = 400 ºF

220 ºC = 425 ºF

LIQUID MEASUREMENTS

CONVERSION CHART

8 fluid ounces = 1 cup = ½ pint = ¼ quart

16 fluid ounces = 2 cups = 1 pint = ½ quart

32 fluid ounces = 4 cups = 2 pints = 1 quart = ¼ gallon

128 fluid ounces = 16 cups = 8 pints = 4 quarts = 1 gallon

BAKING IN GRAMS

1 cup flour = 140 grams

1 cup sugar = 150 grams

1 cup powdered sugar = 160 grams

1 cup heavy cream = 235 grams

VOLUME

1 milliliter = 1/5 teaspoon

5 ml = 1 teaspoon

15 ml = 1 tablespoon

240 ml = 1 cup or 8 fluid ounces

1 liter = 34 fluid ounces

WEIGHT

1 gram = .035 ounces

100 grams = 3.5 ounces

500 grams = 1.1 pounds

1 kilogram = 35 ounces

US TO METRIC COOKING CONVERSIONS

1/5 tsp = 1 ml

1 tsp = 5 ml

1 tbsp = 15 ml

1 fluid ounces = 30 ml

1 cup = 237 ml

1 pint (2 cups) = 473 ml

1 quart (4 cups) = .95 liter

1 gallon (16 cups) = 3.8 liters

1 oz = 28 grams

1 pound = 454 grams

BUTTER

1 cup butter = 2 sticks = 8 ounces = 230 grams
= 16 tablespoons

WHAT DOES 1 CUP EQUAL

1 cup = 8 fluid ounces

1 cup = 16 tablespoons

1 cup = 48 teaspoons

1 cup = ½ pint

1 cup = ¼ quart

1 cup = 1/16 gallon

1 cup = 240 ml

BAKING PAN CONVERSIONS

9-inch round cake pan = 12 cups

10-inch tube pan =16 cups

10-inch bundt pan = 12 cups

9-inch springform pan = 10 cups

9 x 5 inch loaf pan = 8 cups

9-inch square pan = 8 cups

BAKING PAN CONVERSIONS

1 cup all-purpose flour = 4.5 oz

1 cup rolled oats = 3 oz

1 large egg = 1.7 oz

1 cup butter = 8 oz

1 cup milk = 8 oz

1 cup heavy cream = 8.4 oz

1 cup granulated sugar = 7.1 oz

1 cup packed brown sugar = 7.75 oz

1 cup vegetable oil = 7.7 oz

1 cup unsifted powdered sugar = 4.4 oz

APPENDIX 3:
THE DIRTY DOZEN AND CLEAN FIFTEEN

The Environmental Working Group (EWG) is a widely known organization that has an eminent guide to pesticides and produce. More specifically, the group takes in data from tests conducted by the US Department of Agriculture (USDA) and then categorizes produce into a list titled "Dirty Dozen," which ranks the twelve top produce items that contain the most pesticide residues, or alternatively the "Clean Fifteen," which ranks fifteen produce items that are contaminated with the least amount of pesticide residues.

The EWG has recently released their 2021 Dirty Dozen list, and this year strawberries, spinach and kale – with a few other produces which will be revealed shortly – are listed at the top of the list. This year's ranking is similar to the 2020 Dirty Dozen list, with the few differences being that collards and mustard greens have joined kale at number three on the list. Other changes include peaches and cherries, which having been listed subsequently as seventh and eighth on the 2020 list, have now been flipped; the introduction – which the EWG has said is the first time ever – of bell and hot peppers into the 2021 list; and the departure of potatoes from the twelfth spot.

DIRTY DOZEN LIST

* Strawberries
* Spinach
* Kale, collards and mustard greens
* Nectarines
* Apples
* Grapes
* Cherries
* Peaches
* Pears
* Bell and hot peppers
* Celery
* Tomatoes

CLEAN FIFTEEN LIST

* Avocados
* Sweet corn
* Pineapple
* Onions
* Papaya
* Sweet peas (frozen)
* Eggplant
* Asparagus
* Broccoli
* Cabbage
* Kiwi
* Cauliflower
* Mushrooms
* Honeydew melon
* Cantaloupe

These lists are created to help keep the public informed on their potential exposures to pesticides, which then allows for better and healthier food choices to be made.

This is the advice that ASEQ-EHAQ also recommends. Stay clear of the dirty dozen by opting for their organic versions, and always be mindful of what you are eating and how it was grown. Try to eat organic as much as possible – whether it is on the list, or not.

APPENDIX 4: RECIPES INDEX

Made in the USA
Coppell, TX
04 October 2023

22393706R00072